Advance Praise for God of Empowering Love

What a supremely loveable book! David Polk brings home the great process theological liberation of divine love from its brutalization by power. With a love that does not overpower but empowers, God is, reciprocally, empowered. What Polk offers that no process theologian has yet done is a comprehensive, vividly readable map of the scriptural sources, the theological transmutations, and the history of struggles between omnipotence and love—until now. And because he poses the challenge with his constructive resolution on the horizon, the book moves forward with grip and momentum. Here at last is the book we have needed not just to clinch the matter of theodicy for ourselves—but to help all those students and friends who want to pursue this burning question of questions further.

~Catherine Keller, George T. Cobb Professor of Constructive Theology, Drew University, The Theological School, author of *Cloud of the Impossible: Negative Theology and Planetary Entanglement.*

David Polk's *God of Empowering Love* demonstrates that in the process community he is the outstanding student of the history of theology. Since we believe that the present cannot be understood in separation from the past, the work he has done is of immense importance in understanding ourselves and the challenges we face. Historical understanding and even knowledge of the past gets far too little attention in contemporary society and in the church as well as it is shaped by that society. Polk's book might help to renew historical awareness and the recognition of its importance.

~John B. Cobb, Jr., Professor Emeritus, Claremont Graduate University and Claremont School of Theology

David Polk presents an impressive overview and critique of the understanding of the God-world relationship in the Hebrew and Christian Bible, in the writings of Church Fathers in the early Christian centuries, those of notable medieval theologians, and of Christian theologians from the early modern period to the present day. His focus is on the historical shift from heavy emphasis on the power of God understood

as transcendent of creation in the Patristic and Medieval period to an equally strong contemporary emphasis on the compassionate love of God for all creatures within a cosmic process based on trial and error. Given that many contemporary Christians still think of God more in terms of unilateral power than of mutual love, this book makes a strong case for reversing that priority. As Polk incisively notes, the proper theological question is not how an all-powerful God is also a loving God but how a loving God also effectively exercises power.

~Joseph A. Bracken, S.J., Emeritus Professor of Theology, Xavier University, Cincinnati

The path that through the centuries led Christian theology away from the dynamic and interactive God of the biblical writings to the immutable deity of classical theologians also involved a de-emphasis upon divine love in favor of divine power. David Polk traces this path with great care in remarkably accessible language, showing how at numerous points the ideas of creative thinkers, pointing to a better way, were largely ignored. With equal care and lucidity, Polk traces the eventual turn, still in progress, toward a new understanding that recovers what was lost and provides the groundwork for a creative resolution to age-old theological conundrums appropriate to our contemporary situation. Concluding with a resolution of the love-power question through a concept of empowering love, the book makes an important contribution to contemporary theological reflection. I can heartily recommend it not only as a textbook for college and seminary students but also as material for advanced-level adult study groups in local churches. It is not an easy task to speak to such a wide spectrum of persons, and we should be grateful to Polk for having done so.

~Russell Pregeant, Professor of Religion and Philosophy and Chaplain, Emeritus, Curry College

David Polk has written a tour de force on the issue of God's power and love, citing major figures in the past and present. This book should be a powerful resource to those pondering the all-important questions pertaining to God's empowering love.

~Thomas Jay Oord, Author of *The Uncontrolling Love of God*

This book has long needed to be written. Polk takes on the paradoxical theodicy question of: how can God be both all powerful and all loving in the face of evil? In a wonderfully detailed, logically argued, and reader-friendly style, Polk traces the "living, loving empowering God of the biblical witness" to the Greek influenced theism that dominated Christian history—God as absolute Lord of all, eternal, immutable, passionless, into which love had to be "shoe-horned" as a mere attribute of this almighty God, a wrong turn from which the church has suffered for centuries. Following the theological twists and turns of this paradox down the centuries, Polk notes early twentieth century challenges to divine immutability in favor of a loving suffering God and contemporary moves to a redefinition of power, but argues that the dilemma cannot be resolved from the side of power but by starting with God as fully and unconditionally love and then asking, "What does power mean when applied to a loving, relational God?" In the tradition of process theology, Polk concludes, "We are created in the image of God who is empowering Love." This highly recommended gem of a book is a must for anyone, scholar or layperson, who has ever wrestled with this question in the light of their experiences.

~Dr. Val Webb, Australian theologian, author of eleven books, including *Testing Tradition and Liberating Theology: Finding Our Own Voice*.

David Polk masterfully combines academic rigor with lively readability to produce the most thoroughgoing and compelling study of God, power, and love in our time.

~Patricia Adams Farmer, author of *Embracing a Beautiful God*

Polk's vision of God's power as empowering the world rather than controlling it is a valuable contribution to theological and spiritual reflection. He has offered us a rich historical survey of the interplay between love and power in our religious history.

~Bob Mesle, Professor of Philosophy and Religion, Graceland University, Lamoni, Iowa

A book forty years in the making (and worth the wait!), David Polk offers readers two invaluable gifts. First, he presents an accessible history of both the development of and dissatisfaction with the "wrong turn" the church took when it substituted the God of the philosophers—that is, God defined as omnipotent, immutable, impassive, apathetic, and so forth—for the God revealed by Jesus of Nazareth. Second, and more importantly, Polk offers a fresh way to conceive of God's power: empowering love.

~Ronald L. Farmer, author of *Beyond the Impasse: The Promise of a Process Hermeneutic*

Dreams of "ice cream castles in the air" at one extreme and nightmares of fire and brimstone wrath at the other, conscientious Christians have constantly wrestled like Jacob and Job to discern the ways of God's saving love and compassion amid the hurts, sufferings, and transience of all creatures great and small. Polk's is a fresh, wide-ranging, and mercifully well-written unfolding of theology's dealings with questions of "God and the problem of evil" from biblical times to today's new voices. It's a welcome resource for clergy and laity concerned, as well as teachers and students.

~James O. Duke, The I. Wylie and Elizabeth M. Briscoe Professor of History of Christianity and History of Christian Thought
Brite Divinity School, Texas Christian University

Wow! This book will help pastors preach with greater clarity and conviction that love is the true power of God. The history of Christian thought juxtaposing love and power will be an invaluable resource for students and pastors.

~Jan Linn, retired founding pastor of Spirit of Joy Christian Church, St. Paul, MN, and former professor, Lexington Theological Seminary

The book was like having David Polk in the room explaining what he studied. The Table of Contents and Introduction are a sampling of his scholarship on many of the theologians in his adult life. The final chapters on the 20th-century scholars are a wonderful study of religion and philosophy, bringing the reader up to our current time. A study group with David is as exciting and reassuring as ever, even long distance and years later. Remnants of a process theology group are awaiting publication for study and discussions.

~Karen Kral, artist, ALC lay leader, Cedar Rapids, Iowa

GOD of EMPOWERING LOVE

GOD *of* EMPOWERING LOVE

A History and Reconception
of the Theodicy Conundrum

David P. Polk

ANOKA, MINNESOTA 2016

God of Empowering Love: A History and Reconception of the Theodicy Conundrum

© 2016 Process Century Press

All rights reserved. Except for brief quotations in critical publications and reviews, no part of this book may be reproduced in any manner without prior permission from the publisher.

Process Century Press
RiverHouse LLC
802 River Lane
Anoka, MN 55303

Process Century Press books are published in association with the International Process Network.

New Revised Standard Version Bible, copyright 1989, Division of Christian Education of the National Council of the Churches of Christ in the United States of America. Used by permission. All rights reserved.

Cover design: Susanna Mennicke

VOLUME I: THEOLOGICAL EXPLORATIONS SERIES
JEANYNE B. SLETTOM, GENERAL EDITOR

ISBN 978-1-940447-14-8
Printed in the United States of America

SERIES PREFACE: THEOLOGICAL EXPLORATIONS

This series aims to explore the implications of Whiteheadian philosophy and theology for religious belief and practice. It also proposes that process religious thinkers, working from within many different traditions—Buddhist, Confucian, Christian, Hindu, Indigenous, Jewish, Muslim, and others—have unique insights pertinent to the critical issues of our day.

In 1976, we published a book, *Process Theology: An Introductory Exposition,* in which we aimed to "show the creative potentiality of a process perspective in theology." In addition to its explanation of process concepts and their application to Christian doctrine, the book noted the contribution of Whiteheadian thought toward "intercultural and interreligious understanding" and took an early stance on the ecological threat, claiming that process theology was prepared to "make a distinctive contribution" to this challenge.

Since the publication of that book, we have seen many others explore these and other themes in articles, books, and conferences. At the same time, the threat to planetary health and the need for "intercultural and interreligious understanding" has only accelerated. This series is an effort to support theologians and religious philosophers in their ongoing exposition of possible Whiteheadian solutions.

John B. Cobb, Jr.
David Ray Griffin

To

John B. Cobb, Jr.,

mentor and friend,
one who embodies
empowering love

IN GRATITUDE

Elizabeth Johnson, author of *She Who Is*, kindly reviewed my book on Pannenberg's theology (*On the Way to God*) with the proposal that I turn my attention to pursuing the clues I had surfaced in developing more explicitly the notion that God's power is indeed to be conceived as a power of love. Here, a quarter of a century later, is the result of that endeavor. Thank you, Elizabeth Johnson, for setting me on a fruitful path, even though the gestation period turned out to be exceedingly long.

I also acknowledge a grateful debt to the following:

To Mary Elizabeth Moore for facilitating my access to borrowing privileges at the library of Candler School of Theology, Emory University, and to the extremely helpful staff of that library, as well as my brother Jim and his wife Cara for their gracious hospitality on those occasions when I traveled to Atlanta.

To the staff of the Interlibrary Loan desk at the North Port branch of the Sarasota County Library in Florida, for enabling me to access obscure texts that were of vital importance to the research behind this book, as well as the staff of the British Library, London.

To Marjorie Suchocki for stimulating my creative passion to bring this project finally to completion.

To Joseph Bracken, John Cobb, Jan Linn, Tom Oord, Bob Mesle, Russ Pregeant, Jon Berquist, Terence Fretheim, Ron Allen, David Lull, Patricia Farmer, Ron Farmer, Val Webb, and James Duke for providing critical feedback on all or parts of the manuscript-in-process.

To my editor and publisher Jeanyne Slettom for believing in this project and shepherding it into existence, and for extraordinary dedication to making Process Century Press soar.

And finally to my wife Kitty for longsuffering patience as I invested the early years of my retirement in the extended pursuit of this writing venture.

Table of Contents

IN GRATITUDE
INTRODUCTION, *i*

PART I: BIBLICAL EXPRESSIONS OF GOD'S POWERFUL LOVE

1 WITNESS TO A LIVING GOD: THE OLD TESTAMENT, 1

    Testimony to God's Power, 1
    Testimony to God's Love, 16
    The Conjoining of God's Power and God's Love, 19

2 WITNESS TO A LIVING GOD: THE NEW TESTAMENT, 26

    The Announcement of God's Inbreaking Reign, 28
    Power in Weakness, 30
    "God Is Love" 31

PART II: THE TRIUMPH OF POWER OVER LOVE

3 ENCOUNTERS WITH THE PHILOSOPHERS' GOD, 37

    The Assurance of Divine Omnipotence, 38
    A Philosophical Counterpoint, 42
    "What's Love Got to Do with It": Divine Impassibility, 45
    What Has Been Lost? 48

4 THE ESTABLISHMENT OF ALMIGHTY GOD, 53

    Trinitarian Consolidations in the East: Gregory of Nyssa, 54
    The Victorious Synthesis: Augustine of Hippo, 56

5 REFINEMENTS OF AN OMNIPOTENT GOD, 72

   A Love So Great: Richard of St. Victor, 72
   The New Aristotelian Synthesis: Thomas Aquinas, 74
   Potentia Absoluta, Potentia Ordinata: William of Ockham, 79
   God's Defense Attorney: John Calvin, 80

6 REARRANGINGS OF A TITANIC GOD, 87

   A Consciousness of Absolute Dependency:
     Friedrich Schleiermacher, 87
   God Who Loves in Freedom: Karl Barth, 89
   God as Being-Itself: Paul Tillich, 92
   God as the Power of the Future: Wolfhart Pannenberg, 95

7 THE VICTORY OF A STOIC GOD, 101

   The Philosophy of Stoicism, 101
   A Stoic Theology, 103
   Moving Forward by Going Back, 104

PART III: THE EVENTUAL COLLAPSE OF THE UNTENABLE

8 MUSINGS ON THE MYSTICS' GOD, 109

   The Primacy of Love: Dionysius and Bonaventure, 110
   Repressed Voices: the Contributions of Women Mystics, 114

9 CHALLENGES TO AN UNCHANGING GOD, 124

   J. K. Mozley's Surprising Discovery, 124
   Jürgen Moltmann's Crucified God, 126

10 ODES TO A SUFFERING GOD, 130

   The "Hardest Part": G. A. Studdert-Kennedy, 130
   Tragedy in God: Nicolas Berdyaev, 133
   Voices from East Asia: Kazoh Kitamori and Jung Young Lee, 134
   The God Who Suffers with the Suffering: Dorothee Sölle, 136

11 MOURNING OVER A DEAD GOD, 141

    A Projection of Human Wishing: Ludwig Feuerbach, 141
    "Returning the Ticket": Fyodor Dostoyevsky, 144
    "We Have Killed God": Friedrich Nietzsche, 145
    God's Self-Annihilation: Thomas J. J. Altizer, 148

12 OBITUARIES FOR A PATRIARCHAL GOD, 153

    The Unmasking of Patriarchy's Dominant Sway: Mary Daly, 154
    Toward a God of Mutual Relations: Carter Heyward, 155
    Erotic Power: Rita Nakashima Brock, 156
    She Who Is: Elizabeth Johnson, 157

13 INKLINGS OF AN IMPOTENT GOD, 163

    When Bad Things Happen: Harold Kushner, 164
    Earlier Predecessors in the Christian Tradition, 165
    A God of Limited Power: Edgar Brightman, 167

14 BREAKTHROUGHS TO A LOVING GOD, 171

    Reclaiming the Insight that God *Is* Love, 172
    The Power of Omnipotent Love, 178
    The Transforming Power of Love: Teilhard de Chardin, 184
    Letting Love Fully Redefine Power, 186

15 HUNGER FOR A LIBERATING GOD, 201

    A Black Theology of Liberation: James Cone, 202
    God's Preferential Option for the Poor:
        Latin American Voices, 205

16 OVERTURES TO A RELATIONAL GOD, 216

    Philosophical Underpinnings: Whitehead and Hartshorne, 217
    A Process Theology of Love: Daniel Day Williams, 222
    Unilateral and Relational Power: Bernard Loomer, 224
    God as Creative-Responsive Love: John B. Cobb, Jr., 226

    A God Who Is Omni-Amorous: Catherine Keller, 228
    Transition: From Challenge o Reconstruction, 230

Part IV: The Reunification of Love with Power

17 Glimpses of a Revealed God, 237

    God Is Love: Reaffirming 1 John, 238
    God's Empowering Reign of Love: Reaccessing Jesus, 240
    Power in Weakness: Re-viewing the First Easter, 242

18 The Love of an Empowering God, 246

    Envisioning a Fresh Alternative: Key Components, 246
    Weaving a New Tapestry: Contributions from the
       Countertestimony, 249
    The Movement of Eros: The Gift of New Possibility, 251
    The Movement of Agape: The Gift of Divine Embrace, 256

For Further Reading, 259

Indices

Scripture Index, 261

Author Index, 265

Subject Index, 268

Introduction

I begin at Dachau.

At Buchenwald. Bergen-Belsen. Auschwitz. Anne Frank, who did not make it home. Dietrich Bonhoeffer, executed days before the liberation. Elie Wiesel's father. So many millions more.

The classical Christian synthesis of the power of God and the love of God—forged in those formative years of contact with Greek philosophy, hammered out by Augustine and Aquinas and other giants of Christian thought, fractured by the critiques of Dostoyevsky and Nietzsche and their comrades in intellectual arms—was smashed to pieces by the overwhelming human devastation that was the Holocaust. No longer could any reflective person in the church pretend that the God of power in the traditional sense was truly loving—or that a God of love had any significant power in the world we actually live in. One or the other, it seemed—or the very being of God—had to go.

This is, of course, the issue addressed on a more personal level in Rabbi Harold Kushner's highly popular *When Bad Things Happen to Good People*, reassessing a conflict at least as ancient as the biblical Book of Job. It seems that more and more people are taking Kushner's option of choosing a good and caring God, who does not control events, over the traditional God of power. It is almost as though the God of power was tried for over two thousand years and found wanting, so now we are trying the God of love instead.

This book is an assertion that the choice between God's love and God's power is one that we are not required to make.

The prevailing voices in two milennia of Christian tradition asked, "How is an all-powerful God loving?" They answered in a variety of unsatisfying ways, but essentially the problem is that *they asked the wrong question*. I am asking, instead, *"How is an all-loving God powerful?"* or *"How is God, who is essentially love, powerful?"* Therein lies all the difference. I maintain we must allow love to redefine power, rather than allowing power to redefine love. Similarly: *To ask how God's power is loving, and how God's love is powerful, is not to ask the same question in two different ways; it is to ask two different questions.*

I contend that God has all the genuine power that God can possibly have without ceasing to be Love. That is the heart of the issue. And it leads me to affirm the central thesis of this extended exploration into the history of theological debate: that the God we worship and try to comprehend is no other than a God who is *Empowering Love*.

My initial forayin Part One is into the biblical witness to One characterized very explicitly as a "living" God, tracing the dynamic interrelationship between God and God's creation, God's people, through the Old Testament into the New. The centrality of *hesed* in the former and *agape* in the latter gives us a handle on understanding the God powerfully at work in us and among us in ways we still struggle to grasp.

Part Two covers the initial encounter of biblical content with the widespread influence of Greek intellectual ideas in the milieu of the Roman Empire, leading to accommodations to the biblical message that proved problematic. What became the predominant synthesis of Christian theism in Augustine of Hippo can be seen to have endured through ensuing centuries down to the present, with subsequent modifications but no essential alteration of the fundamental position on God's power and love initially formulated. Absolute power won out over love. Love, wherever and however possible, had to be "shoehorned" in, somehow.

In Part Three, I introduce multiple challenges to the Augustinian synthesis that eventually brought about its collapse, ranging from the mystics' elevation of divine love to a questioning of God's immutability and essential apathy, including the call for a post-patriarchal understanding of a God who is more than merely male, and arriving eventually at a renewed witness to the absolute importance of elevating love to the center of divine reality and determining this to involve God in essential relationality not just with Godself, through the Trinity, but with all that comes into being under God's impetus.

The final part of this book is a reconstructive one, the objective toward which all that precedes has been aiming. There, I attempt to explicate the precise meaning I have in mind when I name God the God of Empowering Love.

I fully perceive that there is nothing even remotely final or definitive about this reconstructive effort. Every human construct of thought is subject to deconstruction as a step on the way to a new reconstruction. This is offered as a step in that ongoing process, with no claim greater than perhaps it proves informative and helpful to others who are wrestling with the same problem I am concerned with. I fully expect others to make important advances over what I present here, and that is how it should be.

I also do not deny for one moment that my own perspective is shaped by my social situation. The reach for objectivity is always limited by the reality of one's own very specific subjectivity. I am a European American male, a Protestant, of some considerable years. My writing is colored by my contextuality. That can only be acknowledged, not surmounted. But I hope that the reflections offered here are expandable into other formulations by those with different cultural settings that inform them.

I have made a conscientious effort to let the voices of the Christian tradition speak for themselves in their own—though often translated—words, rather than interpose my own paraphrasing that can introduce unintentionally a personal bias. Even so, I acknowledge two clear aspects of subjectivity: my particular selection of quotations, and my lifting of them out of their original context. That is, obviously, unavoidable. My claim to fairness is justifiable only by appeal to the reader to delve further into those original sources on your own, should you so choose. My limited attempt to overcome my subjective particularity is to be found only in the range of voices to which I have tried to listen as attentively as possible.

The project for which this book is a culmination had its beginnings four decades ago, when I first published a short essay defining and exploring what I called a "Gospel of Empowering Love." This is finally a putting to rest of notions that would not let go of me for forty years. I offer it here as a gift.

Part I

Biblical Expressions of God's Powerful Love

I

Witness to a Living God: The Old Testament

TESTIMONY TO GOD'S POWER

High up on the slopes of Mount Carmel, the conflict is joined. Two factions are present: the numerous representatives of Baal, and a single proponent of Yahweh by the name of Elijah. The issue to be decided is a simple but far-reaching one: whose god has power—which means, of course, whose god is *really* God?

As the story is recounted (1 Kings 18:20–40), Elijah proposes a contest: prepare two sacrificial bulls as burnt offerings, but let God provide the fire. The challenge is accepted. But the intense and extensive efforts of the prophets of Baal prove to be of no avail. After half a day of the best they can muster, the result of their pleading is "no voice, no answer, and no response" (18:29).

Then Elijah takes center stage. Obstacles are piled on by the narrator—jars of water soaking the wood to the core, poured on not once but three times. At last, the time of resolution is at hand.

> At the time of the offering of the oblation, the prophet Elijah came near and said, "O LORD, God of Abraham, Isaac, and Israel, let it be known this day that you are God in Israel, that

I am your servant, and that I have done all these things at your bidding. Answer me, O LORD, answer me, so that this people may know that you, O LORD, are God, and that you have turned their hearts back." Then the fire of the LORD fell and consumed the burnt offering, the wood, the stones, and the dust, and even licked up the water that was in the trench. When all the people saw it, they fell on their faces and said, "The LORD indeed is God; the LORD indeed is God." (18:36–39)

This notion that the god who is truly God is the one who manifests *power* is hardly original to the Israelites. It is widespread, and ancient. As Wolfhart Pannenberg has observed, it is generally recognized that "the being of the gods is their power."[1] That is our point of departure for evaluating the biblical witness to God, but it is only that: a jumping-off point.

Immediately after this incident, the biblical record provides us with another and startlingly different divine/human encounter. God's prophet has had to flee from the wrath of the king's wife, his life now in jeopardy. At Mt. Horeb Elijah experiences the powerful and empowering presence of God in an unexpected manner.

[God] said, "Go out and stand on the mountain before the LORD, for the LORD is about to pass by." Now there was a great wind, so strong that it was splitting mountains and breaking rocks in pieces before the LORD, but the LORD was not in the wind; and after the wind an earthquake, but the LORD was not in the earthquake; and after earthquake a fire, but the LORD was not in the fire; and after the fire a sound of sheer silence. (19:11–12)

The key phrase is also translatable as "the sound of a soft whisper" or, in the RSV, "a still, small voice." The narrative provides stirring testimony that convictions about God's power conveyed in the literature of the Old Testament move well beyond what the ancient Israelites inherited from their cultural surroundings. Let us begin with that inheritance before moving on to what is distinctive about the hebraic testimony.

VIEWS OF GOD'S POWER ADOPTED FROM ISRAEL'S NEIGHBORS

That the biblical witness to God's power includes notions common to the religious environment of the day is widely recognized. In writing specifically about creation accounts, Terence Fretheim takes notice of "a widespread fund of images and ideas upon which Israel drew."[2] I regard that as more broadly applicable in regard to other notions of God's power as well.

The power to create. "Ah, Lord God!" Jeremiah proclaims, "It is you who made the heavens and the earth by your great power and by your outstretched arm!" (Jer 32:17).[3] What is narrated at the very beginning of the biblical record, God's creating of all that is, also pervades the subsequent literature down through the prophets and the Wisdom tradition.[4]

> I made the earth,
>   and created humankind upon it;
> It was my hands that stretched out the heavens,
>   and I commanded all their host. (Is 45:12)

So far, what we are encountering is a raw manifestation of God's unilateral power, the absolute might to bring into being—and impose order on—an unresisting cosmos. The object of God's activity, the "creation," is purely passive and receptive. This is in common with creation myths present throughout the ancient Middle East. But as we shall see shortly, that only begins to scratch the surface of Israel's own understanding of God as Creator.

Power over the forces of nature and over human and animal behavior. This is an explicit example of Pannenberg's observation. God not only brings the cosmos into being but continues to exercise power, even control, over all that is within it. Isaiah proclaims that:

> the Sovereign , the LORD of hosts,
>   will lop the boughs with terrifying power . . .
> He will hack down the thickets of the forest with an ax. (Is. 10:33f.)

Second Isaiah's God, who "formed the earth and made it," and "did not create it a chaos" (Is. 45:18), uses Cyrus, king of Persia, as a tool to effect God's goals (45:1, 13), generating weal as well as woe (45:7). The psalmist's God:

covers the heavens with clouds,
> prepares rain for the earth,
> makes grass grow on the hills.
. . . gives to the animals their food,
> and to the young ravens when they cry. (Ps. 147:8–9)

God asks Moses the rhetorical question, "Is the LORD's power limited?" (Num. 11:23), with the very clear implication that it definitely is not. Even as they reflect the particularities of Israel's covenantal relationship with Yahweh, these passages bear the clear imprint of borrowed notions about God's unchallengeable sway over the whole of creation.

Power to dictate the outcome of struggles and warfare. This is a subset of the preceding theme. Understanding God as triumphant in battle was a fundamental conviction throughout the ancient Near East. God may seem opposable in the short term but not in regard to the eventual outcome. Israel is reminded by the chronicler that "God has power to help or to overthrow" in battle (2 Chr. 25:8). The psalmist reassures the faint of heart that God "will shatter kings on the day of his wrath" and "execute judgment among the nations, filling them with corpses" (Ps. 110:5–6). The narrative of Gideon bringing only three hundred warriors into battle against the combined might of the Midianites and Amalekites, blowing trumpets that resulted in God setting "every man's sword against his fellow" among the enemies' army (Judges 7:22), is a colorful expression of God's capacity to shape the result of any human conflict.

God as divine monarch. Although there are particular ways in which the notion of God as divine monarch takes on a distinctive character with Israel, its roots can readily be traced throughout the ancient Near East, from Egypt to Babylonia. In Egypt, the sun god Amun-Re was regularly conceived as the true heavenly lord and father of the reigning pharaoh.[5] In Babylonia the human ruler was understood to be "the earth-bound bearer of the heavenly dignity, a mortal container of the immortal kingly essence."[6]

The Gideon story culminates in a refusal of the Israelites' offer of kingship: "I will not rule over you, and my son will not rule over you; the LORD will rule over you" (Judges 8:23). King David's hymn of praise at the conclusion of 1 Chronicles echoes this theme.

> Yours, O LORD, are the greatness, the power, the glory, the victory, and the majesty; for all that is in the heavens and on the earth is yours; yours is the kingdom, O LORD, and you are exalted as head above all. Riches and honor come from you, and you rule over all. In your hand are power and might. (1 Chr. 29:11–12)

Isaiah's call vision sees God as the heavenly king sitting on his throne (Is. 6:1,5). Psalms 93–100 have as their common theme *YHWH malak*, "the LORD reigns," "the LORD is king."[7] God is the king everlasting, robed in majesty (Ps. 93:1–2), "a great King above all gods" (95:3).

> Say among the nations, "The LORD is king!
> The world is firmly established; it shall never be moved. (96:10)

> The LORD is king! Let the earth rejoice;
> let the many coastlands be glad! (97:1)

> Mighty King, lover of justice,
> you have established equity;
> you have executed justice
> and righteousness in Jacob. (99:4)

God is king not only of all the earth but specifically "over the nations"; the "shields of the earth," i.e., the means of defense of earthly realms, are none other than God's very own property (Ps. 47:7-9).

Personal power. "To some degree or other," Bernhard Anderson has observed, "anthropomorphism appears in all circles and periods of OT tradition."[8] God walks in the Garden in the cool of the evening (Gen. 3:8). God's "voice" is "powerful . . . full of majesty" (Ps. 29:4).[9] God's mighty "hand" (*yad*) is typical language for expressing the exercise of God's power, in examples far too numerous to bear mentioning. The Old Testament unhesitantly and consistently views Yahweh as a distinct person.... Anthropomorphism is indigenous to a faith which views God in terms of historical actions and relationships rather than in terms of natural power or impersonal being.... [To Yahweh] are ascribed the characteristics of personality: wisdom, will, purpose, love, anger, anguish, patience, hatred, jealousy, joy, etc.[10]

This is hardly unique to the biblical record. The anthropomorphizing of God and of God's power was a common notion readily available for appropriating. But Israel separated this out from the equally common tendency to envision God in animal form, especially prevalent in ancient Egypt. And as we will see, the notion of divine personal power takes on a very particular character in the context of the Mosaic covenant.

VIEWS OF GOD'S POWER DISTINCTIVE TO ISRAEL

To observe what the people of the Old Testament shared with their varied religious environment in regard to the concept of divine power constitutes no more than a prelude to the full symphony of ideas yet to be encountered. In some respects, the biblical witness took existing notions and gave them a distinctive character all its own. In other respects, it brought entirely new understandings into focus. To both of these I now turn.

God's power is exercised in the context of a divine/human covenant. "Constantly present behind all the testimonies to Yahweh's marvelous power is one particular presupposition," Walther Eichrodt insisted half a century ago. "This power is the power of the God of the covenant."[11] In God's covenant with Moses and, through Moses, with the people of the exodus, the being of God acquired "an explicitly personal character"[12] that countered anthropomorphizing tendencies "primarily through the experience of *the infinite superiority of the divine nature* to all merely human attributes and capacities—an experience which marks every encounter with the divine in the Old Testament."[13]

The heart of this covenant is found in the promise, "I will take you as my people, and I will be your God" (Ex. 6:7). Commitments are verbalized on both sides: God is "the faithful God who maintains covenant loyalty with those who love him, and keep his commandments" (Deut. 7:9). So, obviously, human faithfulness and loyalty are fully expected in return. Deut. 28 details blessings that flow upon those who are obedient to God's precepts as well as curses unleashed upon those who are not.

Walter Brueggemann's perspective on Israel's core testimony is "that it is Yahweh's sovereign power and covenantal solidarity that mark the God to whom Israel bears witness. . . . *What is important is the recognition that for Israel, power and solidarity are held together, and that both are crucial for Israel's normative utterance about Yahweh.*"[14]

God is a single center of power. The Old Testament is chock full of references to other gods, to Yahweh presiding over a council of gods.[15] Explicit monotheism clearly arrived on the scene only belatedly. Whereas the Decalogue begins with the prohibition that "you shall *have* no *other gods* before me" (Ex. 20:3, Deut. 5:7, emphasis mine), it remains for Second Isaiah to insist that there simply are no other gods, period. The gods to whom Israel's neighbors (and enemies) pray are "a delusion," their accomplishments "nothing," their images "empty wind" (Is. 41:29). A typically recurring phrase in Isaiah is simply, "I am God, and there is no other" (46:9; 45:5, 6). It is this God and this God alone who is "mighty in power, great in strength" (Is. 40:26). So also does Jeremiah maintain that the gods of the other nations "are no gods" at all (Jer. 2:11), and Hezekiah prays to the God of Israel that "you are God, you alone, of all the kingdoms of the earth" (2 Kings 19:15).

God's powerful creative activity is ongoing. "Do not remember the former things, or consider the things of old," God is heard to say by Second Isaiah. "I am about to do a new thing" (Is. 43:19). Terence Fretheim is by no means alone in maintaining that this is more than just the divine oversight of the created order. God's ongoing work of creating involves "the emergence of genuinely new realities in an increasingly complex world."[16]

This is already implicit in the opening text of the biblical witness. Creation is not simply the "making" of a cosmos and its contents. It is the bringing of design out of formlessness, order out of chaos (Gen.

1:2). And this process is hardly finished when the initiating acts of creating are over. Chaos threatens even the tranquility of the Garden in the disrupting antics of the serpent (Gen. 3:1). Chaos in the form of raging waters, originally contained and restrained (Gen. 1:6), is allowed to overwhelm the earth as prelude to a fresh start with Noah and his descendents (Gen. 6–8). The rainbow signifies a divine promise, but it does not negate the ongoing capacity of the forces of chaos to subvert the tenuous emergence of greater and more complex order. It is rather an assurance that God's power cannot and will not be defeated by chaos.

Psalm 104, which Brueggemann calls "perhaps the fullest rendition of creation faith in the Old Testament,"[17] appropriates the Hebrew word for original creation, *bara'*, for the activity of continuing creation. According to Bernhard Anderson: "Creation is not just an event that occurred in the beginning, at the foundation of the earth, but is God's continuing activity of sustaining creatures and holding everything in being."[18]

This capacity to continue to create the genuinely new is a significant motif in the testimony of Second Isaiah (e.g., 41:17–20), culminating in his disciples' envisioning of the creation of "new heavens and a new earth" (65:17; cf. 66:22), holding within itself the promise of the eventual championing of divinely intended order over all that threatens to inhibit it.

Divine power is conjoined with righteousness. "I am the LORD" says God to Jeremiah in the prophet's testimony; "I act with steadfast love, justice, and righteousness in the earth" (Jer. 9:24) The identity of Israel's God is explicitly characterized here by qualities of absolute reliability. This is no god of arbitrary power and capricious action, as Israel's neighbors repeatedly resorted to. The Psalms ring with assertions of God's steadfast righteousness (7:9–11; 11:7; 116:5; 119:137), which, like God's *hesed*,[19] "endures forever" (111:3).

There is no question but that Israel's understanding of the righteous power of God is distinctly developed within the context of the covenant God has established with God's people. Zechariah makes that point with unmistakable clarity, in words that echo the covenant's very foundation: "They shall be my people, and I will be their God, in faithfulness and in righteousness" (Zech. 8:8).

God exercises power in a manner that invites participation by those whom God's power has created. Terence Fretheim has dug deeper than anyone else in bringing this theme to light. The first divine words to human beings (Gen. 1:28, exercise "dominion," *radah*), he has written, "constitute a sharing of the exercise of power (dominion). From the beginning God chooses not to be the only one who has or exercises creative power. . . . God establishes a power-sharing relationship with humans."[20]

In this regard, then, Fretheim understands God's power as portrayed in the Old Testament to be fundamentally interactive and essentially, not coincidentally, *interrelational*, a conviction that thoroughly pervades his *God and World in the Old Testament*.[21] God so enters into relationships:

> that God is not the only one who has something important to say . . .
> that God is not the only one who has something important to do and the power with which to do it . . .
> that God is genuinely affected by what happens to the relationship . . .
> that the human will can stand over against the will of God . . .
> that the future is not all blocked out.[22]

That "God will take into consideration human thought and action in determining what God's own action will be" is what Fretheim calls the "divine consultation."[23]

The first creation story in Genesis dares to proclaim that human beings are created "in the image of God" (Gen. 1:27). I regard this as critical for comprehending the scope of God's sharing of power. As God is powerful, so are we—who bear God's image—expected to exercise power. The language of Gen. 1:26–27, explicitly occurring only here in the Old Testament, is a fundamental shift of orientation, a "democratizing," of the ancient Near East's notion of the earthly ruler as being God's image on earth.[24] The history of attempts to embody this democratized notion shows how easy it is to get it wrong. If God's power is perceived to be all controlling, dominating, impositional, so will humans aspire to be controlling and dominating over others in God's name, imposing their own will on others on the understanding that they are only fulfilling their God-given destiny. The thesis undergirding this book is that this behavior actualizes a false notion of the power of the God in whose image we are created, with calamities both large and small the result.

One final note remains to be offered. If the original but also continuing act of creating is one of bringing increasing order out of the swirl of chaos that threatens to engulf it, then it is surely clear by now that this is an ongoing creative process in which human beings are actively, and powerfully, invited by God to participate. We are not merely passive. We contribute, substantively.

God's power is a* liberating *power that* empowers *the weak and the powerless. Heschel observed that according to the Roman historian Tacitus "The gods are on the side of the stronger." To the contrary, Israel's prophets "proclaimed that the heart of God is on the side of the weaker. God's special concern is not for the mighty and the successful, but for the lowly and the downtrodden, for the stranger and the poor, for the widow and the orphan."[25]

This is first encountered definitively in God's leading of the descendents of Abraham out of bondage in Egypt. God's covenant with Israel and God's "surprising liberation of a poor and oppressed people"[26] are intimately linked. Moses sings of God's terrifying displays of power, hazaq, in destroying the Pharaoh's military might (Ex. 15:1–18).

> When the Egyptians treated us harshly and afflicted us, by imposing hard labor on us, we cried to the Lord, the God of our ancestors; the Lord heard our voice and saw our affliction, our toil, and our oppression. The Lord brought us out of Egypt with a mighty hand and an outstretched arm, with a terrifying display of power. (Deut. 26:6–8)

Divine power undergirding the powerless is visible in tales as varied as the deliverance of the baby Moses in the waters of the Nile and the reversal of odds in David's conquest of Goliath. It is particularly emphasized in the Old Testament passage that prefigures Mary's Magnificat, the prayer of Hannah.

> The bows of the mighty are broken
>   but the feeble gird on strength . . .
> [The LORD] raises up the poor from the dust;
>   he lifts up the needy from the ash heap,
> to make them sit with princes
>   and inherit a seat of honor. (1 Sam. 2:4, 8)[27]

God exercises power in a manner that leaves God at risk and vulnerable. A God who shares power with others is a God who relinquishes the illusion of control for the sake of an openness in regard to what transpires within the cosmos. This engenders, according to Fretheim, "a divine vulnerability, as God takes on all the risks that authentic relatedness entails."[28]

This is clearly a controversial notion, but it appears to follow from what has previously been examined about the understanding of God's power in the Old Testament. Fretheim states that "the future of the created order is made dependent in significant ways upon the creaturely use of power," and how Israel responds to the divine lure contributes even also to "the future of God," not just to its own future.[29]

But Fretheim is by no means the first or only biblical scholar to become cognizant of this motif. Heschel was aware that God is "moved and affected by what happens in the world, and reacts accordingly. . . . This notion that God can be intimately affected, that he possesses not merely intelligence and will, but also pathos, basically defines the prophetic consciousness of God,"[30]

Furthermore, in the divine encounter with Moses at the burning bush, God discloses God's name: "I AM WHO I AM" (Ex. 3:14). In the traditions of Israel's era, to have a name for someone is to have some degree of power over that individual. In that understanding, then, God's revealing of God's name to Moses represents God's willing relinquishment of invulnerability. This correlation of naming and divine vulnerability has been widely recognized for some time.[31]

Human beings can challenge God's exercise of divine power and accuse God of abusing that power. When the wanderers in the wilderness lose faith in their Deliverer and mold a golden calf to worship in God's place, God's wrath waxes hot against them and God expresses to Moses the intent to consume them utterly (Ex. 32:1–10). But Moses dares to intercede on the people's behalf.

> "O LORD, why does your wrath burn hot against your people, whom you brought out of the land of Egypt with great power and with a mighty hand? Why should the Egyptians say, 'It was

with evil intent that he brought them out to kill them in the mountains, and to consume them from the face of the earth'? Turn from your fierce wrath; change your mind and do not bring disaster on your people." (Ex. 32:11–12)

Job rails against the manner in which divine power has been directed explicitly against his wellbeing (Job 6–7, 16–17).

> I will not restrain my mouth;
>   I will speak in the anguish of my spirit;
>   I will complain in the bitterness of my soul. (7:11)

The testimony of the Book of Job is a troubling one because there is in fact no satisfactory resolution of Job's challenges at all. In the end, God simply overwhelms Job—in essence, shouts him down, reversing the text just quoted: "I lay my hand on my mouth" (40:4). But the challenge itself remained in the canon for all to read and take note of.

The most extreme instance of a challenge to God's power in the Old Testament is no less than the charge of rape and defilement made by Jeremiah. The language in Jer. 20:7, "O LORD, you have enticed me . . . you have overpowered me," utilizes the terminology (*patah*) of "manipulative or violent sexual exploitation."[32] The point of the testimony is not that God is a manipulative or deceiving deity; it is that it is not beyond the pale of possibility to *accuse* God of so behaving. That is but one more expression of the consequences of the power-sharing relationship between God and world.

God is capable of a change of mind. Fretheim has called attention to nearly forty references to "divine repentance" in the Old Testament.[33] This is now more typically translated from the Hebrew as having a "change of mind" (e.g., Ex. 32:12 quoted above). The theme is a continuation of the preceding section: The consequence of a challenge to how God exercises power can indeed be a reversal of intent on God's part.

And so the culmination of Moses' reminder of how much Yahweh has already invested in the children of Abraham is that "the LORD changed his mind about the disaster that he planned to bring on his people" (Ex. 32:14). In the Jonah narrative, it is not the prophet but the outsider, the king of Ninevah, who surmises, "Who knows? God may relent and change his mind" about destroying the city, and, indeed, God does just that (Jonah 3:9–10). The writings of Jeremiah are replete with instances where God changes God's mind about disasters God had intended to bring about (Jer. 18:8, 10; 26:3, 13,19).

The underlying conviction in this pair of themes is that the God of the Old Testament is a living, dynamic power who interacts with creation often in fresh and direction-reversing ways. This is not a static power "locked in stone," a mindless supracosmic force grinding inevitably toward its intended ends. God's power is one that is ever interactive specifically with what emerges day to day in response to what God has initially set into motion.

God's interactive power is not defeated by human wrongdoing but finds unexpected ways to wring the good from out of the bad. In the extended Joseph story that brings Genesis to a close, a fascinating interpretation of events emerges. Joseph's brothers have sold him into slavery in Egypt, intending great harm to befall him. When they meet again, Joseph is hardly a slave. He has become essentially the Pharaoh's vice-regent. And he tells his brothers that he sees the hand of God in shaping the preceding course of events (Gen. 45:4–9).

A simple way of unpacking this would turn God into the divine puppet-master and Jacob's children merely puppets unknowingly carrying out the divine intent. An alternative understanding that is more faithful to the biblical witness overall is that this is one poignant instance of God's capacity to turn what humans intend for evil into something empowering. Gerhard von Rad considers this "the primary subject of the whole story: God's will to turn all the chaos of human guilt to a gracious purpose."[34]

God's power can also be experienced as destructive, as a manifestation of God's wrath. Brueggemann is one who has given extended attention to Israel's "unsolicited" testimony that the God who creates is also a God who can and does wreak destruction.[35] Beyond the wholesale destruction brought on by the Great Flood comes the devastating of Sodom and Gomorrah and all their inhabitants (Gen. 19:24–25) and the unleashing of a host of plagues against all of Egypt, guilty and innocent alike (Ex. 7:14–12:32). One way of receiving this testimony is to observe Israel's absolute resistance to the notion that any divine power other than Yahweh's is ever at work in destructive events. But it is also an acknowledgment that Yahweh's wrath is fierce and can have vivid consequences. The prophecies of Isaiah begin with this jolting reminder:

> Hear, O heavens, and listen, O earth;
>   for the Lord has spoken:
> I reared children and brought them up,
>   but they have rebelled against me . . .
> Therefore says the Sovereign, the LORD of hosts,
>   the Mighty One of Israel:
> Ah, I will pour out my wrath on my enemies,
>   and avenge myself on my foes! (Is. 1:2, 24)

The prophets proclaim God's wrath to be the consequence of Israel's failure to live faithfully within the covenant. It is the flip side of God's love, the result of the recipients of that love failing abysmally to live up to their part of the covenantal bargain. Even so, Patrick Miller observes the "priority of the Lord's compassion" as the context in which divine wrath is presented. "The intercession of the prophet works precisely because it is grounded in the character of God who is bent toward mercy and compassion, not toward anger and punishment."[36] And Second Isaiah assures his readers that wrath does not have the last word; it shall eventually cease.

> Thus says your Sovereign, the LORD,
>   your God who pleads the cause of his people:
> See, I have taken from your hand the cup of staggering;
> you shall drink no more
>   from the bowl of my wrath. (Is. 51:22)

God may elect to withhold power until it is to be exercised at some later time. Apocalyptic visions supplanted prophetic hearings toward the end of the Old Testament period and on into the Intertestamental era. They show up in Daniel and Ezekiel and elsewhere, and even put in an early appearance in the collection of oracles in Isaiah 24–27. The collapse of prophetic voices interpreting God's work among the people leads to the psalmist's lament:

> We do not see our emblems;
> > there is no longer any prophet,
> > and there is no one among us who knows how long.
> How long, O God, is the foe to scoff?
> > Is the enemy to revile your name forever?
> Why do you hold back your hand;
> > why do you keep your hand in your bosom? (Ps. 74:9–11)

The "holding back" of God's "hand" clearly expresses a sense that somehow the mighty hand of God can no longer be discerned in the course of human events. Among the welter of specific and often conflicting details, this is an overarching theme of the apocalyptic point of view: God has withdrawn. God can no longer be counted on in making sense of what is happening.

But this is understood to be only a temporary lapse. There will eventually come the "day of the Lord" (Joel 1:15; 2:11, 31; Eze. 30:3; Zep 1:7) when the power of God is promised to return, to overtrump all earthly adversity. That understanding is a significant part of the background to the Gospel witness in the New Testament.

All of these individual subthemes are expressions of the power of a living God. The various aspects of Israel's testimony to the power of God in the Old Testament can hardly be boiled down to one all-encompassing statement. But this much can be observed: They all witness to the understanding of a God who is dynamically alive. "My soul thirsts for God, for the living God," says the psalmist (Ps. 42:2); "my heart and my flesh sing for joy to the living God" (84:2). "But the LORD is the true God; he is the living God," Jeremiah proclaims (Jer. 10:10). It is this characteristic of God's being that we must be wary of losing sight of as we continue our conceptual journey.

TESTIMONY TO GOD'S LOVE

Hosea is outraged. The covenant people of the northern kingdom have proven unfaithful. The monarchy is in chaos. The powers that be, such as they are, continually attempt alliances with foreign nations, be it Egypt or Assyria. Into such a morass steps the earliest of the "writing prophets" of the Old Testament with a trio of extended metaphors that warn of God's visitation of wrath but culminate with an incredible and wholly unexpected reassurance: God's love will triumph!

The first two metaphoric narratives in chapters 1–3 are probably parallel versions of the same symbolic event. Hosea understands himself to be called to take as wife a woman of ill repute—a whore, an adulteress—by whom he fathers three children with symbolic names: the Punished One (*Jezreel*), No Mercy (*Lo Ruuhamah*), and Not My People (*Lo Ammi*) (1:6–9). The allusions are obvious ones: So have God's liberated covenant-partners behaved. They have gone whoring after other gods (1:2; 9:1). The covenant has been violated to the degree that the relationship seems forever severed: "for you are *not* my people and I am *not* your God" (1:9, emphasis added; also 1:10).

The terms of the metaphor in chapter 11 shift from faithful husband and faithless wife to dismayed father and rebellious child.

> When Israel was a child, I loved him,
> and out of Egypt I called my son.
> The more I called them,
> the more they went from me . . .
> I led them with cords of human kindness,
> with bands of love.
> I was to them like those
> who lift infants to their cheeks.
> I went down to them and fed them. (11:1–2, 4)

The intimacy of these verses is striking. God's tender love in the exodus and the wilderness years is akin to the actions of a nurturing, nursing mother. But God's people have now turned away, and the consequences in terms of the execution of God's terrifying wrath are sure to be catastrophic.

> They shall return to the land of Egypt,
> and Assyria shall be their king,
> because they have refused to return to me.
> The sword rages in their cities,

> it consumes their oracle-priests,
>   and devours because of their schemes.
> My people are bent on turning away from me.
>   To the Most High they call,
>   but he does not raise them up at all. (11:5–7)[37]

However, Hosea's understanding of God is far too complex simply to let divine anger and wrath have the final say. On the way to a resolution, there is, as it were, a pause, to ponder the scope of God's vexation. It is as though, for Hosea, God is wrestling with Godself, is almost agonizing over how to find the right way forward.

> Shall I ransom them from the power of She'ol?
>   Shall I redeem them from Death?
> O Death, where are your plagues?
>   O She'ol, where is your destruction?
> Compassion is hid from my eyes. (13:14)

It does not stay hidden. Hosea's witness in the midst of all this turmoil is the bold affirmation that the *hesed* of God is finally going to prevail above all else.

> How can I give you up, E'phra·im?
>   How can I hand you over, O Israel? . . .
> My heart recoils within me;
>   my compassion grows warm and tender.
> I will not execute my fierce anger;
>   I will not again destroy E'phra·im;
> for I am God and no mortal,
>   the Holy One in your midst,
>   and I will not come in wrath. (11:8–9; cf. 14:4–9)

Hosea contrasts God's steadfast *hesed* with human love, which is variable and unreliable, saying to the people, "Your love is like a morning cloud, like the dew that goes away early" (6:4), whereas the first story of Israel as faithless wife culminates with the husband-God expressing the intent to "take you for my wife in righteousness and in justice, in steadfast love, and in mercy" (2:19).

The most important Hebrew word for love, *hesed*, is typically translated into English with the qualifier "steadfast." But that adjective alone hardly exhausts the scope of its meaning. This is particularly an understanding of God's love that is rooted in the covenant, so that it may also be identified as "covenant love." In the very ancient Song of Moses, this is quite clear. "In your steadfast love you led the people whom you redeemed" (Ex. 15:15). God's loving relationship with God's people in the covenant is so vital that this aspect of God alone is offered up as a resolution to the mystery of "why." Why this people? Why the children of Abraham? The Deuteronomist's answer is that Israel was chosen simply "because the Lord loved you" (Deut. 7:8; see also 10:15).[38]

And so we see that, from God's side, *hesed* is love that endures through all adversity. It is the overarching context within which the merely temporary consequences of God's righteous wrath are experienced.[39] In contrast to the behavior of the covenant people, it is love that is not fickle or transient. And it is surely a love that is not dependent upon the lovability, or lack of it, of the one who is loved.

Hesed is also understandable as the fundamental motive in the act of creation itself. The unflagging endurance of *hesed* becomes the staccato refrain punctuating the recital of God's creating and liberating activity in Psalm 136. The theologian Jürgen Moltmann is the one to whom I'm indebted for using the phrase *creatio ex amore*, "creation out of love."[40] I regard this as an avenue of thought well worth pursuing, and I consider it a far more biblical notion than the traditional *creatio ex nihilo*, which misinterprets Gen. 1:1–2. It is not at all inappropriate to see God's *hesed* as underlying the very act of initial as well as continuing creation. And so God's *hesed* is also "creative love."

It is no doubt within that context that we can appreciate the testimony of the psalmists that "the earth is full of the steadfast love of the Lord" (Ps. 33:5)[41] The psalmists and others speak of the "abundance" of God's *hesed* throughout the lands (Ps. 106:45; Neh. 9:17; Lam. 3:32). Although rooted for Israel in the experience of covenant, God's love flows out from there into the whole of God's cosmic realm. It is boundless.

THE CONJOINING OF GOD'S POWER AND GOD'S LOVE

The Psalms abound with intentional juxtapositions of divine power and love.

> Once God has spoken;
> > twice have I heard this:
>
> that power belongs to God,
> > and steadfast love belongs to you, O Lord. (Ps. 62:11–12)
>
> So I have looked upon you in the sanctuary,
> > beholding your power and glory.
>
> Because your steadfast love is better than life,
> > my lips will praise you. (63:2–3)[42]

Psalms 98 and 100 particularly integrate the kingly power of God with God's *hesed*. The hymns to God's mighty deeds are not limited to past and present actions: "with the Lord there is steadfast love, and with him is great power to redeem" (Ps. 130:7). Edwin Good went so far as to conclude, concerning such passages as these, that for the Old Testament witness and for the psalmists in particular, "love is the character of God's judgment and is *the mode in which he exercises his power.*"[43]

Walther Eichrodt went further than any other recent Old Testament scholar in focusing on this important interrelationship of power and love. He saw that Hosea lifts up admirably "*the quite irrational power of love as the ultimate basis of the covenant relationship.*"[44] For Hosea, "love is part of the perfection of Yahweh's nature and a basic element in holiness. . . . in the end, it is *the incomprehensible creative power of love which marks Yahweh as the wholly 'other',* the one whose nature is in complete contrast to that of the created cosmos."[45] Eichrodt utilized provocative but undeveloped phrasing to identify this union, writing of Hosea's "vision of love as the ultimate and decisive power"[46] and insisting that "Love is the effective power in the saving stipulations of the covenant."[47]

Eichrodt never unpacked this coupling to characterize any understanding of how God's love itself is also power. But I am indebted to him for daring to articulate the notion as part of his analysis of the Old Testament witness.

More recently, Walter Brueggemann has pushed the conceptual envelope with his commentary on two parallel formulae that assert Yahweh's "incomparability": "Who is like you?" (e.g., Ex. 15:11), a rhetorical question addressed to Yahweh, and the echoing answer, "There is none like you" (Ps. 86:8).[48] Bruegggemann considers the divine incomparability to be a fundamental uniting of power and solidarity, and maintains not that it is expressed throughout the Old Testament but "only that it is Israel's most extreme witness about God," assumed though not verbalized everywhere in Israel's testimony.[49]

I would maintain that the formula is equally expressible as a union of power and *hesed*. Consider the wording of the first text Brueggemann puts forth in support of his analysis, a portion of the Song of Moses:

> "Who is like you, O LORD, among the gods?
>   Who is like you, majestic in holiness,
>   awesome in splendor, doing wonders?
> You stretched out your right hand,
>   the earth swallowed them.
> In your steadfast love you led the people whom you redeemed;
>   you guided them by your strength to your holy abode."
>   (Ex. 15:11–13)

The explicit terminology of God's love does not appear in the next two texts he identifies (Ps. 35:10, 113:5–8), though that is implied in the delivering of the weak and needy, the raising of the poor from the dust. It does return, however, in the final text, Micah 7:18–20, where God is promised to "again have compassion on us" (Mic. 7:19).

The conjoined language of power and love occurs once again in two of the three texts Brueggemann discusses in regard to the second formulaic expression, "There is none like you," absent only from Jer. 10:1–16 (specifically, 10:6). Power is the prevailing theme in this hymn of praise; solidarity with Israel is mentioned only at the end (10:16). But it is explicit in Solomon's prayer of dedication: "O LORD, God of Israel, there is no God like you in heaven above or on earth beneath, keeping covenant and steadfast love for your servants who walk before you with all their heart" (1 Kings 8:23). And the conjunction is strong also in Psalm 86:

> There is none like you among the gods, O Lord,
>   nor are there any works like yours . . .
> For you are great and do wondrous things,
>   you alone are God . . .
> For great is your steadfast love toward me. (Ps. 86:8, 10, 13)

In my estimation, Brueggemann's work on the paired formulae provides a vital key to understanding the Old Testament's witness to God's power and love. Power is not divine power unless it is characterized by *hesed*. Love is not divine love unless it is potent, efficacious. The two are *essentially* inseparable.

One very important consideration yet remains. The multiple meanings of *hesed* have not yet been exhausted. The still unexplored one could only surface after *hesed*'s vital conjunction with God's power has been presented. The God of covenanting, creating, enduring love is the God who "gives power and strength to his people" (Ps. 68:35). Micah is "filled with power" to proclaim God's justice (Mic. 3:8). Second Isaiah expresses this in soaring poetry:

> Have you not known? Have you not heard?
> The Lord is the everlasting God,
>   the creator of the ends of the earth.
> He does not fait or grow weary;
>   his understanding is unsearchable.
> He *gives power to the faint,*
>   *and strengthens the powerless.*
> Even youths will faint and be weary,
>   and the young will fall exhausted;
> but those who wait for the Lord shall renew their strength;
>   they shall mount up with wings like eagles,
> they shall run and not be weary,
>   they shall walk and not faint. (Is. 40:28–31, ital. mine)

Such passages as these lead me to the inescapable conclusion that the *hesed* of God in the Old Testament is understandable as no less than *empowering love*.[50] We do not have to await the life and message of Jesus of Nazareth to encounter this fundamental theme. The New Testament, and Jesus in particular, do not strike out in a radically new direction in regard to the juxtaposition of God's power and love, but bring a number of Old Testament tendencies to integrated completion. The seeds have already been sown.

ENDNOTES

1. Wolfhart Pannenberg, *Theology and the Kingdom of God* (Philadelphia: The Westminster Press, 1969), 55.

2. Terence E. Fretheim, *God and World in the Old Testament* (Nashville: Abingdon Press, 2005), 65 (hence, *GWOT*).

3. See also Jer 10:12, 27:5, 51:15. The Hebrew language did have words for the abstract concept we name "power," namely, *koch*; *hazaq*, generally translated as "be strong"; and *me'od*, "strength." But anthopomorphized language is more prevalent, such as "God's outstretched arm" and "God's mighty hand" (Jer 21:5.) I am indebted to Jon Berquist for this information.

4. The exposition of these texts forms the structure of Fretheim's *GWOT*.

5. Martin Buber, *Kingship of God*, tr. Richard Scheimann (New York: Harper & Row, 1967), 87f.

6. Buber, 89.

7. See James Luther Mays, "The God Who Reigns," in *The Forgotten God*, ed. A. Andrew Das and Frank J. Matera (Louisville: Westminster John Knox Press, 2002), 31f.

8. Bernhard Anderson, "God, OT Views of," in *The Interpreter's Dictionary of the Bible*, vol. E-J:417–30 (Nashville: Abingdon Press, 1962), 423 (hence, *IDB*).

9. Cf. the creation story in Gen. 1, where "God said . . . and it was so."

10. Anderson, 423.

11. Walther Eichrodt, *Theology of the Old Testament*, tr. J. A. Baker (Philadelphia: The Westminster Press, 1961), 231.

12. Eichrodt, 206.

13. Eichrodt, 213, ital. orig.

14. Walter Brueggemann, *Theology of the Old Testament: Testimony, Dispute, Advocacy* (Minneapolis: Fortress Press, 1997), 143, ital. orig. The conjoining of power and solidarity will be addressed further, below.

15. This is seen particularly in Gen. 1:26 where God addresses the divine council, saying "Let us" create humans in "our image, according to our likeness," though the language shifts to the singular in the following verse.

16. Fretheim, *GWOT*, 7.

17. Brueggemann, 155.

18. Bernhard W. Anderson, *From Creation to New Creation: Old Testament Perspectives* (Minneapolis: Fortress Press, 1994), 89.

19. See below.

20. Fretheim, "The Book of Genesis: Introduction, Commentary, and Reflections" (*The New Interpreter's Bible, vol. I*) (Nashville: Abingdon Press, 1994), 345f. See also *GWOT*, 49.

21. See esp. 13-22 for crucial summary statements. Abraham Heschel, in his trailblazing work on the prophetic literature, already lifted up this theme in Old Testament analysis half a century ago in his *The Prophets*, 2 vol. (New York: Harper & Row, 1962). "What the prophets proclaim is God's intimate relatedness to man" (1:219). God does not reveal godself to the prophet "in an absolute abstractness, but in a personal and intimate relation to the world" (2:3). God is "moved and affected by what happens in the world, and reacts accordingly. . . . This notion that God can be intimately affected, that he possesses not merely intelligence and will, but also pathos, basically defines the prophetic consciousness of God" (2:4).

22. Fretheim, *GWOT*, 22f. The numerous biblical texts that undergird these statements are provided there.

23. Fretheim, *The Suffering of God: An Old Testament Perspective* (Philadelphia: Fortress Press, 1984), 49.

24. Fretheim, "The Book of Genesis," 345.

25. Heschel, *The Prophets*, 1:167. See, e.g., Is. 40:29: "He gives power to the faint, and strengthens the powerless."

26. Daniel L. Migliore, *The Power of God and the Gods of Power* (Louisville: WJK Press, 2008), 43. The original is italicized.

27. Similarly Psalm 35 proclaims: "O Lord, who is like you? You deliver the weak from those too strong for them, the weak and needy from those who despoil them" (35:10). See Hans-Ruedi Weber's helpful analysis of these texts in his *Power: Focus for a Biblical Theology* (Geneva: WCC Publications, 1989), 125-31.

28. Fretheim, *The Suffering of God*, 76.

29. Ibid., 74, 47. See also 55, 75.

30. Heschel, *The Prophets*, 2:4.

31. See, e.g., Eichrodt, *Theology of the Old Testament*, 207; Walther Zimmerli, *Old Testament Theology in Outline*, tr. David E. Green (Atlanta: John Knox Press, 1978), 18: "Those who are named are vulnerable."

32. Brueggemann, *Theology of the Old Testament*, 360.

33. Fretheim, *The Suffering of God*, 17.

34. Gerhard von Rad, *God at Work in Israel*, tr. John H. Marks (Nashville, Abingdon Press, 1980), 32. See the culminating statement in Gen. 50:20: "Even though you intended to do harm to me, God intended it for good." See also Fretheim's helpful discussion of this theme in "The Book of Genesis," 646.

35. Brueggemann, *Theology of the Old Testament*, 534-51.

36. Patrick Miller, "'Slow to Anger': The God of the Prophets," in A. Andrew Das and Frank J. Matera, eds., *The Forgotten God: Perspectives in Biblical Theology* (Louisville: Westminster John Knox Press, 2002), 43f. Heschel emphasized that same point: God's *wrath* is an aspect of God's continual *care*: "God's heart is not of stone." God's intent (so Isaiah 27:3) is to have no wrath. (*The Prophets*, 2:73f.)

37. See also Hosea 2:9-13; 4:5-10; 5:1-15; 8:7-14; 10:13-15.

38. See Brueggemann, *Theology of the Old Testament*, 414-17, on God's "originary love for Israel."

39. See Ex. 34:6-7, where God is "abounding in steadfast love and faithfulness, keeping steadfast love for the thousandth generation," whereas God's anger over iniquity and sin is held only through four generations.

40. Jürgen Moltmann, *God in Creation: A New Theology of Creation and the Spirit of God* (Gifford Lectures, 1984-85), tr. Margaret Kohl (San Francisco: Harper & Row, 1985), 75f., where he quotes Dante: "From the Creator's love came forth in glory the world" (*Inferno*, I:39f.).

Thomas Oord proposes his own modified version in *The Nature of Love: a Theology* (St. Louis: Chalice Press, 2010), 133–38.

41. See also Ps. 36:5; 119:64; 145:9.

42. See also Ps. 89:1–14; 106:7–8.

43. Edwin M. Good, "Love in the OT," *IDB*, vol. K-Q:167, ital. mine.

44. Eichrodt, *Theology of the Old Testament*, 251, ital. orig. See also 253.

45. Eichrodt, 281, ital. orig.

46. Eichrodt, 253.

47. Eichrodt, 256. He continued there: "As distinct from the prophetic conception, in which the love of God is pressing forward to a completely new world order, that love is here understood as *the power which upholds the present order*, and which maintains the covenant in the character of a *restauratio*, not a *renovatio omnium*. . . . Such love shines forth unalterably like the sun in heaven and constitutes the inner strength of the eternal divine order." (ital. orig.)

48. Brueggemann, *Theology of the Old Testament*, 140–44.

49. Brueggemann, 143.

50. Fretheim takes note of the theme of "divine empowerment" in *The Suffering of God*, 75.

2

Witness to a Living God: The New Testament

The writers of the New Testament followed the precedent of the Greek translators of the Old Testament some 250 years earlier. "In classical Greek the meaning for *agape* was broad," Bernard Brady reminds us. It "was used to suggest a variety of loves, such as affection, fondness, and contentedness. The translators [of the Septuagint] probably chose this term because its use was less common and its meaning more unspecified than either *philia* or *eros*. The irony here is that a classic Greek word with a relatively unspecified meaning becomes the most well-known Greek word in the Christian vocabulary."[1]

It is not possible simply to collate *hesed* and *agape* into a single understanding, even though they are closely interrelated—and even though the New Testament language of *agape* clearly owes more to the meanings of love in the Old Testament than to the ordinary meanings of the word in the Hellenistic environment. Much of what is said about God's *agape* is consistent with the Old Testament notion of God's *hesed*, even as we notice that the scope of the covenant has been radically altered and expanded, with a new basis in the work and words of Jesus. And what we have uncovered in the depictions of God's *hesed* is given significantly new dimensions in reflecting on the role of the crucifixion in comprehending

God's power and love—no longer just a basis for power "to the weak," as we will see, but now a focus on power *in weakness* itself.

New Testament language for "power" is less anthropomorphic than what we have previously encountered. The "mighty hand" of God recedes into the background. The Greek word most commonly used to denote power is *dunamis*, from which the English word "dynamic" is derived. The *dunamis* of the "Most High" coming upon Mary generates her conception of Jesus (Lk 1:35). Jesus challenges the Sadducees that they know neither the scriptures nor the *dunamis* of God (Mt 22:29). The disciples are bidden by their risen Lord to remain in Jerusalem until they are clothed with *dunamis* "from on high" (Lk 24:49). Paul states that believers live in the *dunamis* of God (2 Cor 6:7; 13:3). And in Mt 26:64, *dunamis* is even identified as synonymous with God: "you will see the Son of Man seated at the right hand of Power."[2]

The second term, *exousia*, is slightly ambiguous, bearing the meaning both of power and of authority. Whoever receives Jesus receives from him the *exousia* to become his child (Jn 1:12), i.e., both the *authority* to be such but also the *power* so to live. Jesus granted his twelve disciples the power/authority, *exousia*, to "cast out demons" (Mk 13:15).

The conjunction of divine power and divine love that we saw emerging in the Old Testament witness comes to fruition in the New. Constants in the manner in which God is perceived in the Old are, according to Fretheim, "unsurpassably exemplified" in the New, and specifically "in the life and death of Jesus Christ."[3] Jesus is the image of the invisible God (Col. 1:15), reflecting the glory of God and bearing the very stamp of God's nature (Heb. 1:3), having become Emmanuel, God With Us (Mt. 1:23). In his uncompromised transparency to God's will, Jesus becomes the embodiment of that which was lost to humankind in the fall from innocence. Jesus is the *imago Dei* uncorrupted, so that John's Gospel can insist that, for Jesus, "Whoever has seen me has seen the Father" (14:9).[4]

In light of this realization, three provocatively new foci will occupy our immediate attention: the proclamation of the impending arrival of the *basileia tou theou*; the significance of the crucifixion (and resurrection) of Jesus for understanding the nature of divine power; and the Johannine conviction that love characterizes the very essence of God.

THE ANNOUNCEMENT OF GOD'S INBREAKING REIGN

A significant element in the background to the Gospel accounts of Jesus is the tradition of apocalyptic literature in which God has come to be viewed as temporarily absent from the current flow of history. The prevailing Synoptic Gospel focus in Jesus' teaching[5] on the inbreaking of God's powerful and empowering reign on earth cannot be fully understood without this conceptual backdrop. Jesus shatters this theme of divine withdrawal with both a message and a lifestyle that proclaims God's intimate nearness[6] and participates in a "prolepsis"[7] of what is yet to come in fullness: The outcast is brought back into the fold, the physically impaired are made whole, the eschatological banquet of inclusivity is experienced here and now.[8] And yet, these are only foretastes.

Luke echoes Hannah's prayer in his recounting of Mary's song of praise, the "Magnificat," but with significant new nuances. Hannah had observed that "the LORD makes poor and makes rich; he brings low, he also exalts" (1 Sam. 2:7). Mary makes the reversal of exalted and lowly, powerful and powerless, far more explicit:

> He has brought down the powerful from their thrones,
>   and lifted up the lowly;
> he has filled the hungry with good things,
>   and sent the rich away empty. (Lk 1:52–53)

It is as much promise as past fact, and its scope is far wider than what Mary is experiencing about her own radically reversed situation.

This reversal is at the heart of her son Jesus' ministry. His parables frequently end with a "punch line" that presents a challenge to conventional expectation: the scorned Samaritan is the "good" one who proves neighbor to the victim on the Jericho Road; those who come to work late at the harvest are provided the same reward as those who toiled all day; the wayward prodigal son is the one who is feasted; the prayer of a repentant sinner is more acceptable to God than that of a righteous Pharisee.[9] Shorter sayings make the same point: A camel could pass through a needle's eye more easily than a person of great wealth can enter into God's inbreaking realm (Mt 19:24).

The Synoptic Jesus' focus on the urgency of human readiness to receive God's promised *basileia* on earth is a subject of much scholarly debate regarding the tension between the signs of its arrival—the blind see, the crippled walk, as proleptic manifestations of Jesus' mediation of God's rule here and now—and the promise of a fullness of that reign yet to be consummated. In my perspective, it is not all that complicated. It is a matter of both/and, not either/or. In Jesus' message and activity, God's powerful and empowering reign of love is already making itself felt, but only in the midst of ongoing conflict between God's power of love and the forces of chaos widely at work to thwart it. On the one hand, Luke can present Jesus in the synagogue at Nazareth as proclaiming Isaiah's prophecy of release to captives, liberation of the oppressed, recovery of sight, as already fulfilled in him (Lk 4: 16–21). But, on the other hand, Mark's Jesus maintains that some within his hearing will still be alive in the near future when the *basileia* arrives *en dunamei*, "with power" (Mk 9:1), a promise unsurprisingly not repeated in the somewhat later texts of Matthew and Luke.

I have resisted using the English word "kingdom" here. I do not regard that as an adequate term for doing justice to the full meaning of *basileia*. I prefer to use "reign" or even "realm" because I believe they more fully embody the basic thrust of Jesus' teaching. If the power as well as the presence of God has been seen to be missing from the ongoing historical drama in the apocalyptic writings, there is now a concentration on this reclaimed power and presence in a strikingly novel way. It is elusive. It cannot be pinned down. It can be "lived out" symbolically in Jesus' activity in feasting with sinners, and in repudiating conventional emphases on earthly power (e.g., Jn 14:30). But it does not hold full sway. That remains but a promise. And, as we will see, Jesus' fate threatens to cancel out the validity of the promise.

Specifically, I consider it fully appropriate to characterize this inbreaking manifestation of God's power as an offer, embodied in Jesus, of the possibility that the love of God can be received in an empowering way by those open to it. It is the conjoining of power and *hesed* once again, but now in the form of an invitation to participate in God's reign of love by saying "yes" to it and being empowered to live "as if" that reign were all-in-all even though it is not.¹⁰ Love is what is expected of the recipients of God's offer: loving one another as a new covenantal commandment (Jn 13:34), love that is so embracing that it even includes one's enemies (Mt 5:43–44).¹¹

POWER IN WEAKNESS

And the promise of the arrival of God's reign of empowering love all comes crashing down, so it would appear, in Jesus' ignominious and seemingly impotent fate. He dies the death of an enemy of the state, horribly crucified at the hands of the occupying Romans.

The vital importance of the New Testament witness about Jesus' resurrection is an insistence that the work of destruction does not have the final word. God overtrumps the opposition. I cannot presume, as so many theologians do, to be able to read God's mind and insist that the cross was God's plan all along. In fact, I refuse to endorse a doctrine of divine child abuse. An early instance of the church's attempt to make sense of all this was to set forth a striking contrast of powers at work: Peter twice offers testimony in Acts that "*they* put him to death by hanging him on a tree; but *God* raised him on the third day" (10:39–40, emphasis mine; see also 5:30). Powers of control act; God counteracts.

Attention must be paid to the telling reversal of ordinary concepts of power that Paul presents in his first letter to the church at Corinth. Daniel Migliore has expressed this very cogently:

> Among the New Testament writers, it is Paul who ponders most deeply the way in which *Jesus' suffering, death, and resurrection redefine the power of God*. Paul knows well and takes with utmost seriousness the violent powers of this world. . . . In the light of the cross of Christ, however, Paul declares an even greater power. God has shown his power in a completely unexpected form. This man Jesus, crucified in weakness, is the Lord. What to human eyes is shameful, weak, and ineffective is God's own glory and strength. In a startling phrase, Paul proclaims 'God's weakness' (1 Cor. 1:25). This is an unprecedented way of speaking of the power of God, and it yields a highly paradoxical account of true power."¹²

The key texts are these: For those who are being saved, the cross is "the power of God" (1:18). Jesus Christ himself is both "the power of God and the wisdom of God" (1:24). And most critically of all, "God's weakness is stronger than human strength" (1:25). This is echoed later in the second letter to Corinth in Paul's remark that "power is made perfect in weakness" (2 Cor 12:9).

I am disappointed in most critical exegetical work on these passages that tends to gloss over the revolutionary character of Paul's insight. One exception is Victor Furnish's claim that "for Paul the saving power of God revealed in the cross is the power of God's self-giving love (cf. 2 Cor. 5.14; Rom. 5:8)," and that "in proclaiming that the cross is the place of God's definitive self-disclosure he [Paul] has identified the power that is proper to God's own being as the saving power of love."[13] That is, at least, a good start.

Finally, in this section, one further Gospel text merits comment. On Golgotha the leaders mocked the dying Jesus, taunting him: "He saved others; let him save himself if he is the Messiah of God, his chosen one" (Lk 23:35). But that is precisely the nature of the point being made here. The power of God flowing through Jesus is not something to be turned inward upon his own assurance of well-being. As Migliore has noted, "the conception of power held by those who mock Jesus is exactly the bondage from which he wants to set them free."[14] God has surrendered the illusion of over-powering control. We are still learning so to do.

"GOD IS LOVE"

John's Gospel is the one that highlights most extensively the character of God as love. It is the entire world that God loves that is understood to motivate God's having given to the world "his only Son" (3:16). "As the Father has loved me, so I have loved you" (15:9), Jesus tells his disciples. The prayer of Jesus in the Upper Room culminates in a drumbeat of repetitions concerning "the love with which you [God] have loved me" (17:26; cf. 23–25). The Father not only loves others by loving the Father's Son, but also directly "loves you" (16:27), i.e., the disciples, the ones who abide in Jesus' love.

The high point of this uniting of God and God's love comes in the first epistle attributed to John, specifically in the pronouncement in the fourth chapter that "God *is* love" (1 Jn 4:8, 16, emphasis mine). Indeed, the identity between God and love is so strong that John can maintain that we only have a capacity to love because of a sense of having first been loved by God (4:19). Love, in John's understanding, is original with God, derivative with us.

I have encountered no stronger advocate of the importance of these statements than C. H. Dodd, who insisted in light of 1 John that the Gospel is the proclamation "of God himself as love."[15] He concluded that:

> to say "God is love" implies that *all* His activity is loving activity. If he creates, He creates in love; if He rules, He rules in love; if He judges, He judges in love. All that He does is the expression of His nature, which is—to love. The theological consequences of this principle are far-reaching."[16]

I find Dodd persuasive on this point. To pass over this witness as irrelevant for theology is highly suspect, although much of the history of Christian theology betrays just this oversight.

I wish to wrap up this section by returning once again to Paul, and specifically to the tantalizing depiction in 1 Corinthians 13 of what love is and how love operates. Among other things, love is patient. Love "rejoices in the truth." Love "endures all things." And perhaps most importantly of all, love "does not insist on its own way" (13:4, 6, 7, 5).[17] This last proposition cannot be overlooked. If, indeed, God is love and God's power is characterized above all by being a power of love, then we can begin to discern that *God* does not insist on God's own way! That is not how God's power operates. It can only be seen as invitational, not impositional; offering, not controlling; undergirding, not dominating; and finally, *em*powering, not *over*powering.

How well did the church, over the centuries, maintain this key element of the biblical witness to a living, loving, empowering God? As we shall see, not well at all.

ENDNOTES

1. Bernard Brady, *Christian Love* (Washington, D.C.: Georgetown University Press, 2003), 54. Brady points out that *agape* along with its other forms occurs 341 times in the New Testament, in every single book, *philia* seldom, *eros* not at all. But he is mistaken on one key point: The translators of the Septuagint more often chose the Greek word *eleos*, "mercy," not *agape*, for the rendering of *hesed*. Having said that, it is also true that most New Testament uses of *agape* reflect *hesed* more than they reflect the other Old Testament words for love, such as the verb *'ahav* and the noun *'ahavah*. (From an email to the author from Jon Berquist, 2 Feb. 2012.)

2. Mk 14:62: "the Power." Lk 22:69 spells it out in full: "the power of God."

3. Fretheim, *The Suffering of God*, 5.

4. Pannenberg insists as a theologian that "as Christians we know God only as he has been revealed in and through Jesus. All other talk about God can have, at most, provisional significance," and "if God is revealed through Jesus Christ, then who or what God is becomes defined only through the Christ event." *Jesus—God and Man*, tr. Lewis L. Wilkens and Duane Priebe (Philadelphia: The Westminster Press, 1968), 19, 140. I contend that this is a perspective worthy of continuous attention as these investigations proceed. It is often lost sight of, even by those who promote it.

5. No attempt is intended here to establish a "historical Jesus" behind the church's telling of the Jesus story in the New Testament texts. My concern at this juncture is with the biblical witness itself, as crucial springboard for—and basis for judgment of—subsequent developments in the church's theologizing.

6. Consider the centrality of Jesus' address of God as "Father," as in the Lord's Prayer, Mt 6:9. In Mk 16:34, when Jesus is praying in Gethsemane, the original Aramaic term, *abba*, is kept in the Greek text. And *abba* is a *child's* way of addressing a father, as intimate as the English word "daddy."

7. A *prolepsis* is a sort of "happening in advance." For both Pannenberg and Moltmann, as we will encounter later, it is a "breaking in" of God's future into our present.

8. For a more extended analysis of the apocalyptic context of Jesus'

relationship to the *basileia*, see my *On the Way to God: An Exploration into the Theology of Wolfhart Pannenberg* (Lanham, Maryland: University Press of America, 1989), 187–96, 215–20.

9. See Lk 10:29–37; Mt 20:1–15; Lk 15:11–32; Mt 18:9–14.

10. Walter Wink writes of the future of God's reign as an invitation to live in God's "domination-free order" in contrast to the "domination system" to which we fallen mortals are typically in thrall, *Engaging the Powers: Discernment and Resistance in a World of Domination* (Minneapolis: Fortress Press, 1992), 46f.

11. George Johnston noted in his *IDB* article on "Love in the NT" that in the Synoptics, Jesus never explicitly states that God loves. But the implication of that is widely discernible. Jesus' observation that God cares for the lowly sparrow and that the very hairs on our head are numbered (Lk 12:6-7) "is not quaint, poetic hyperbole so much as a tender declaration of the universal and intimate character of the divine love as Jesus knew it." Vol. K–Q:169.

12. Migliore, *The Power of God and the gods of Power*, 53, ital. orig.

13. Victor Furnish, *The Theology of the First Letter to the Corinthians* (NY: Cambridge University Press, 1999), 74, 118. See also Hans-Ruedi Weber, in *Power*: "The scandal, weakness and folly of the cross turn upside down all the traditional concepts of wisdom and power," constituting a "radical reinterpretation of what true wisdom and power are" (85, 86).

14. Migliore, *The Power of God and the gods of Power*, 52.

15. C. H. Dodd, *The Johannine Epistles* (The Moffatt New Testament Commentary, vol. 14) (London: Hodder and Stoughton, 1946), 112.

16. Dodd, 110, ital. orig. See also 109, 116.

17. Furnish writes of this chapter: "the *agape* Paul commends in chapter 13 is nothing else than the enduring reality of God's own love, which the apostle understands to be revealed in the cross as God's saving power. For the apostle, this love is the reality that is proper to God's own being, and therefore an eschatological power that belongs to an order of reality which is utterly different from the passing realities of this present age" (103).

Part II

The Triumph of Power over Love

3

Encounters with the Philosophers' God

"What indeed has Athens to do with Jerusalem? What concord is there between the Academy and the Church?" Tertullian famously queried around the turn of the third century C.E. (*Prescription Against Heretics*, 7).[1] The question might just as well be turned on its head: What has Jerusalem to do with Athens?

The early encounter of the Christian witness with prevailing Hellenistic philosophical notions about the nature of God was of crucial importance in establishing the universal relevance of the Judeo-Christian story about God's dealings with humanity. To confirm its credibility, the message had to move beyond its initial eastern Mediterranean ghetto by engaging the broader social context into which it was continually expanding. *That* this interaction between biblical testimony and Greek philosophy occurred could therefore be considered a critical, even necessary, development. *How* it turned out can be seen to have corrupted essential elements of the biblical vision, especially the central notion of a dynamic, living deity for whom love is at the core of divine manifestations of power. And that, in turn, spun out unfortunate consequences that have held sway for two millennia.[2]

The focus of my investigation here was not of paramount concern to early Christian theologians and apologists. Their primary objective was to establish God's relation to Jesus, or rather, how Jesus could somehow be both visibly and fully human yet fundamentally divine, which led eventually to the development and refinement of a doctrine of the Trinity. At the same time, there were concentrated efforts to confirm God as "uncreated creator" of all that is, to recognize God's lordship over all that God has created, and to defend God's power over death by virtue of Jesus' resurrection. The climate was one of ferment and conflict, so that corrupting alternatives, such as Marcionism and other dualisms, were ardently opposed. To this short list, Jaroslav Pelikan would add the protecting of God's "otherness," particularly in regard to God's "sovereign independence."[3]

It seems at first glance that understanding God as *love* was simply a given, not requiring any special defense, because that love was so clearly manifest in the person of Jesus Christ as well as in the grace of redemption. But Robert Grant half a century ago took notice of how difficult it was for early Christian theologians "to make sense of the basic affirmation that God is love." Although, according to Grant, what characterizes the God of the gospels is "all-inclusive love," the theme of love was one that philosophical theologians treated "only with difficulty"; after the New Testament, we encounter "relatively few references to God's love" in the early Christian literature.[4] The subject of God's power, however, is an altogether different matter.

THE ASSURANCE OF DIVINE OMNIPOTENCE

EARLY EFFORTS TO CHARACTERIZE GOD'S POWER

A defense of God's absolute and unopposable omnipotence over all that God has created came to dominate non-canonical Christian theologizing from early on, even though other avenues were available to be pursued. Writing early in the second century C.E., Clement of Rome identified God as the "Master of the universe" (*1 Clement* 8:2) who oversees without dissension or opposition the divinely ordained orderliness of all that transpires in creation (20:1–12). "Nothing is impossible to God except for lying . . . By his majestic word he established the universe, and by his word he can bring it to an end" (27:2, 4) God "will do everything when he wants to and as he wants to" (27:5).[5]

Aristides of Athens, ca. 125, appears to have been the first to articulate this for Christians in specifically philosophical form. Drawing on Aristotelian tradition, Aristides wrote: "I perceived that the world and all that is therein are moved by the power of another, and I understood that he who moves them is God, who is hidden in them, and veiled by them. And it is manifest that that which causes motion is more powerful than that which is moved" (*Apology*, sec. 1). And later on he observed that Christians take from their Jewish forebears the understanding that God is "one, the Creator of all, and omnipotent" (14).[6]

A generation passed without any explicit reinforcement of a doctrine of divine omnipotence. Writers struggled to frame their understanding in more ambiguous terms. Justin Martyr lifted up the Logos of God as the means, or bridge, by which an absolute and unchanging deity can have relations with the created order. Jesus Christ is presented as the "first Power after God the Father and Master of all" (*1st Apology* 32). But this is not unlimited: Humans have "free choice" and "power of choice," within the embrace of God's perfect foreknowledge (43f.). So also, Justin's onetime pupil Tatian restricted the phrase "all power" to God's initial creative activity; God's creation, especially humanity, is not without power altogether but simply is not "of equal power with God" (*Address to the Greeks*, 5).

In his *A Plea for Christians* (177 CE), Athenagoras employed philosophical abstractions to identify God through negations of observable features of creation: God is "uncreated, eternal, invisible, impassible, incomprehensible, illimitable" (sec. 10). In respect to divine power, all Athenagoras could posit is that it is "indescribable" (10). He then went on to acknowledge that "there are other powers which surround matter and pervade it," but nothing is opposed to God to such an extent that it can obviate God's intentions: "if anything did manage to set itself up against God, it would cease to exist. It would fall to pieces by the power and might of God" (24).

So far, this appears to be the championing of divine power as superior to, though not exclusive of, all other centers of power. That is found also in the contemporaneous *Apology* that Theophilus of Antioch wrote *To Autolycus* (180 CE), where he identified God as "in power incomparable" (1.3), and "more powerful than man" (2.4). To illustrate that relationship more vividly, Theophilus drew attention to the heavenly bodies: "For the sun is a type of God, and the moon of man. And as the sun far surpasses the moon in power and glory, so far does God surpass man. And as the sun remains ever full, never becoming less, so does God always abide perfect, being full of all power . . . But the moon wanes monthly" (2.15).[7]

UNQUALIFIED OMNIPOTENCE: THE CONTRIBUTION OF IRENAEUS

It is only when we turn to Irenaeus of Lyons that we encounter full blown a philosophical defense of divine omnipotence, but precisely in Irenaeus we are dealing with a leading Christian thinker of his time whose influence was extensive.[8]

When he became bishop of the church of Lyons, in Gaul, Irenaeus saw as his primary task the championing of legitimate Christian doctrine against the corruptions of Gnostic thought, primarily by attacking the errors of Valentinus and his followers. Valentinus was active ca. 120–160 CE, from Alexandria to Rome. Irenaeus summarized Valentinus' basic position in *Against Heresies* (2.11.1) as particularly full of intermediate entities between a perfect God and this world's creation, who constitute a "Pleroma" of secondary but powerful beings that account for the far less than perfect state of creaturely affairs.

This supplies the context for Ireneaus' unequivocal insistence on the all-encompassing omnipotence of the true God of Christianity. God is "the Omnipotent" (*AH* 2.5.4), free and independent, "the Lord Omnipotent" (4.17.3,5).[9] And this is especially reflected in God's act of initial creation. For Irenaeus, in contrast to his heretical opponents, God worked with nothing already extant when God began to create. The "raw materials" were of God's own formulating. "God, according to His pleasure, in the exercise of His own will and power formed all things . . . out of what did not previously exist" (2.10:2). "God (being powerful, and rich in all resources) created matter itself" (2.10:3). God "Himself called into being the substance of His creation" (2.10:4). So therefore, if God the Creator "made all things freely, and by His own power, and arranged and finished them, and His will is the substance of all things, then he is discovered to be the one only God who created all things, who alone is Omnipotent" (2.30.9).[10]

The manner in which Irenaeus attempted to integrate God's omnipotence with God's love was essentially limited to God's redemptive activity through Jesus Christ: The love of God is manifest in that God does not leave us to our just desserts but ultimately saves us from the folly of our ways. In that respect, by far the most extensive references in Irenaeus to divine love name not the Father but the Son; the one who is "a most holy and merciful Lord, who loves the human race" is precisely the Savior (3.18.6). Even so, one passage does tie the two foci together: It is explicitly through God's "love and power" that God "shall overcome the substance of created nature" (4.38.4). The distinction that later follows this is that the Creator "is, in respect to His love, the Father; but in respect to His power, He is Lord" (5.17.1).

THE FLOWERING OF THE PHILOSOPHICAL DIALOGUE AT ALEXANDRIA

For Clement of Alexandria, writing toward the end of the second century C.E., philosophy is "the handmaid of theology," given to the Greeks as preparation for Christ in a manner similar to the Law being given to the Hebrews (*Stromata*, 1:5). In this perspective he was following a trail first blazed by a fellow Alexandrian a century and a half earlier, the Jewish philosopher Philo, a contemporary of Jesus who attempted to clothe the Septuagint in amenable patterns from Greek philosophy, particularly Platonism.[11] His synthetic effort is echoed throughout the corpus of Clement's writings, which are far less systematic in approach than one would wish; the *Stromata* ("Miscellanies") is less an orderly treatment of theological topics than a series of notes woven into a tapestry whose warp and woof are difficult to discern.[12]

Concerning God, Clement pursued two fundamental principles: that God is beyond the reach even of abstract human language and therefore must be identified by what God is not, but that, at the same time, God must be understood as "the omnipotent God" (*Stromata*, 1.24): "Nothing withstands God, nothing opposes Him: seeing He is

Lord and omnipotent" (1:17). This is cogently articulated in a passage meriting quotation at length because of how it summarizes in one place the relationship of these two basic affirmations:

> This discourse respecting God is most difficult to handle. For since the first principle of everything is difficult to find out, the absolutely first and oldest principle, which is the cause of all other things being and having been, is difficult to exhibit. For how can that be expressed which is neither genus, nor difference, nor species, nor individual, nor number, nay more, is neither an event or that to which an event happens? No one can rightly express Him wholly. For on account of His greatness, He is ranked as the All, and is the Father of the universe. Nor are any parts to be predicated of Him.
>
> For the One is indivisible; wherefore also it is infinite, not considered with reference to inscrutability, but with reference to its being without dimensions, and not having a limit. And therefore it is without form and name.
>
> And if we name it, we do not do so properly, terming it either the One, or the Good, or Mind, or Absolute Being, or Father, or God, or Creator or Lord. We speak not as supplying His name; but for want, we use good names, in order that the mind may have these as points of support, so as not to err in other respects. For each one by itself does not express God, but all together are indicative of the power of the Omnipotent. (5.12)

The crux of the matter is that God is conceived to be beyond division or parts, beyond dimensions, beyond individuation, beyond form, not properly identified by any name—but wholly *power* without qualification or limitation.

A PHILOSOPHICAL COUNTERPOINT

ORIGEN AND THE LIMITS ON DIVINE POWER

Clement's successor and theological superior at Alexandria was Origen, who began teaching at the tender age of eighteen when his tutor had to flee to avoid the latest round of persecutions. He eventually penned the systematic treatise that his teacher had aspired to but never completed, entitled *On First Principles*. In it, toward the outset (1.2.10), Origen offered an extended analysis of the nature of divine omnipotence. Since there was never a time when God was not almighty, and since God must have something over which to exercise power in order to be deemed omnipotent, then God already contained the universe somehow within Godself. Quoting Psalm 104:24 that "'thou has made all things in wisdom'," and identifying that wisdom with the Christ, Origen could maintain that "wisdom, through which God is called Almighty, has a share even in the glory of omnipotence. For it is through wisdom, which is Christ, that God holds power over all things." So the omnipotence of Father and Son "is one and the same," and Jesus as Lord is "glorified as being the effluence of omnipotence." And what is this "glory of omnipotence"? It is God the Father holding "dominion over all things," a dominion he "exercises through his Word." Thereupon Origen concluded by asserting: "this is the purest and brightest glory of omnipotence, that the universe is held in subjection *by reason and wisdom, and not by force and necessity*."[13]

This implicit modification of divine omnipotence, subjugating it to divine "reason and wisdom," hints at the direction in which Origen was moving. Sheer exercise of power somehow does not get at the heart of what characterizes God's activity. "This blessed and ruling power," he went on to declare, "is the good God and kindly Father of all, at once *beneficent power and creative power*, that is, *the power that does good and creates and providentially sustains* . . . these powers which are in God, nay, which *are* God."[14] Therefore, divine omnipotence does not compel or overpower. God "has so ordered everything that each spirit or soul . . . should not be compelled by force against its free choice to any action except that to which the motions of its own mind lead it."[15] With all these caveats against unqualified omnipotence being laid down like stepping stones to a new horizon of view, Origen finally arrived at a provocative conclusion: "we must maintain that even the power of God is finite, and we must not, under pretext of praising him, lose sight of his limitations."[16] Therefore he warned toward the very close of his treatise, "let no one take offence at the saying, if we put limits even to the power of God."[17]

A PATH NOT TAKEN: PERSUASIVE POWER IN PLATO'S *TIMAEUS*

Origen's mental wrestling with the qualified character of divine power already had a close kinsman in Plato in the dialogue known as the *Timaeus*, from the sixth century BCE. The work was in wide circulation among the philosophically minded Christians of the period under discussion here, although I have found no indication that Origen drew on its intriguing propositions.

Plato presented two orders of existence: that which *is*, i.e., *being*, which is unchanging and eternal and is "always real" (e.g., the Platonic forms), and that which becomes (*génesis*) "and is never real."[18] He then introduced a concept of initial creation of "that which becomes" that echoes closely the insights of Genesis 1:1–2 far to the south in Judea: creation as an act of bringing order out of chaos. "Desiring, then, that all things should be good and, so far as might be, nothing imperfect, the god [Demiurge] took over all that is visible—not at rest, but in discordant and unordered motion—and brought it from disorder into order."[19]

We have already seen how defending God's omnipotence required the development of a doctrine of *creatio ex nihilo* in Theophilus and Irenaeus, a notion not at all explicit in Genesis 1:2 where, when God began to create, all was "a formless void." The terms Plato used are very different: "Reason" and "Necessity." Necessity is responsible for that which arises by chance, "at random and without order."[20] In a very real sense, it is the "given" upon which the Demiurge worked his "rational" activity of bringing order out of chaos. Thereupon Plato wrote: "the generation of this universe was a mixed result of the combination of Necessity and Reason. Reason overruled Necessity by *persuading* her to guide the greatest part of things that become toward what is best; in that way and on that principle this universe was fashioned in the beginning by *the victory of reasonable persuasion over Necessity.*"[21]

This focus on divine power as persuasive, not coercive or controlling or overpowering, is harmonious with what we have already observed in the biblical witness, though it is a path not trod by any but a few of the early Christian synthesizers of Hellenistic philosophical thought. The one place where the exception is clearly visible is in the anonymous *Letter to Diognetus* from the mid-second century CE, where

God's use of persuasive and not coercive power is affirmed in regard to how God leads wayward humanity to salvation: The invisible God, the Ruler and Creator of all, sent "the Designer and Maker of the universe himself, by whom he created . . . like a king sending his son who is himself a king. He sent him as God; he sent him as man to men. He willed to save man by persuasion, not by compulsion, for compulsion is not God's way of working."[22]

"WHAT'S LOVE GOT TO DO WITH IT"[23]—DIVINE IMPASSIBILITY

OPENINGS TOWARD THE RETENTION OF GOD AS LOVE

Nowhere in the biblical witness do we find an assertion that "God is power." Power is certainly something that God wields, as we have encountered from the very outset. But 1 John does contain the bold proclamation, "God is love" (4:8,16), as we have seen. And the everlasting love that God has for God's covenant people, articulated throughout the Old Testament, comes to fruition for Christians in the embodiment of divine love manifest in Jesus Christ. What, then, became the fate of this key element of biblical understanding when his followers attempted to incorporate the insights of Hellenistic philosophy into their worldview? Did it remain at the center of the being and activity of a dynamic, living deity, or did it become reduced to something quite otherwise?

Let children be taught that love itself has power, Clement of Rome proposed (*1 Clement* 21:8). He went on to sing love's praises (49, 50) with phrases that echo 1 Corinthians 13, observing that "the bond of God's love" (49:2) is what unites God and us, so that "you see, brothers, how great and amazing love is, and how its perfection is beyond description" (50:1). A very soft expression is found in Aristides of Athens who observed that Christians "know the loving-kindnesses of God toward them" (*Apology*, XVI). And the writer of the *Letter to Diognetus* noted that God gave up God's Son "to show at last his goodness and power. O the overflowing kindness and love of God toward man!" (9:2).

Intriguingly, the most extensive assertions of the preeminence of God's love seem to have been made by those whom the church came to vilify as proponents of heresies. Hippolytus of Rome, early in the third century c.e., referenced the gnostic Valentinus as having followed 1 John in naming God as "wholly love," in relation to which "love is not love unless there is something loved."[24]

The case of Marcion is somewhat complex. He was active early in the second century CE and is well known for having posited not one but two Gods, one represented in the Old Testament and seen as responsible for the world's creation, the other encountered only in the New Testament in the teaching of Jesus and specifically in the theology of Paul. Our access to his work is essentially through the writings of those who opposed him, most extensively in Tertullian's *Against Marcion*.

Over a century ago, Adolf von Harnack interpreted this contrast in terms of "the good God of love" over against the creator God.[25] But Harnack also noted that Marcion's recurring Latin expression for the former was "solius bonitatis,"[26] that is, "only good." Are "goodness" and "love" synonymous terms? Jaroslav Pelikan is more cautious, recognizing that Marcion's God of "simple goodness," per Tertullian, is characterized by "serenity and mildness"[27] and not by any active expression of powerful love. Even so, Marcion clearly tried to lift up a God of sublime benevolence for the alternative church he founded, but he was able to do so only by sacrificing the essential unity between love (his Supreme God) and power (his unloving Creator God).[28]

THE HEAVY BURDEN OF THE DOCTRINES OF GOD'S IMMUTABILITY AND IMPASSIBILITY

The prevailing winds that blew through the doctrinal formulations of the early centuries of the church were jarring nor'easters insofar as any biblical insight into a dynamic and interactive God of love is concerned. Conceptual wreckage was left in their wake. This is especially apparent when questions of change and passion were raised concerning the essential being of God.

The issue arose early.[29] Justin wrote of the "impassible God" in his *First Apology* (sec. 25). The Greek word is *apathes*, akin to the English "apathetic," conveying an absence of passion, an unfeeling indifference. Athenagoras, as we saw earlier, echoed this in his identifying of God through negations of the known world (*A Plea for Christians*, sec. 10). Irenaeus championed this understanding explicitly: "The Father of all" is no less than "He who is impassible" (*Against Heresies*, 2.12.1).³⁰ For Clement of Alexandria, this is true both for the nature of God (*Stromata*, 2.16) and for the highest achievable good of those who would truly embody the divine image: "Endurance also itself forces its way to the divine likeness, reaping as its fruit impassibility" (2.20). In sharp contrast to the Old Testament testimonies to the wrath of God and the yearning of God for the covenant people to mend their ways, Clement wrote, "God is impassible, free of anger, destitute of desire" (4.23).

We have concentrated here on impassibility but that theme is tightly interlocked with its companion, immutability, i.e., changelessness. That God is constant in God's purposes goes without saying insofar as the biblical narratives are concerned. But we have had occasion to observe the frequency of testimony that God "changed God's mind" about this or that. So what is at work here in insisting on applying abstract philosophical concepts of immutability and impassibility to the Christian's God?

For the Greeks, change was problematic and ephemeral, less than "truly real." That can readily be discerned in Plato's notion of the eternal Forms or Ideas, which come to be varyingly embodied in passing moments but which themselves are unchanging and unaffected by how the world momentarily incarnates them. We have encountered this already in Plato's *Timaeus*.

A very close corollary has to do with how the attribute of *perfection* can be applied to divine reality. Capacity for change is impossible to a Being characterized as perfect for the simple reason that movement would necessarily occur from the less to the more perfect, or the converse. But either direction would deny any constancy of absolute perfection.

Thus, the trap the integrators of Bible and philosophy set for themselves: Inasmuch as God can never be properly conceived as less than perfect, all the qualities of ongoing dynamic interaction of God with God's creation got subsumed under categories of pure thought. Any tinge of affectedness or alteration on the part of God must be dutifully rejected. And, it was.

So, what *does* love have to do with it, insofar as God is concerned? A kernel remains, but stripped of its satisfying richness. God's love has been reduced to a stance God takes unswervingly toward the creation and fallen humanity, bereft of passion and particularity, an eternal and unchanging love utterly unaffected by the responses of the beloved. The question remains: Is that truly love?

ANOTHER PATH NOT TAKEN: INSIGHTS OF THE LATER ORIGEN

Once again, an alternative avenue of possibility presented itself to the church as a way of breaking through this conceptual logjam. Toward the end of his long career, Origen apparently experienced a change of heart of major proportions. In his *Homily on Ezekiel*, he wrote:

> What is that affection whereby on our account He [Christ] is affected? It is the affection of love. The Father Himself, too, the God of the Universe, long suffering, and of great compassion, full of pity, is not He in a manner liable to affection? Are you unaware that, when He orders the affairs of men, He is subject to the affections of humanity? . . . The very Father is not impassible [*Ipse pater non est impassibilis*], without affection. If we pray to him, He feels pity and sympathy. He experiences an affection of love. He concerns himself with things in which, by the majesty of His nature, He can have no concern, and for our sakes He bears the affections of men. (6.6)[31]

This rejection of *apatheia* as not an appropriate stance for God or for God's people was sadly bypassed as the church's thinking continued to move onward through time. The "affection of love" held insufficient appeal to those whose heads had been irreversibly turned toward idealized abstractions. Origen, for this and other idiosyncrasies such as his universalist doctrine of apokatastasis,[32] came to be identified not as orthodox but heterodox by the church's official leadership. His time would have to come later.

WHAT HAS BEEN LOST?

Colin Gunton has astutely observed that "the Christian doctrine of God is for much of its history a hybrid of two organisms," namely the biblical understanding of God as living and dynamic, and the Greek categories of absolute perfection. The doctrine of divine attributes "has often been approached using the wrong method; developing the wrong content; and even when that has not been entirely the case, treating things in the wrong order," resulting in a "tangled web" of relations between Hebrew and Greek notions.[33] This was certainly true in those initial centuries of conceptual reflection.

Wolfhart Pannenberg concluded his incisive overview of the period with the observation that one must "spare the Christian doctrine of God from the gap between the incomprehensible *essence* and the historical *action* of God, by virtue of which each threatens to make the other impossible," and went on to state that "in the recasting of the philosophical concept of God by early Christian theology considerable remnants were left out, which have become a burden in the history of Christian thought."[34]

What we have seen in this chapter is a critical loss of any incipient uniting of divine power and divine love that the biblical record endeavored to convey, with overwhelming power coming to the fore and love being reduced to something less than its biblical richness of insight and imagery. An absolutely powerful God for whom love is but one attribute among many is neither palatable nor biblical. The establishment of the doctrine of divine omnipotence has set the stage for problematic attempts to shoehorn love back into the portrayal of divinity without doing injustices either to the notion of love or the understandings of power. As we shall have occasion to see, those attempts were doomed from the start.

ENDNOTES

1. Quotations from the original sources in this chapter are taken from the huge trove of English translations on the easily accessible website "www.earlychristianwritings.com."

2. Wolfhart Pannenberg has rightly pointed out that Christian theology cannot subsume Christian motifs into a status of mere illustrations of a philosophical idea of God. The task of the theologian, he contends, is to engage philosophy with its own "assimilative, transforming power." "Christian theology can link up with the philosophical idea of God only

by breaking through it at the same time . . . Theology must push on to the basic elements of the philosophical idea of God and transform those elements in the critical light of the biblical idea of God." ("The Appropriation of the Philosophical Concept of God as a Dogmatic Problem of Early Christian Theology," in *Basic Questions in Theology, Volume II*, trans. George H. Kehm [Philadelphia: Fortress Press, 1971], 140, 139.) My pivotal question is indeed whether, in those initial formative centuries of theological reflection, it was rather the core of the Christian witness itself that became transformed, to its ongoing detriment. As Daniel Day Williams expressed it, "the fusing of Christian faith with Greek metaphysics was, if not a disaster, a wrong turn from which theology has yet to recover." (*The Spirit and the Forms of Love* [New York: Harper & Row, 1968], 17.)

3. Jaroslav Pelikan, *The Christian Tradition: A History of the Development of Doctrine, Vol. I: The Emergence of the Catholic Tradition (100–600)* (Chicago: The University of Chicago Press, 1971), 52.

4. Robert M. Grant, *The Early Christian Doctrine of God* (Charlottesville: University Press of Virginia, 1966), 2–4.

5. Although the technical term is nowhere used by Clement, Pannenberg—correctly, I believe—calls this "the freedom of God's active omnipotence" (op. cit., 175f.).

6. Aristides characteristically named the deity as "God Almighty"—*theos pantokrator*, in the Greek. *Pantokrator* explicitly means "ruler of all."

7. Theophilus neglected to push the analogy further in the direction that the moon (humankind) has no light/power of its own but shines only with the reflected light/power of the sun (God).

8. Pannenberg praises Irenaeus' attempts at a Christian philosophical synthesis as superior even to the Alexandrians (Clement, Origen) who followed (op. cit., 178f.).

9. For an insightful critique of Irenaeus' theology of God's power, see Richard Norris, "The Transcendence and Freedom of God: Irenaeus, the Greek Tradition and Gnosticism," in William R. Schoedel and Robert L. Wilken, eds., *Early Christian Literature and the Classical Intellectual Tradition: In Honorem Robert M. Grant* (Paris: Editions Beauchesne, 1979), 87–100.

10. Colin Gunton identifies Irenaeus as the first explicitly to expound the doctrine of *creatio ex nihilo*, in *Act and Being: Towards a Theology*

of the Divine Attributes (London: SCM Press, 2002), 26. Certainly he was the first to give it extensive emphasis, although the notion may well have been "in the air" in the latter half of the second century CE. Already Theophilus, far to the East in Antioch, wrote around the same period of time that "the power of God is manifested in this, that out of things that are not He makes whatever He pleases" (*To Autolycus*, 2.4).

11. Philo's body of work is available in English translation at www.earlyjewishwritings.com/philo.html. See also the Philo entry in the "Internet Encyclopedia of Philosophy" at www.iep.utm.edu/philo/.

12. See Justo Gonzalez, *A History of Christian Thought* (Nashville: Abingdon Press, 1970), 1:196f.

13. The quotations here are from Origen, *On First Principles*, tr. G. W. Butterworth (New York: Harper & Row, 1966), Book 1, chapter 2, paragraph 10, found on pp. 23–25. The emphasis is mine.

14. Ibid., 1.4.3 (p. 41). Again, the emphasis is my own.

15. Ibid., 2.1.2 (p. 77).

16. Ibid., 2.9.1 (p. 129). This wording is found only in an original Greek manuscript; Rufinus altered it in his Latin translation.

17. Ibid., 4.4.8 (p. 323). This so scandalized Rufinus that he omitted the passage altogether.

18. Francis M. Cornford, *Plato's Cosmology: The* Timaeus *of Plato translated with a running commentary* (London and Henbley: Routledge & Kegan Paul, 1937), 27D-28A (22).

19. Ibid., 30A (33).

20. Ibid., 46E (157).

21. Ibid., 48A (160), emphasis mine. Cornford recognized that Plato's Demiurge is anything but omnipotent (36f., 165). "The creation of the world—said Plato—is the victory of persuasion over force," according to Alfred North Whitehead in *Adventures of Ideas* (New York: Macmillan, 1933), 90. Plato "does finally enunciate without qualification the doctrine of the divine persuasion" (170).

22. "Letter to Diognetus," tr. Eugene R. Fairweather, 7.2,4, in Cyril C. Richardson, ed., *Early Christian Fathers,* vol. I of *The Library of Christian Fathers* (Philadelphia: The Westminster Press, 1953), 218f.

23. The quote is the title of a song written by Terry Britten and Graham

Lyle (1984) and made famous by the singer Tina Turner.

24. Hippolytus, *Against All Heresies*, 6.29.6. See Grant's brief discussion in *The Early Christian Doctrine of God*, 35.

25. Harnack, Adolf, *History of Dogma*, tr. Neil Buchanan (NY: Dover Publications, 1961), I:272.

26. Ibid., 272, ft. 2.

27. Pelikan, *The Christian Tradition*, I:74, quoting Tertullian, *Against Marcion*, 1.25 (see also *AM* 1.6). See Pelikan's excellent summary of Marcion's theology, I:71–81.

28. Tertullian's own position over against the errors of Marcion was the championing of the one God who is both "wholly goodness" and completely "omnipotent . . . able both to help and to hurt." Such a God is both "perfect father" and "perfect master: a father in His mercy, a master in His discipline; a father in the mildness of His power, a master in its severity; a father who must be loved . . . a master who must needs be feared" (*AM* 2.13). This is wholly alien to the observation in 1 John 4:18 that "there is no fear in love, but perfect love casts out fear."

29. See the brief summary of this topic in Grant, *The Early Christian Doctrine of God*, Appendix II, "The Impassibility of God," 111–14.

30. See also *AH* 2.18.6 Even though he acknowledged that Christ truly suffered (*AH* 3.18.6), Irenaeus found himself having to affirm that the Logos, consistently with the Father, "must be perfect and impassible" (2.17.7) as well.

31. This will come back onto play only in the late twentieth century, particularly in the work of Jürgen Moltmann.

32. This is the doctrine of the universal restoration of all in God's creation that has fallen from grace. A shorthand way of expressing it is that, in the end, "even the Devil will be saved." It is a provocative but propitious point of view because it asserts, in essence, that anything less can be understood to be a denial of the all-encompassing power of God's love!

33. Gunton, *Act and Being*, 2, 8.

34. Pannenberg, *BQT* II:181f.

4

The Establishment of Almighty God

The early fourth century CE saw a tectonic shift in the fortunes of the oppressed but ever growing Christian community: The emperor Constantine handed over the reins of religious leadership in his empire to the church.

One might readily surmise that the course of that century would bring forth significant theological developments demonstrating the connection between the power of God reigning in heaven and imperial power being wielded on earth. But that was not the case.[1] The two overriding issues occupying the attention of the church's theologians were the definitive formulating of a doctrine of the Trinity and the resolving of christological issues deriving from that. At the same time, the new official status of the church allowed an imposing of orthodox positions against all the losing sides, backed by imperial Rome. The time for freewheeling explorations into alternative theological possibilities of understanding was now in the past.

This chapter presents and evaluates the relevant contributions of two champions of this victorious theological synthesis: the Cappadocian Gregory of Nyssa in the East, and the brilliant but flawed work of perhaps the West's greatest theologian, Augustine of Hippo.

TRINITARIAN CONSOLIDATIONS IN THE EAST: GREGORY OF NYSSA

Gregory of Nyssa (ca. 334) was the younger brother of Basil of Caesarea and a good friend of another Gregory, of Nazianzus, the three together known in history as the Cappadocian Fathers. All three being elevated to bishoprics, Basil was the abler administrator, and the Nazianzen was the more eloquent orator. But the Nyssen was by far the most outstanding theologian of the three, wherefore it is to his work that I wish primarily to direct our attention.

The Cappadocian Fathers crystallized the trinitarian debates that followed the Council of Nicaea with formulations that found wide favor in ensuing epochs. Their fundamental position can be readily summarized from the *Five Theological Orations* (ca. 380) of Gregory of Nazianzus.[2] There he affirmed the absolute unity of God's essence (*ousia*), discerned by us in an interlocking trio of distinct but equal relations,[3] identified as *hypostases* or "persons." This dance of internal divine relations—accessible to us only by virtue of the incarnation of God in Jesus the Christ and the subsequent witness of the church to the gifts of God's enlivening Spirit—is between the unbegotten Father and the begotten Son, but also equally and essentially including the Holy Spirit who "proceeds" from the Father. In this understanding, there is no "before" of God that does not entail this Trinity of divine relations.

Does this positing of a unified God impacting us and the world in a Trinity of relations provide helpful insights into the subject of this inquiry, the relationship between God's power and God's love? The first point that must quickly be conceded is that whatever may be said of the attributes of one person in the relational triad must be affirmed of all three. The Father alone is not powerful, even in initial creation, which occurred according to John 1:3 as in and through the Word (Son). The Son alone is not loving, and so on.[4] "Christ," Gregory of Nyssa affirmed in *An Answer to Ablabius* (ca. 380), "is the power of God," but by this same principle, "power is a unity in Father, Son, and Holy Spirit."[5]

Gregory then went on to maintain that "the divine nature is unlimited and incomprehensible . . . altogether infinite," and that "infinity entirely transcends limitation."[6] His explorations surrounding this claim center on divine activity and the power by which that activity is operative. Infinite power, by extension, utterly transcends limitation.

Does this also apply to *love*? Does God's infinite love utterly transcend limitation? That focus is absent from the discussion here, but it receives attention elsewhere, where Gregory tried to integrate these two aspects of divine reality. In his *Address on Religious Instruction* some three years later, he recognized the *self*-limiting dimension of God's unlimited power:

> It is universally agreed that we should believe the Divine to be not only powerful, but also just and good and wise and everything else that suggests excellence. It follows, therefore, in the plan of God we are considering, that there should not be a tendency for one of his attributes to be present in what happened, while another was absent. For not a single one of these sublime attributes by itself and separated from the others constitutes virtue. What is good is not truly such unless it is associated with justice, wisdom, and power . . . Power, too, if it is separated from justice and wisdom, cannot be classed as virtue. Rather it is a brutal and tyrannical form of power.[7]

God's inherent *goodness* is a far more typical emphasis in Gregory (and in these early centuries overall) than God's love. Even so, the conjoining of power and love explicitly is identified several paragraphs later. In the Gospel story, Gregory wrote,

> *the union of power with love* for man is displayed. In the first place, that the omnipotent nature was capable of descending to man's lowly position is a clearer evidence of power than great and supernatural miracles. For it somehow accords with God's nature, and is consistent with it, to do great and sublime things by divine power. It does not startle us to hear it said that the whole creation, including the invisible world, exists by God's power, and is the realization of his will. But descent to man's lowly position is a supreme example of power—or a power which is not bounded by circumstances contrary to its nature.[8]

In these reflections, Gregory saw the love of God displayed rather particularly in God's activity through the Son to grant eternal salvation beyond our mortal life on Earth by virtue of the "superabundance of Omnipotence" displayed in the resurrection.[9] But this activity in no way affects God's own being, which is eternally perfect and therefore not subject to change.[10] This doctrine of divine immutability denies any interactivity on the part of God's love (except internally, in the relations of the Trinity), which led him to conclude: "in order that the Supreme Being may not appear to have any connection whatever with things below, we use, with regard to His nature, ideas and phrases expressive of His separation from all such conditions; we call . . . that which is unreceptive of change, or sufferance, or alteration, *passionless*, changeless, and unalterable."[11]

And therein lies the rub. The full-blown championing of Greek categories of static supremacy has denied utterly the biblical witness to a God sublimely interactive with the cosmic forces God set in motion. Fundamental convictions have been stood on their head: God cannot appear to have *any* connection with "things below" that would reflect back on God's utter self-sufficiency. Power flows only in one way, outward from the divine. Love, similarly, flows only one way, outward from a "passionless" God who is not all affected by what and whom God loves because that would necessarily diminish God's unalterable perfection.

What we have seen bubbling to the surface in the previous centuries of Christian thought has now resulted in a distillation of pure uncontaminated divinity: power without real opposition,[12] love without real interactive engagement. One recalls the old quip about the farmer being asked directions to a traveler's destination and replying, "Well, you can't really get there from here." That's the dilemma the church set for itself. It so defined the nature of power, divine power, that one can no longer move from that place to a destination that includes any meaningful understanding of the full nature of divine love. The church, and the Western world, suffered for centuries from that wrong turn.

THE VICTORIOUS SYNTHESIS: AUGUSTINE OF HIPPO

There is no denying the astonishing breadth, depth, and brilliance of Augustine's body of work. He was the one who put it all together in a way that the church in the West has had to live with, and write footnotes on, ever since. The simple equation is that the Bible/Gospel + Plato = Augustine. The devil, of course, is in the details.

Born in 354, Augustine came late to Christian faith (age 30), as he spelled out in his *Confessions* (398). His was an intensely philosophical mind, and he struggled with the dualism and essential corporeality of Manichaeism before finding conceptual liberation in the neo-Platonism of Plotinus, who enabled him for the first time to envision a sublime reality unaffected by material corruption.[13] Apart from a few years in Italy in the 380s, he lived his life chiefly in Tagaste, Hippo (where he served as bishop), and Carthage on the Mediterranean coast of northern Africa, adjacent to today's city of Tunis. By the time he died in 430, the barbarians had sacked Rome twenty years earlier and would capture his own city shortly after his death.

In regard to the vast body of original resources available to us, Augustine recognized and called attention to his own tendency toward excessive verbiage—an exhaustiveness that itself is exhausting to the reader—in the prayer with which he closed *On the Trinity*: "I am not silent in thoughts, even when silent in words . . . set me free from such multitude of speech."[14] Of all that is varyingly valuable in the corpus of Augustine's insights, it is essential here only to lift up those components that contribute to his attempt to reconcile convincingly God's power and love. The task is not unlike that of Arthur Conan Doyle's famous detective Sherlock Holmes, who repeatedly observed the necessity of separating what is of critical importance (i.e., to our inquiry) from what is merely interesting or incidental. Much that is vitally interesting in Augustine will not receive attention here. I propose that we embark upon four intersecting avenues of exploration, with a concluding caveat.

A TRINITY OF EQUAL RELATIONS

The understanding of a triune God is at the very heart of Augustine's reflections on divinity. He did not substantially advance the Cappadocians' formulation of the doctrine of one divine essence in three "persons" or hypostases, nor was his grasp of the Greek language all that strong,[15] though he did champion emphatically the overarching significance of the *unity* of the three. His major contributions seem to lie in the numerous summations he penned but also in the way in which he defended the absolute *equality* of Father, Son, and Spirit in their relations to one another and the co-reality of *all* God's attributes in *each* member of the Trinity.

In regard to the latter, "whatsoever is said of each in respect to themselves, is to be taken of them, not in the plural in sum, but in the singular," so that it must be said, concerning greatness, or goodness, and so forth, "not three greats, but one great . . . not three goods, but one good . . . So the Father is omnipotent, the Son omnipotent, and the Holy Spirit omnipotent; yet not three omnipotents, but one omnipotent."[16]

In regard to the former, Augustine's lack of facility with Greek terminology allowed him to concentrate on the trifold distinctions within the unity of God as a matter of internal divine *relations* as opposed to the positing of three distinct "persons." At the very outset of his treatise on the Trinity, he championed both the Son's equality with the Father as well as the equality of the Holy Spirit with both. We teach, he said,

> this doctrine, that the Father, and the Son, and the Holy Spirit intimate a divine unity of one and the same substance in an indivisible equality; and therefore that they are not three Gods, but one God; although the Father hath begotten the Son, and so He who is the Father is not the Son; and the Son is begotten by the Father, and so He who is the Son is not the Father; and the Holy Spirit is neither the Father nor the Son, but only the Spirit of the Father and of the Son, Himself also co-equal with the Father and the Son, and pertaining to the unity of the Trinity.[17]

He insisted emphatically that there can be no subordination of Father over Son, reading all scriptural indications of the Son's varied limitations—e.g., John 14:28, "the Father is greater than I"—as having only to do with the human aspect of the divine-human Jesus.[18]

Further along, Augustine returned to this theme with a renewed emphasis on the internal relationships of the Holy Spirit: "So also the Holy Spirit is one with them, since these three are on . . . for the same Spirit is not without reason said to be the Spirit both of the Father and of the Son . . . For the Spirit of God is one, the Spirit of the Father and of the Son, the Holy Spirit, who worketh all in all."[19]

A TRINITY OF UNCHANGEABLE TIMELESSNESS

God's triune immutability stands at the very forefront of Augustine's pilgrimage of faith. His extended flirtation with Manichaeism had led him to struggle with the corruptibility of all substantial reality, which became a dilemma for him. He poured out his confusion to God in his *Confessions*:

> with all my heart I believed You incorruptible and inviolable and immutable, for though I did not see whence or how, yet I saw with utter certainty that what can be corrupted is lower than what cannot be corrupted, that the inviolable is beyond question better than the violable, and that what can suffer no change is better than what can be changed . . . I could not but think of You as some corporeal substance, occupying all space . . . Yet even at this I thought of You as incorruptible and inviolable and immutable, and I still saw those as better than corruptible and violable and mutable.[20]

The breakthrough came for Augustine when he read "some books of the Platonists translated from Greek into Latin."[21] He found himself liberated to a non-corporeal understanding of this divine incorruptibility, "and there was from that moment no ground of doubt in me."[22]

This became a pivotal conviction from which Augustine would not waver for the rest of his life and is the conceptual axis around which Western theology has been spinning ever since. In the corpus of Augustine's works the subject is not so much argued, through logical procession, as posited, through a myriad of analogies presumably demonstrating the superiority of immutability over being subject to change.

The strongest presentations of this theme are to be found in Books 4 and 5 of *On the Trinity* (400–428). "For the essence of God, whereby He is, has altogether nothing changeable, neither in eternity, nor in truth, nor in will; since there truth is eternal, love eternal; and there love is true, eternity true; and there eternity is loved, and truth is loved."[23] Necessarily, then, "that is not properly called eternal which undergoes any degree of change."[24] Truth itself, in true neo-Platonic understanding, "remains immortal, incorrupt, unchangeable."[25] The ultimate conclusion follows: "He who is God is the only unchangeable substance or essence, to whom certainly being itself . . . most especially and most truly belongs."[26]

Out of this central proclamation arises the corollary of God's essential *timelessness*. Time, of course, is the arena in which change continually occurs. But if God were subject to the sequentially of time, would God not then be subject to change? Absolutely: "nothing happens accidentally to God in time, because He is incapable of change,"[27] Augustine affirmed in his magisterial *City of God* (413–426). Rather, God is outside of and, of course, not affected by time, working "visible miracles" consistent with "his unchanging counsel, in whose plan all future events are already present. For he moves events in time, while himself remains unmoved by time. He knows what is to happen as already having happened."[28]

It is only our faulty perspective that subjects God to the vagaries of time. We experience creation by a triad of memory, awareness, and anticipation or will. Not so for God. God's triune eternity is in no way circumscribed by three modes of relating to the passing of time. Rather, God "sees all without any kind of change" and "comprehends all . . . in a stable and eternal present" that simultaneously embraces all of time's finite flow.[29] "There was no time before times began . . . that which begins to be spoken of God in time, and which was not spoken of Him before, is manifestly spoken of Him relatively; yet not according to any accident of God."[30]

So the Father is Father and the Son is Son and the Spirit is Spirit in a timeless eternity of unchanging relationships that affect all of time without being affected by any of time, wherefore God is not in any way liable to "passions" insofar as that involves God's timeless essence.[31] The triune God "lives" unchangingly in the sufficiency of the divine interrelations.[32]

Finally, here, it is relevant to note that Augustine affirmed rather curiously the doctrine of God's *simplicity*: "There is then one sole Good, which is simple, and therefore unchangeable; and that is God."[33] Immutability and simplicity clearly go hand in hand. "What is meant by 'simple' is that its being is identical with its attributes . . . The reason why a nature is called simple is that it cannot lose any attribute it possesses, that there is no difference between what it *is* and what it *has*."

Accordingly, he concluded, "the epithet 'simple' applies to things which are in the fullest and truest sense divine, because in them there is no difference between substance and quality."[34]

GOD'S UNOPPOSABLE OMNIPOTENCE

I have already had occasion to quote Augustine's statement that "the Father is omnipotent, the Son omnipotent, and the Holy Spirit omnipotent; yet not three omnipotents, but one omnipotent."[35] This theme is a repetitive drumbeat in his *City of God*, where he asserted that, regardless of our finite sense of historical developments occurring under the sway of merely human forces:

> It is therefore this God, the author and giver of felicity, who, being the one true God, gives earthly dominion both to good men and to evil . . . he gives in accordance with the order of events in history, an order completely hidden from us, but perfectly known to God himself . . . he is himself in control, as the master of events, and arranges the order of things as governor.[36]

We must attribute to the one true God alone the power to direct the fortunes of empires. It is none other than God who "rules and guides these events, according to his pleasure."[37]

We recognize that God is called "Almighty" for the very reason that God's unopposable omnipotence entails the power to do whatever God wills,[38] without obstruction or counterpotency. The immutable God is unchangingly in control of all that comes to be, without qualification.

Writing about initial creation, Augustine affirmed that God is "the one Creator, by whose unspeakable power it comes to pass."[39] When creation began, time began. When creation reaches its end, time will cease. And all that creation is composed of cannot be out of God, which would make God mutable, and it cannot be out of other pre-existing components, which would set up an eternal co-existent with God.[40] Therefore creation can only be comprehended as *ex nihilo*, "out of nothing." And it is God alone who created from nothing all things both spiritual and corporeal.

In that creative activity, God has bestowed on humans a freedom of the will to choose between the good of God and the lack of good not of God. Without such a freedom, there is no meaning in any divine action of condemning us for our waywardness. But is this nothing more than a chimera? Augustine endeavored valiantly to hold free will and God's omnipotence in union, particularly in regard to God's unlimited foreknowledge of what, from our time-bound perspective, is yet to occur but from God's eternal perspective does not truly possess the character of a "not yet."

> we confess his [God's] supreme power and foreknowledge. We are not afraid that what we do by an act of will may not be a voluntary act, because God, with his infallible prescience, knew that we should do it.[41]

God foreknew, of course, that we would sin; God "knew beforehand how evil the man would become whom God himself had created good; he also knew what good, even so, he would bring out of man's evil."[42]

> Evil men do many things contrary to the will of God; but so great is his wisdom, and so great his power, that all things which seem to oppose his will tend towards those results or ends which he himself has foreknown as good and just.[43]

In spite of all the inherent tensions, Augustine could not surrender an insistence that, although God is eternally powerful over everything and knows from a timeless perspective all decisions arising within creation, we and not God are nonetheless responsible for our own misdeeds. It is a curious logic that has bedeviled the church for centuries.

The supratemporal reality of God's unchanging essence required Augustine to champion the apostle Paul in insisting that whatever our post-mortal fate may turn out to be has been *predestined* by God from all eternity. It is, once again, God's unopposable omnipotence that underlies the argument.

> [God] promised not from the power of our will but from His own predestination. For He promised what He Himself would do, not what men would do. Because, although men do those good things which pertain to God's worship, He Himself makes them to do what He has commanded; it is not they that cause Him to do what He has promised. Otherwise the fulfillment

of God's promises would not be in the power of God, but in that of men.[44]

So, in regard to the "two societies of human beings" that Augustine named the City of God and the City of Man, one "is predestined to reign with God for all eternity, the other doomed to undergo eternal punishment with the Devil."[45]

The dilemma is of colossal magnitude. We have earned our own damnation through our perverted utilization of our God-given free will, but God in God's ineffable mystery not only knew of our corruption from all eternity but even ordained it in the exercise of God's all-embracing power. Albert Outler has summarized this problematic enigma in a helpful way:

> Against all who minimize grace or who assert man's abilities and power, after the Pelagian fashion, he [Augustine] opposes a harsh doctrine of God's omnipotence, which allows not the slightest qualification, or even paradox. In this 'polemical mood', Augustine declares that God's grace is irresistible and inexorably effectual in accomplishing the divine purposes. Salvation is a sheer miracle wrought by God's inscrutable will on behalf of a part of ruined mankind and is in no way congruent with human action or ability. Damnation is, likewise, sheer justice wrought by the same inscrutable will. God's mercy and justice are both alike beyond human questioning. The elect rejoice in God's mercy; the damned must acknowledge His justice. Both take their destiny from His choice and by His fixed decree.[46]

I will return to this issue in the next section, in raising once again the question of how this understanding of divine power is coordinated with divine love. First, however, one remaining topic merits our attention here, and that is the matter of how the overarching power of God is not at all responsible for the existence of *evil*.

Augustine's position, like that of Gregory of Nyssa,[47] is that evil is nothing in itself, nothing at all substantial, but is conceivable only as a *privation* of the good, an absence of something rather than anything real—and therefore, it is in no way a component of God's creative activity. To God, Augustine wrote in his *Confessions*, "evil is utterly not."[48]

An apt analogy would seem to be that blindness is not some substantial reality but an absence of sight.

Although "theodicy" as a conceptual term only arose in the eighteenth century with Gottfried Leibniz, the issue it identifies is certainly as old as the Book of Job, to wit, how can God be perceived as both good and powerful if evil exists? Augustine essentially swept the ground out from under theodicy's moorings by maintaining that evil in fact has no independent existence at all. To the extent that we experience evil, that is due to the perversion of our wills in our failure to actualize God's intentions for us[49]—which of course, unsatisfyingly, leads us right back to the previous threads of the omnipotent God's foreknowledge and predestination. The enigma remains.

GOD AND LOVE

Over a century ago the German scholar Otto Sheel recognized that, for Augustine, "the idea of absolute causality and omnipotence is raised to a position of greater importance than the Father's love."[50] There are understandable reasons for that. Augustine read his Bible in a Latin translation and was not directly conversant with the Hebrew and Greek terms *hesed* and *agape*. He had to rely on what was available to him in his native Latin, primarily, *caritas*, from which the English "charity" is derived, but which for Augustine contained the meaning of "desiring."

In one of his earliest works, *On Christian Doctrine* (397), Augustine proposed that God can love us in only two possible ways: by *enjoying* us (*frui*), or *using* us (*uti*). This seems to be an unfortunate distortion of the biblical meaning of love as willing—and acting for—the well-being of the beloved. But for Augustine:

> If He [God] enjoys us, He needs some good of ours, but no sane person would say this. For every good of ours either is God or comes from God . . . Therefore He does not enjoy us but uses us. For if He did neither, I cannot see how He could love us.[51]

But God, being utterly impassive and wholly self-contained, truly has "no use" for us either, after all. God, strictly speaking, *needs* only God.[52] As Thomas Oord has concluded, regarding Augustine's view,

"God has no desires we could possibly satisfy. We do not contribute to a God who has all value eternally in God's unchanging person."[53]

In searching for a clear path through this conceptual morass, we return to the centrality of focus with which this section began, God's Trinity of equal relations. God as trinitarian is eternally "One [the Father] who loves Him [the Son[who is from Himself, and One [the Son] who loves Him [the Father] from whom He is, and Love itself [the Holy Spirit]."[54] Accordingly, Augustine maintained that the Holy Spirit is none other than "the bond of love that exists between the Father and the Son,"[55] and the "person" within the Trinity to which we are indebted for the gift of God's love outward to us and to all of creation.[56] "Therefore the Holy Spirit, of whom He hath given us, makes us to abide in God, and Him in us; and this it is that love does. Therefore He is the God that is love."[57] But the gift of love we receive from the Holy Spirit is not so much God's love of us as it is our own God-derived ability to love. As is expressed in 1 John 4:16, "We love because he [God] first loved us."[58]

Augustine could pen eloquent paeans to this facet of God. In his sermon on 1 John 4, he waxed poetic:

> I do not know whether love could be commended to us more magnificently than in the words, 'God is pure love'. Brief praise and great praise! Brief in word and great in meaning. How quickly one says it: 'God is love'. And this is brief: if you were to count it, it is one thing; if you were to weigh it, how substantial it is![59]

Would that he had stayed true to this insight. But because God in God's self-sufficiency desires nothing from us and has no constitutive use for us, affirming any substantial meaning to the notion that God "loves" us becomes problematic. There is certainly a component of love in God's sanctifying grace that saves (some of) us from eternal damnation. But nothing within creation can be *worthy* as a recipient of God's perfect love because that love can have as its true object only that which is also perfect—namely, God's trinitarian self.

The key implication is an obvious one, discerned by many: The only valid object of God's love . . . is God! And that is because only God is truly and perfectly worthy of God's love. John Burnaby saw rightly that "Augustine in his zeal for the divine self-sufficiency is too fearful of representing the loving will of God as a real seeking of our human love. Perfect love must be eternally in the Holy Trinity."[60] God's love of anything and anyone not God can only be a wholly disinterested love,[61] which renders the meaning of such love problematic. Oord concludes that for Augustine, "God ceaselessly loves Godself in contemplation and enjoyment in the Trinity's inner life."[62] It is only the understanding of the threefold interrelationship of persons within the Trinity that allows Augustine barely to escape the charge that his position amounts to a sort of divine narcissism.

POWER AND LOVE: THE PERILOUS FLAW

Augustine erected the conceptual edifice that dominated the landscape of Christian thinking for a millennium and a half, with doctrines reaching far beyond the select focus presented here. But in this critical arena of the relationship between God's power and God's love, he established a structure of thought that proved problematic to the extreme. In his overarching concentration on God's absolute immutability, the living God of the biblical witness "lives," now, only in a timeless eternity of trinitarian interrelatedness, *sans* passion, *sans* timely interaction, *sans* any affect creation can have on God.

In particular, Augustine's position on predestination, necessitated by his championing of God's unopposable omnipotence, gives one pause. Did God create us out of love? Why, then, are most souls damned to eternal Hell by the justice of God while only some are saved by the grace of God? What kind of God deliberately creates subjects that are foredoomed to be the eternal victims of God's powerful and righteous wrath? For Pelikan, the "sovereignty of divine power and divine grace" was the double focus of Augustine that led to his presenting his doctrine of double predestination, which protected the absoluteness of God's power while denying the absoluteness of God's love![63] And Burnaby saw that "Augustine never realized that his own conception of grace required nothing less than a revolution in his thought of the divine omnipotence."[64]

Power has triumphed. Love has been truncated, soaring flames reduced to mere ash. Must it ever be so? Let us explore how this theological architecture held up or was extended and modified over the ensuing centuries.

ENDNOTES

1. The doctrine of the divine right of kings, for example, was not explicity promulgated until the reign of James I of England in the seventeenth century.

2. See *The Library of Christian Classics*, vol. III: *Christology of the Later Fathers*, ed. Edward Rochie Hardie (Philadelphia: The Westminster Press, 1954), 113–214.

3. This critical emphasis on internal triune *relatedness* in God is explicitly spelled out in *Oration* 3:16 (LCC III, 171).

4. Gregory of Nyssa, *An Answer to Ablabius*, LCC III, 262.

5. Ibid., 263. All subsequent references to "Gregory" in this chapter are to Gregory of Nyssa.

6. Ibid., 264.

7. Gregory of Nyssa, *An Address on Religious Instruction*, LCC III, 296 (sec. 20).

8. Ibid., 300f. (sec. 24), emphasis mine. He went on to say: "God's transcendent power is not so much displayed in the vastness of the heavens, or the luster of the stars, or the orderly arrangement of the universe or his perpetual oversight of it, as in his condescension to our weak nature . . . We marvel at the way the Godhead was entwined in human nature and, while becoming man, did not cease to be God" (301).

9. Gregory of Nyssa, *On the Soul and Resurrection*, in Philip Schaff and Henry Wace, eds., *A Select Library of the Nicene and Post-Nicene Fathers of the Christian Church, 2nd Series* (Edinburgh: T&T Clark, 1893), 5:465. Available online in the Christian Classics Ethereal Library at www.ccel.org/ccel/schaff/npnf205.toc.html

10. See particularly Gregory's presentation of this notion in his *Against Eunomius*, in Schaff and Wace, op. cit., sections 1:22 and 2:2.

11. Gregory of Nyssa, *Answer to Eunomius' Second Book*, in Schaff and Wace, op. cit., 5:308, emphasis mine.

12. Gregory denied that evil has any positive existence. Understood as

the absence of the good, it is therefore not anything God created or is in any way responsible for. See *An Address on Religious Instruction*, LCC III, 282, 285 (sec. 7, 8).

13. See Augustine's *Confessions*, the whole of Book 7.

14. Augustine of Hippo, *On the Trinity*, tr. Arthur West Haddan, in Philip Schaff, ed., *A Select Library of the Nicene and Post-Nicene Fathers of the Christian Church,* Vol. 3 (Edinburgh: T&T Clark, 1886), Book 15, Ch. 28, Para. 51. Available online at www.ccel.com.

15. Ibid., 3.Preface.

16. Ibid., 5.8.9.

17. Ibid., 1.4.7.

18. Ibid., 1.11-12.

19. Ibid., 4.20.29. See also the preceding paragraphs in this chapter.

20. Augustine, *Confessions*, 7:1. This and subsequent quotes are from the translation by F. J. Sheed, *The Confessions of St. Augustine: Books I–X* (New York: Sheed & Ward, 1942); here, p. 107.

21. Ibid., 7:9 (Sheed, 116). See also 7:20: "Now that I had read the books of the Platonists and had been set by them towards the search for a truth that is incorporeal" (Sheed, 123.)

22. Ibid., 7:10 (Sheed, 118).

23. Augustine, *On the Trinity*, 4.Preface.

24. Ibid., 4.18.24.

25. Ibid.

26. Ibid., 5.2.3.

27. Ibid., 5.16.17.

28. Augustine, *The City of God*, X.12. The translated quotes are by Henry Bettenson in the Penguin edition (Baltimore: 1972), 390f. Toward the end of this massive tome, Augustine challenged the biblical narratives on God's having a change of mind or will by affirming that "it is the people who change, rather than God; and they find him, in a sense, 'changed' in their experience." Whatever we perceive as new from our perspective within history "has been prepared from all eternity in his [God's] unchanging will." XXII.2 (Bettenson, 1023, 1025).

29. Ibid., XI.21 (Bettenson, 452).

30. Augustine, *On the Trinity*, 5.16.17.

31. Ibid., 5.8.9.

32. See Augustine, *On Christian Doctrine*, 1.8; tr. J. F. Shaw, in Philip Schaff, ed., *A Select Library of the Nicene and Post-Nicene Fathers of the Christian Church*, Vol. 2. (Edinburgh: T&T Clark, 1886). Online at www.ccel.org.

33. Augustine, *The City of God*, XI.10 (Bettenson, 440).

34. Ibid. (Bettenson, 440–42, ital. original).

35. Augustine, *On the Trinity*, 5.8.9. (Footnote 16, above.) See also *The City of God*, XI.24.

36. Augustine, *The City of God*, IV.34 (Bettenson, 176). Augustine interpreted God's activity in relation to the sack of Rome by Alaric and his Goths. "God's providence constantly uses war to correct and chasten the corrupt morals of mankind." Ibid., I.2 (Bettenson, 6).

37. Ibid., V.22 (Bettenson, 215f.)

38. Ibid., XXI.7 (Bettenson, 977).

39. Augustine, *On the Trinity*, 3.9.17.

40. See Augustine, *Confessions*, 12.7-8. See also Scott MacDonald, "The Divine Nature," in Eleonore Stump and Norman Kretzmann, eds., *The Cambridge Companion to Augustine* (New York: Cambridge University Press, 2001), 84; and William A. Christian's cogent discussion on Augustine's doctrine of creation out of nothing in his essay on "The Creation of the World," in Roy W. Battenhouse, ed., *A Companion to the Study of St. Augustine* (New York: Oxford University Press, 1955), 332–36.

41. Augustine, *The City of God*, V.9 (Bettenson, 190).

42. Ibid., XIV.11 (Bettenson, 568).

43. Ibid., XXII.2 (Bettenson, 1023).

44. Augustine, *On the Predestination of the Saints*, X.19, tr. Peter Holmes and Robert Ernest Wallis, tr. rev. Benjamin B. Warfield, in Philip Schaff, ed., *A Select Library of the Nicene and Post-Nicene Fathers of the Christian Church*, Vol. 5. (Edinburgh: T&T Clark, 1886). Online at www.ccel.org.

45. Augustine, *The City of God*, XV.1 (Bettenson, 595).

46. Albert C. Outler, "The Person and Work of Christ," in *A Companion to the Study of St. Augustine*, 360.

47. See ft. 12, above.

48. Augustine, *Confessions*, 7:13. So also, in *The City of God*, XII.7, he wrote: "The truth is that one should not try to find an efficient cause for a wrong choice. It is not a matter of efficiency, but of deficiency; the evil will itself is not effective but defective" (Bettenson, 479).

49. Augustine's position on God and evil is insightfully spelled out by John Hick in his *Evil and the God of Love*, rev. ed. (New York: Harper & Row, 1977), chs. 3-4, 8, cogently summarized by Tyrone Inbody, *The Transforming God* (Louisville: Westminster John Knox Press, 1997), 40–42.

50. Otto Sheel, *Die Anschauung Augustins über Christi Person und Werk*, 145, as quoted (and translated) by Jaroskav Pelikan, *The Christian Tradition: A History of the Development of Doctrine*, 1:295.

51. Augustine, *On Christian Doctrine*, Bk 1, Ch. 31, tr. D. W. Robertson, Jr. (Indianapolis: The Bobbs-Merrill Co., 1958), 27.

52. Ibid., 1.32: "That use which God is said to make of us is made not to His utility but to ours" (Robertson, 27).

53. Thomas Jay Oord, *The Nature of Love: a Theology* (St. Louis: Chalice Press, 2010), 68.

54. Augustine, *On the Trinity*, 6.5.7.

55. Ibid.

56. Ibid., 15.18–19.

57. Ibid., 15.17.31.

58. See, e.g., Augustine, *Ten Homilies on the First Epistle of John*, 7.6, tr. H. Browne, in Philip Schaff, ed., *A Select Library of the Nicene and Post-Nicene Fathers of the Christian Church*, Vol. 7. Online at www.ccel.org. John Burnaby saw perceptibly that when Augustine wrote of the love of God, he meant *our love of God*, not God's love of us. But this is, indeed, "God's own love which is ours by His gift." Burnaby, *Amor Dei: a Study of the Religion of St. Augustine* (London: Hodder & Stoughton, 1938), 99.

59. Ibid., 9.1.

60. Burnaby, op cit., 166.

61. Ibid., 167.

62. Oord, *The Nature of Love*, 69, referencing Augustine, *On the Trinity*, 9.2.

63. Pelikan, *The Christian Tradition: A History of the Development of Doctrine*, 1:297.

64. Burnaby, 230. So also, Daniel Day Williams noted that Augustine's "determination to keep all time and becoming apart from God led to disastrous consequences for the understanding of God's love," particularly including the loss of genuine human freedom. See *The Spirit and the Forms of Love* (New York: Harper & Row, 1968), 75.

5

Refinements of an Omnipotent God

The "Dark Ages" were anything but dark insofar as ongoing theological inquiry is concerned. While following Augustine's lead, new threads were woven into the fabric of his tapestry, including both a refined understanding of the character of God's power and fresh reflections on the nature of God's love. All of that came to a head in the rediscovery of Aristotle in the West and the work of the second great synthesizer of Christian faith, Thomas Aquinas. This was followed by the challenges wrought by the Protestant Reformation and especially by the formulations of the lawyer-turned-theologian John Calvin, who "updated" Augustine's work with a vengeance.

It is also worth remembering here that feudal society in the Middle Ages was characterized by a descending hierarchy of greater and lesser lords, all the way down to tenant serfs. Much that was articulated in this period was considerably conditioned by this social context.

A LOVE SO GREAT: RICHARD OF ST. VICTOR

In his *Proslogion* (1078), Anselm of Canterbury defined God as "a being than which none greater can be thought"[1] and went on to perceive that greatness in terms of ultimate power: "O Lord God, thou art more truly almighty just because thou canst do nothing through lack of power, and nothing has power against thee."[2] God is understood here as "at once [both] compassionate and impassible," but also both compassionate and *not* compassionate! How? "Thou art compassionate according to our sense, but not according to thine . . . we feel the effect of thy compassion, but thou dost not feel emotion."[3] So once again the unqualified championing of impassible divine power limits the scope and meaning of divine love. We bask in God's love, but that love does nothing to augment God's being. It is, as it were, disinterested love.

Richard of St. Victor, a century later, offered a propitious correction to Anselm. In his *On the Trinity* (*ca.* 1170), he argued that God loves with a love "so great that nothing greater can exist and . . . of such a kind that nothing better can exist."[4] Richard, however, remain locked in an Augustinian framework that negated the force of his observation, turning it inward upon the relational Trinity: "A divine person, then, could not have the highest charity toward a person who was not worthy of the highest love . . . no person could be wholly deserving of the love of a divine person if he were not God."[5]

Even so, there are hints of an understanding that can move us forward. Denis Edwards notes that:

> Richard lived in a century that was marked by the discovery of romantic love and by an intense interest in friendship in the new monastic movements. Richard's unique contribution was in his application of reflection on Christian friendship to the central mystery of the Trinity . . . Richard's trinitarian theology suggests that relationships of mutual love are the foundation of all reality. It argues that all creation springs from this dynamism of mutual love. Relationality is the source of creaturehood."[6]

This recognition of the supreme importance of the mutuality of love is clearly a propitious move in the right direction. It remains to be spelled out, however, beyond the innertrinitarian being of God into the fullness of relations between God and God's creation.[7]

THE NEW ARISTOTELIAN SYNTHESIS: THOMAS AQUINAS

The "Dumb Ox"[8] of the thirteenth century may have been shy and quiet and slow, preferring the solace of his books and his writing to the demands of oration and teaching, but his effect on all subsequent theologizing was profound and rather all-encompassing, particularly insofar as the Roman Catholic Church is concerned. Thomas Aquinas[9] (1225–1274) did not reintroduce Aristotle to Western theology. That had already been occurring from the time Muslims, who had kept his writings alive in Greek and Arabic, conquered Sicilty and Spain and the work of translation into Latin ensued. But Aquinas was surely the one who brought Aristotle's philosophy into a fresh new synthesis that rivaled the output of Augustine eight and a half centuries before.

The basic contrast between Aristotle and his mentor Plato is that Plato taught that the search for true knowledge involved turning from the senses inward to truths known by the soul. Aristotle taught that all knowledge begins with sense observation. Certainly Aquinas traded Platonic notions for Aristotelian ones, but that unfortunately may be seen to have been merely a different route to the same flawed destination, arriving at almost identical conclusions clothed in a different philosophical language. I now turn our attention to that development insofar as the relationship between divine power and divine love is concerned.

ACTIVE AND PASSIVE POWER

Even before he finished his comprehensive *Summa Theologica* (1265–72), Aquinas articulated his key understanding of God as *actus purus*, "pure act."[10] In *On the Power of God* (*Quaestiones disputatae de potentia*, 1266), he argued that God's existence and essence are identical,[11] wherefore there can be no admixture in God of both action and potentiality.[12] Equally, as pure act, God cannot be "composite" but must be "utterly simple." True perfection is possible only of that which is simple ("void of all composition").[13]

"God is called almighty [omnipotent] because he can do all things that are possible in themselves."[14] This quality is identified as "active" power, the capacity to act on another. Its corollary, in Aquinas, is "passive" or receptive power, the capacity to be acted upon.[15] As pure act, God is active only. "Is God really related to the creature so that this relation be something in God?" Aquinas answered unequivocally in the negative.[16] Such receptive capacity would be a violation of God's essential and eternal completeness. God impacts the world totally. The world impacts God not at all.

Aquinas extended this focus in the *Summa Theologica*, answering Question 25 on the Power of God. God's essence, God's action, and God's power are not distinct from one another.[17] In his Reply to Objection 4, he wrote:

> Power is predicated of God not as something really distinct from His knowledge and will, but as differing from them logically; inasmuch as power implies a notion of a principle putting into execution what the will commands, and what knowledge directs, which three things in God are identified. Or we may say, that the knowledge or will of God, according as it is the effective principle, has the notion of power contained in it.[18]

And this "active power" is, of course, infinite, unqualified by any power outside itself.[19] The only qualification allowable regarding God's omnipotence is that which involves self-contradiction.

> This phrase, "God can do all things," is rightly understood to mean that God can do all things that are possible; and for this reason He is said to be omnipotent . . . God is called omnipotent because He can do all things that are possible absolutely . . . everything that does not imply a contradiction in terms, is numbered amongst those possible things, in respect of which God is called omnipotent: whereas whatever implies contradiction does not come within the scope of divine omnipotence, because it cannot have the aspect of possibility. Hence it is better to say that such things cannot be done, than that God cannot do them.[20]

Clearly any inclusion of passive power in God would constitute a denial of this understanding of God's omnipotence.

Furthermore, God is understood by Aquinas to be "in all things, innermostly . . . by His power, inasmuch as all things are subject to His power."[21] God's omnipresence is a facet of God's all-encompassing omnipotence.

Finally, passive power in our own selves is what enables our receptivity toward actualizing our potentiality in the direction of perfection,[22] in sharply defined contrast to God's existence as without any unrealized potentiality.

THE UNCHANGED CHANGER

Underlying all these reflections is Aquinas' modification of the doctrine of divine immutability through his appropriation of Aristotle's definition of the Highest Being as the "Unmoved Mover." His first argument for the existence of God is oriented toward "motion," but Timothy McDermott's translation of the *Summa Theologica* brings the pattern more sharply into focus by shifting the discussion in English from motion to "change."

> Some things in the world are certainly in the process of change. This we plainly see. Now anything in the process of change is being changed by something else . . . Moreover, this something else, if in process of change, is itself being changed by yet another thing; and this last by another. Now we must stop somewhere, otherwise there will be no first cause of the change, and, as a result, no subsequent causes . . . Hence one is bound to arrive at some first cause of change not itself being changed by anything, and this is what everybody understands by God.[23]

Aquinas concentrated his attention on the doctrine of divine immutability in Question 9, repeating there that God is "first being" and "pure act, without the admixture of any potentiality." Because to be subject to change is to be open to previously unrealized potentiality, it is obviously the case that "it is impossible for God to change in any way."[24]

God's immutability is also underscored in regard to the relationship of the eternal God to temporality. "Eternity differs from time by virtue of being "simultaneously whole . . . eternity is the measure of a permanent being, while time is the measure of movement."[25] Therefore God as the

One who is not subject to change is the One who is not subject to time either. Eternity is not an infinite progression of temporal moments but that which embraces and encompasses all of time without being subject to before and after.

Can "life," then, be attributed to God? Aquinas answered in the affirmative, in that, "since a thing is said to live in so far as it operates of itself and not as moved by another, the more perfectly this power is found in anything, the more perfect is the life of that thing." And certainly, "a more perfect degree of life is that of intelligent beings, for their power of self-movement is more perfect." Obviously God's "power of self-movement" surpasses that of all others, wherefore "in Him principally is life."[26] But this claim is not augmented by any exploration on Aquinas' part as to what sense can be made of a life that is not dynamic or interactive, the life of an ultimate being characterized by simplicity. Life in God would seem to be something limited to the eternal interrelationships of the members of the Trinity, though that is not explicitly spelled out.

BUT WHAT OF LOVE?

In the non-composite simplicity of God as *actus purus*, it is perfectly feasible for Aquinas to utilize a wealth of expressions equating God with God's power, as realized action; God's will, as unopposable intentions; God's wisdom or knowledge, as transtemporal comprehensiveness. The orientation shifts subtly when the focus is on divine love; the question now becomes "whether love exists *in* God,"[27] not at all whether love itself characterizes the being of God as surely as act and will and power do. Quoting 1 John 4:16, "God is love," Aquinas answered his posited objections by affirming that "*in* God there is love, because love is the first movement of the will and of every appetitive power."[28] Love:

> regards good universally, whether possessed or not. Hence love is naturally the first act of will and appetite; for which reason all the other appetitive movements presuppose love as their root and origin . . . in whomsoever there is will and appetite, there must also be love . . . Now is has been shown that will is in God. Hence we must attribute love to Him.[29]

Love is but an "attribute" of God, as a subset of will. This is, however, necessarily a love that is without passion,[30] because for it to be otherwise would deny God's immutability and impose on God illegitimately an aspect of passive (receptive) power.

But Aquinas did exceed Augustine's limited definition of the nature of love by recognizing that "to love a person is to will good for that person."[31] In that regard, "God does not love some things more than others, because He loves all things by an act of the will that is one, simple, and always the same."[32]

On the other hand, this perspective was curiously applied when it came to defining the relationship between God's love and God's predestining some to eternal salvation and allowing others to suffer their just desserts of God's "abandonment."[33] The full explication by Aquinas is worth our attention:

> Predestination presupposes election in the order of reason; and election presupposes love . . . Whence the predestination of some to eternal salvation presupposes, in the order of reason, that God wills their salvation; and to this belong both election and love:—love, inasmuch as He wills them this particular good of eternal salvation; since to love is to wish well to anyone, as stated above:—election, inasmuch as He wills this good to some in preference to others; since He reprobates some, as stated above. Election and love, however, are differently ordered in God, and in ourselves: because in us the will in loving does not cause good, but we are incited to love by the good which already exists; and therefore we choose someone to love, and so election in us precedes love. In God, however, it is the reverse. For His will, by which in loving He wishes good to someone, is the cause of that good possessed by some in preference to others. Thus it is clear that *love precedes election in the order of reason, and election precedes predestination.* Whence all the predestinate are objects of election and love.[34]

It would seem clear here that the *power* of God is all-encompassing whereas the *love* of God is not, because that love does not result in the effective saving of all of God's human creatures from eternal damnation. Although God has been said to love all equally, that is not so. *Some* are elected and therefore predestined—but not all. John Hick has observed cogently that "if there are finally wasted lives and finally unredeemed sufferings, either God is not perfect in love or He is not sovereign in rule over His creation."[35]

The conclusion seems unavoidable: Aquinas has expanded Augustine's definition of love in a useful direction, but the fundamental problem limiting the meaning of God's love by virtue of God's essential immutability and transtemporality has not been surmounted. Here, also, passive/receptive power has been helpfully introduced, but as something foreign to God. Power as the unopposable actualization of the divine will overtrumps Love as the essential nature of the divine life. The fundamental dilemma has not been resolved.

POTENTIA ABSOLUTA, POTENTIA ORDINATA: WILLIAM OF OCKHAM

One additional debate in the late Middle Ages is worthy of notice, and that is the attempt to distinguish within God an "absolute power," *potentia absoluta*, and an "ordained power," *potentia ordinata*. The terms were not original to William of Ockham (ca. 1285–1347), but he was the one who did the most to explicate their meaning.

> Sometimes we mean by God's power those things which he does according to laws he himself has ordained and instituted. These things he is said to do by ordained power [*de potentia ordinata*]. But sometimes God's power is taken to mean his ability to do anything that does not involve a contradiction, regardless of whether or not he has ordained that he would do it. For God can do many things that he does not choose to do . . . These things he is said to be able to do by his absolute power [*de potentia absoluta*].[36]

The notion of God's absolute power is a way of defending God's total freedom of action. In other words, God is not bound by God's own orderly way of overseeing the flow of historical events. Gordon Leff summarized the distinction in this way:

> God's absolute power (*potentia absoluta*) . . . differed from His ordained power (*potentia ordinata*) in denoting God's omnipotence purely and simply. It was outside all space and time in that it was uncommitted to upholding any set order in the universe. Freedom to will was its only raison d'être. In contrast, God's ordained power was directed to sustaining this world; it constituted God's law of creation, the eternal ordinance by which everything was governed. As given expression in the Bible and interpreted by the Church, it was immutable and irrevocable. Thus while God's ordained power applied less to His own nature than to His creatures, His absolute power referred to Himself, and so, in the final analysis, it could override His ordinances.[37]

This freedom of God to act withput any constraint certainly explained what believers perceived as miracles. But acknowledging the reality of *potentia absoluta* led to a "radical indeterminacy" in which all ordinary assurances about the proper order of things were tossed out the window. "Thus any switch from God's ordained to His absolute power involved throwing all certainty, morality, and indeed probability into the melting-pot: in their place anything could emerge."[38]

This was the real heart of skepticism in the period leading up to the Reformation. God is freed from reason; experience is freed from faith. "Where probability simply questioned, God's absolute power destroyed. Where reason ended, God's *potentia absoluta* began."[39] Because of the potential arbitrariness of God's absolute power, theology was placed beyond reason's reach. Here, attention to the potentially unchecked capacity of God the All-Powerful to direct the affairs of the world reached its conceptual zenith. Love has to fend for itself as best it can; it might be discernible in God's *potentia ordinata*, but it has nothing to do with defining (limiting, directing) the ultimate power of God.

GOD'S DEFENSE ATTORNEY: JOHN CALVIN

In examining the views of the Protestant Reformers I do not find it especially cogent to deal with both Martin Luther and John Calvin. In very many respects, on matters relevant to this inquiry, their theological reflections overlap. But the one who pushed the conceptual envelope to the maximum was Calvin (1509–1564). Therefore it is to his work that I now turn.

It is not coincidental to his corpus of work that Calvin, before he became a reforming theologian, was a lawyer. Bernard Cottret has observed that "Calvin the theologian would be to the end Calvin the jurist. His thought remained permeated with the rigor, the geometry, the fascination, and the memory of the law."[40] He rigorously and without reservation presented and defended all the seemingly radical implications of a God of predestination whose will is absolutely omnipotent.

It was the absolutely unlimited and unchallengable *sovereignty* of God that Calvin was concerned to pronounce, at all costs. Everything else is sacrificed to that overriding proposition. All the quibbling about protecting free will and perceiving double causes in creation's forward movement went by the wayside. Early on in his monumental *Institutes of the Christian Religion* (1536, 1559), he wrote:

> God's providence, as it is taught in Scripture, is opposed to fortune and fortuitous happenings . . . all events are governed by God's secret plan. And concerning inanimate objects we ought to hold that, although each one has by nature been endowed with its own property, yet it does not exercise its own power except in so far as it is directed by God's ever-present hand. These are, thus, nothing but instruments to which God continually imparts as much effectiveness as he wills, and according to his own purpose bends and turns them to either one action or another.[41]

This admits of no diminution of divine omnipotence. It is absolute and all-encompassing.

> And truly God claims, and would have us grant him, omnipotence . . . a watchful, effective, active sort, engaged in ceaseless activity. Not, indeed, an omnipotence that is only a general principle of confused motion . . . but one that is directed toward individual and particular motions. For he is deemed omnipotent . . . because, governing heaven and earth by his providence, he so regulates all things that nothing takes

place without his deliberation . . . there is no erratic power, or action, or motion in creatures, but that they are governed by God's secret plan in such a way that nothing happens except what is knowingly and willingly decreed by him.[42]

Divine foreknowledge is understood to be divine foreordination, from our earthbound point of view.[43] What is emerging here is the most explicit indication to date that God's power is perceived to be the *only* power. Omnipotence admits of no other powers at all; they are mere chimeras. We say or do nothing whatsoever apart from the power of God to produce such effects. All human conditions, rich and poor, lordly or oppressed, are "divinely assigned."[44]

Nothing happens by chance. We judge events "fortuitous" because the true cause of events, i.e., God, is hidden from our eyes.

> [God is] the ruler and governor of all things, who in accordance with his wisdom has from the farthest limit of eternity decreed what he was going to do, and now by his might carries out what he has decreed. From this we declare that not only heaven and earth and the inanimate creatures, but also the plans and intentions of men, are so governed by his providence that they are borne by it straight to their appointed end.[45]

So, in regard to "double predestination," God does not merely "permit" the "wicked" to perish, but "*wills*" it.[46]

Calvin's attempt to maintain that God's providence "does not relieve us from responsibility" failed abysmally inasmuch as his effort to posit "secondary causes" fails the test of common sense. The human will is simply in no way independent of God's all-embracing providential causality.[47] "As far as men are concerned, whether they are good or evil, the heart of the Christian will know that their plans, wills, efforts, and abilities are under God's hand; that it is within his choice to bend them whither he pleases and to constrain them whenever he pleases."[48] The consequent perception that God is ultimately the One responsible even for all evil is "conspicuous."[49]

Calvin dismissed Old Testament passages that speak of God "repenting" by maintaining that these are to be taken figuratively, and yield to our weakness of understanding: "neither God's plan nor his will is reversed, nor his volition altered; but what he had from eternity foreseen, approved, and decreed, he pursues in uninterrupted tenor, however sudden the variation may appear in men's eyes."[50]

The rigorous lockstep of a universe totally under the control of one sole Power continued into Book II: God "bends and turns men's wills even in external things; nor are they so free to choose that God's will does not rule over their freedom . . . your mind is guided by God's prompting rather than by your own freedom to choose."[51]

This selective summary has been decidedly one-sided. I have traced Calvin's championing of a divine omnipotence that is absolute and unqualified, without any vestige of external contribution whatsoever. Nothing has been developed here regarding Calvin's focus on divine love. That is hardly accidental. In a rather exhaustive eighty-page subject index for the *Institutes*, one finds Calvin writing about divine *love* only in four paragraphs.[52] In four columns of citations concerning "Christ," only a single one involves love, God's loving act in Christ.[53] And at no point in his extensive scriptural references did Calvin even deal at all with 1 John 4:8, 16.

Total power. Questionable love. Anna Case-Winters has tellingly perceived that the primary metaphors Calvin used for God—Father, Lord, King—are all *power* metaphors. Even fatherhood was conceived in terms of "a sovereign Father upon whom we are always dependent,"[54] not the intimate *Abba* of the Lord's Prayer.

So the essential architecture of what would come to be known as Christian theism is now fully in place. God is absolute Lord of all, eternal, immutable, passionless. To affirm God equally, if not primarily, to be Love has become conceptually impossible. Love must be "shoehorned" in somehow, as a mere attribute of God Almighty. It is truly revealing in that in the whole history of discussion of the nature of God, nowhere is the prefix "omni" applied to love! God is said to be omnipresent, omniscient, omnipotent, and so forth. Where is the notion that God is "omnilove"? It will take centuries before that seedling takes root and begins to sprout and blossom. In the meantime, footnotes continued to be written to the Augustinian theistic consensus. To that continuation we now turn.

ENDNOTES

1. Anselm of Canterbury, *Proslogion*, ch. 2. This and subsequent quotes are from Eugene R. Fairweather, ed. and trans., *A Scholastic Miscellany: Anselm to Ockham* (*The Library of Christian Classics, Vol. X*) (Philadelphia: The Westminster Press, 1956).

2. Ibid., ch. 7 (Fairweather, 77).

3. Ibid., ch. 8 (Fairweather, 77f.).

4. Richard of St. Victor, *On the Trinity*, III.2. This translation is by Grover A. Zinn in his *Richard of St. Victor* (New York: Paulist Press, 1979), 375. It is superior in its parallel with Anselm to the translation of the lines in Fairweather, *op cit.*, 330.

5. Ibid. (Fairweather, 330).

6. Denis Edwards, "The Discovery of Chaos and the Retrieval of the Trinity," in Robert John Russell, Nancey Murphy, and Arthur R. Peacocke, eds., *Chaos and Complexity: Scientific Perspectives on Divine Action* (Berkeley: The Center for Theology and the Natural Sciences, 1995), 160.

7. For a move in that direction initiated by Bonaventure, a medieval mystical theologian of the following century who was influenced by Richard, see my coverage of his contribution herein in the chapter on the Mystics' God.

8. "You call him a Dumb Ox; I tell you that the Dumb Ox will bellow so loud that his bellowing will fill the world." So said Albert the Great of his modest and most retiring student. See G. K. Chesterton, *Saint Thomas Aquinas* (New York: Doubleday & Co., 1956), Image Books edition, back cover.

9. Scholars are divided in deciding whether to refer to him in shorthand as "Thomas" or as "Aquinas." Certainly his followers are known as Thomists, and "Aquinas" simply designates his origin in the Italian town of Aquino, near Naples. So strictly speaking, he could well be known as "Thomas of Aquino." Even so, because of the distinctiveness and ready recognition of "Aquinas," that is the nomenclature used here.

10. See, e.g., Thomas Aquinas, *On the Power of God (Quæstiones Disputatæ de Potentia Dei)*, Question 3, article 1, paragraphs 12,17; tr. Fr. Lawrence Shapcote (Three Books in One) (Westminster, Md.: Newman Press, 1952). Online at dhspriory.org/thomas. Aquinas' defense of this

point is also found in his *Summa Theologica*, Question 3, articles 1–3.

11. Aquinas, *On the Power of God*, 7.2.

12. Ibid., 3.1.17.

13. Ibid.

14. Ibid., 1.5.7.

15. Ibid., 7.9

16. Ibid., 7.10.

17. Aquinas, *Summa Theologica, Part I*, Question 25, art. 1, in Anton C. Pegis, ed., *Basic Writings of Saint Thomas Aquinas*, Vol. 1 (New York: Random House, 1945),

18. Ibid., 25.1, Reply to Obj. 4.

19. Ibid., 25.2.

20. Ibid., 25.3.

21. Ibid., 8.1,3.

22. Ibid., 9.2.

23. Ibid., 2.3, in the translation by Timothy McDermott (London: Blackfriars, 1964), as quoted in William C. Placher, *A History of Christian Theology* (Louisville: WJK Press, 1983), 154.

24. Ibid., 9.1, from the Pegis translation.

25. Ibid., 10.4.

26. Ibid., 18.3.

27. The focus of Question 20, emphasis mine.

28. Ibid., 20.1, emphasis mine.

29. Ibid.

30. Ibid., 20.1, Reply to Obj. 1.

31. Ibid., 20.1, Reply to Obj. 3.

32. Ibid., 20.3. Aquinas went on to modify this somewhat in Art. 4 in proposing that God "loves better things more."

33. Ibid., 23.3, Reply to Obj. 1: "God loves all men and all creatures, inasmuch as He wishes them all some good; but He does not wish every good to them all. So far, therefore, as He does not wish this particular

good—namely, eternal life—He is said to hate or reprobate them."

34. Ibid., 23.4, emphasis mine.

35. John Hick, *Evil and the God of Love*, 2nd ed. (San Francisco: Harper & Row, 1977), 340.

36. William of Ockham, *Quodlibeta* VI, q. 1, as quoted in Steven Ozment, *The Age of Reform 1250–1550* (New Haven: Yale University Press, 1980), 38. Aquinas had briefly called attention to the distinction in *Summa Theologica*, 25.5.1, Reply to Obj. 1.

37. Gordon Leff, *Medieval Thought from Saint Augustine to Ockham* (Baltimore: Penguin Books, 1958), 288.

38. Ibid., 289.

39. Ibid., 290.

40. Bernard Cottret, *Calvin: A Biography*, tr. M. Wallace McDonald (Grand Rapids: Wm. B. Eerdmans, 2000), 21.

41. John Calvin, *Institutes of the Christian Religion*, I.16.2, tr. Ford Lewis Battles (Philadelphia: The Westminster Press, 1960), 198f.

42. Ibid., I.16.3 (200f.).

43. Ibid., I.16.4 (202).

44. Ibid., I.16.6 (204f.).

45. Ibid., I.16.8 (207).

46. Ibid., III.23.8, emphasis mine (956).

47. See ibid., I.17.3, 9 (214–17, 221f.).

48. Ibid., I.17.6 (218).

49. Anna Case-Winters, *God's Power: Traditional Understandings and Contemporary Challenges* (Louisville: Westminster/John Knox Press, 1990), 71. Calvin used Isaiah 45.7 as a scriptural basis for this.

50. Calvin, *Institutes*, I.17.13 (227).

51. Ibid., II.4.7 (315).

52. Ibid., I.16.1–4.

53. Ibid., II.16.2.

54. Case-Winters, op. cit., 49.

6

Rearrangings of a Titanic God

Titanic: adj., "pertaining to . . . enormous size, strength, power."[1] That the God of Christian theism we have been encountering could be characterized as "titanic" would seem obvious. That this is also the name bestowed on a doomed ocean liner is a provocative coincidence. For me to suggest that much of what followed right into the nineteenth and twentieth centuries was akin to rearranging the deck chairs on the Titanic is not intended to be dismissive of intellectual giants whose efforts far outstrip my own. It is rather to contend that their attempts to shore up the sinking ship of traditional theism were finally to no avail. The ship of Augustinian theism, alas, still sank.

Let us examine a selection of the more important voices.

A CONSCIOUSNESS OF ABSOLUTE DEPENDENCY: FRIEDRICH SCHLEIERMACHER

In the sixteenth century, Nicolaus Copernicus initiated the novel idea in astronomy that the planets and the sun and the stars do not revolve around the Earth but that the planets, including our own, revolve around the sun. Fearing personal consequences once word got out about his revolutionary theory, he delayed publication of his work, reportedly seeing it first in print only on his deathbed in 1543. Two and a half centuries later the German philosopher Immanuel Kant, in the "Preface to the Second Edition" of his *Critique of Pure Reason* (1787), appropriated this "Copernican Revolution" in thought for his own shift from the presumed objectivity of what we know to the act of conscious knowing itself.[2] It remains a contestable assessment because the movement is precisely in the opposite direction: After Copernicus, we humans are no longer understood to be in the center of the universe, whereas Kant concentrated precisely on the subjectivity of individual knowing. Even so, Friedrich Schleiermacher mirrored Kant in the axial shift in his way of approaching theological issues.

Kant had found no access to God through the utilization of pure reason, shifting instead to a moral route through the utilization of "practical reason." In his *The Christian Faith* (2nd ed. 1830), Schleiermacher made a similar but quite different move, concentrating on the human self-consciousness, which he determined to be characterized by "the consciousness of being absolutely dependent, or, which is the same thing, of being in relation to God."[3] This point of departure required, furthermore, that "any proclamation of God which is to be operative upon and within us can only express God in His relation to us," not God as God is in and of Godself.[4]

Even so, Schleiermacher surrendered very little, and his own consciousness's appropriation of God's being, "in relation to us" of course, included and emphasized the traditional attributes of omnipotence, eternity, omnipresence, and omniscience.[5] And for him, "immutability" is already contained within the notion of God's eternity.[6] Causality within the entire system of nature can be exhaustively accounted for by God's causal activity.[7] Following the lead of Aquinas, Schleiermacher declared that there is no distinction between potential and actual in God.[8]

What is decidedly disappointing here is the entire lack of any really fresh probing into the categories of thinking about God that Schleiermacher inherited. The shift to the human consciousness, or "feelings," resulted in no concomitant shift in thinking about the object of those feelings. Might one just as readily experience a "consciousness of *absolute belovedness"* as an initial point of departure for probing God's relation with us? Schleiermacher was unable to move there. Not even a brief appendix on other divine attributes includes the consciousness of God as love.[9] Only at the very end of the enterprise is the notion of the divine love introduced, under the category of "the divine attributes which relate to redemption."[10]

The most curious and distressingly undeveloped notation offered here at the last is an acknowledgment, in commenting on 1 John 4:16, that, indeed, love alone can be understood to be that attribute of God that is in fact an expression "of the very essence of God."[11] This is a wholly unexpected concession. Had Schleiermacher begun here and unpacked this instead of tossing it off as a tantalizing *bon mot*, his work would have been truly revolutionary.

GOD WHO LOVES IN FREEDOM: KARL BARTH

Karl Barth (1886–1968) and Paul Tillich (1886–1965) were exact contemporaries, having been born in the same year, dying only three years apart.[12] Although their approaches to theology and the conclusions at which they arrived were vastly different from one another, I will treat both of them under this rubric of a failure to right the theistic ship.

Barth's theological output concerning the reality of God, especially in his vast, multi-volume *Church Dogmatics* (1936-1962), is rich, verbose, complex, and complicated. But at its core is a simple, straightforward declaration: that God is most basically to be defined as "the One who loves in freedom."[13] This freedom is not conditioned in any way by anything other than Godself: "God loves because he loves; because this act is His being, His essence and His nature . . . God's loving is necessary, for it is the being, the essence and the nature of God," but this is a necessity grounded in God's *freedom* and nowhere else.[14]

"God's act is His loving . . . 'God is' means 'God loves'."[14] That is a refreshing assertion, given the lack of central attention love as a key aspect of God's identity has typically been afforded in the tradition. Even so, this stops short of 1 John 4:8, 16, where God is not merely One who *loves*, but *is* love.[16]

It is also possible to speak of the "multiplicity, individuality and diversity of the perfections of God"[17] as aspects of the one true undivided God. In traditional theology these "perfections" are known as divine "attributes." Barth paired these perfections according to a distinction between God as He is in Himself and God as He is for us,[18] such as righteousness and mercy, or unity and omnipresence. One such pairing is understood to be constancy and omnipotence.[19] But Barth also distinguished between the perfections of the divine loving and those of the divine freedom, and treated power under the latter as, for example, in *Dogmatics in Outline*: "Thus God's power might also be described as God's freedom."[20]

Anna Case-Winters offers a telling critique of Barth's discussion of the interlocking relationship between God's freedom, power, and love:

> At times freedom and power seem almost to be interchangeable terms for Barth. Much of what Barth says concerning power is repeated in his position on freedom. At some points he even seems to reverse things and make freedom a subset of power.[21]

She goes on to assert:

> Barth's location of the discussion of omnipotence under the perfections of freedom rather than the perfections of love proves significant in yet another way. His unfolding development of the doctrine seems more concerned with illustrating divine freedom than with illustrating divine love. The all-determining notion of power which Barth in fact develops demonstrates divine freedom well enough but sometimes makes divine love and even the possibility of genuine divine relationship with a real "other" more difficult to conceive. He does not seem to allow "love" to shape, define, and constitute what power means in the same way that "freedom" shapes, defines, and constitutes the meaning. When it comes to omnipotence, Barth's use of the phrase "the One who loves in freedom" stresses "freedom" more than "love."[22]

This is a real sticking point. Omnipotence has not been allowed to be redefined by Love. God remains "all-powerful, with power over everything that He actually wills or could will,"[23] and Case-Winters notes that, for Barth, power "is still being conceived as the ability to dominate and control."[24] In a somewhat confusing combination of proposals, Barth maintained simultaneously that "God and God alone has real power, all the real power,"[25] but also God "allows what is outside Himself to have power." God's power is "free power over all, the power over all powers."[26] The only way to hold these two statements together would be to acknowledge that all powers other than God's are not, in the final analysis, *real*.

Barth has opened a door, regarding the centrality of love in his defining of the being of God, but it is a door through which he did not fully walk, alas. He insisted that "to define the subject [God] by the predicate [power] instead of the predicate by the subject would lead to disastrous consequences,"[27] and that is, of course, correct. Redefining power as *God's* power, rather than allowing traditional notions of power to control how we understand God, is precisely the step that Barth was not able to take; God's being as love (the subject) has not been allowed to redefine what is meant by the power (the predicate) of God.[28]

With regard to related matters, Barth preferred the term "constancy" to the traditional "immutability" because of his key emphasis on God's essential freedom but that finally amounts to a distinction without a real difference. God, the living, "constant" God, "is not Himself subject to or capable of any alteration."[29] Concomitantly, God's omniscience is not subject to alteration by what occurs in time: "God's knowledge, as omnipotent knowledge, is complete in its range, the one unique and all-embracing knowledge."[30] God's "knowledge of all things is what it is in eternal superiority to all things and *eternal independence of all things*."[31]

Barth's efforts came so close to resolving the power/love relationship in God, particularly in his focus on the implications of Jesus' crucifixion. Commenting on 1 Cor. 1:24 he wrote: "it is Jesus Christ the Crucified who is Himself the power of God,"[32] and later he reflected on the Corinthian theme of God's power in weakness (1 Cor. 1:18).[33] But he failed to allow these concessions to impact his fundamental stance on divine power. Sheila Greene Davaney expresses the problem cogently:

> Although divine power is revealed through powerlessness and passion, this is not the same as identifying God's power with

this impotence and passivity . . . God's power is so unique and so great and superior that it transcends and encompasses what for humanity are so often the oppositions of activity and passivity, power and powerlessness . . . divine power is active in powerlessness but is not to be merely equated with weakness and impotence.[34]

We are left with a sense of deep appreciation for the depths Barth plumbed in his endeavors to place the correlation of divine power and divine love on a new footing, but unfortunately he simply did go far enough to allow the implications of his very own searching to lead him to empowering breakthroughs beyond theism's impasses. The traditional synthesis was still breaking apart in the turbulent sea.

GOD AS BEING-ITSELF: PAUL TILLICH

For Paul Tillich, God does not exist. Even so, Tillich wrote and spoke about God throughout his adult life. This is not the contradiction it would seem to be. To "ex-ist" is to stand out from, to have reality apart from and alongside other similarly "ex-isting" entities. God, rather, is no Supreme Being among beings but that which underlies and holds together all that is separated. In short, God is to be comprehended as the "ground of being" or, equally, "being-itself."[35]

That is the famous revolution in theology that flourished in Tillich's work. With this critical distinction between finite beings and the infinite God as being-itself, Tillich tried to refloat the whole conceptual enterprise on a new hull. How well did he carry it off? Let us investigate that noble prospect.

The crucial ontological statements Tillich made about God were intended to be non-symbolic,[36] in contrast to everything else we try to convey with human words. God as being-itself includes "the power of resisting nonbeing." God is "the power of being in everything and above everything, the infinite power of being."[37] When we speak of God as "living," however, or "personal," we have vacated the non-symbolic premises. God now becomes "the ground of everything personal," the ground of all life.[38] Similarly, for God to be understood to be "in relation"—"external relations between God and the creature"—characterizes a symbolic statement only.[39]

Omnipotence as the power of a "highest being," once again, is rejected. Omnipotence is rather "the power of being which resists nonbeing in all its expressions and which is manifest in the creative process in all its forms."[40] But once again, omnipotence is another symbolic term, though it is retained as an expression of our ultimate courage to have faith in "a victory over the threat of nonbeing."[41] Tillich's non-symbolic statement is simply God as "the power of being."[42]

Following this thread, God as eternal relates to temporality not within it or above it but as the ground of time. "Eternity is the transcendent unity of the dissected moments of existential time."[43] Unaffected by time's passage but underlying it, it would appear to be clear that changelessness is a reliable characteristic of being-itself vis-a-vis changeable, existing beings.

What is to be said of the ground of being as love, or as loving? Tillich actually had a great deal to say about this matter. "Love is an ontological concept . . . And, since God is being-itself, one must say that being-itself is love . . . The process of the divine life has the character of love."[44] But this acknowledgment then has to be qualified: "As is the case of life and spirit, one speaks symbolically of God as love. He *is* love; this means that the divine life has the character of love but beyond the distinction between potentiality and actuality. This means therefore that it is mystery for finite understanding."[45]

How are divine power and divine love interrelated, especially in regard to the demands of justice and the "conflict between the divine love and the divine wrath against those who violate justice"?

> It is not the divine power as such which is thought to be in conflict with the divine love. The divine power is the power of being-itself, and being-itself is actual in the divine life whose nature is love." When justice and therefore love are violated, "judgment and condemnation follow. But they do not follow by a special act of divine wrath or retribution; they follow by the reaction of God's loving power against that which violates love. Condemnation is not the negation of love but the negation of the negation of love. It is an act of love without which nonbeing would triumph over being.[46]

Tillich pursued this relationship further three years after the first volume of his *Systematic Theology*, in a slim volume entitled *Love, Power, and Justice* (1954). The distinction of power and *force* is meaningful only for human beings: "there is indeed a compulsory element in the actuality of power. But this is only one element, and if power is reduced to it and loses the form of justice and the substance of love, it destroys itself."[47]

> Love and power are often contrasted in such a way that love is identified with a resignation of power and power with a denial of love. Powerless love and loveless power are contrasted. This, of course, is unavoidable if love is understood from its emotional side and power from its compulsory side. But such an understanding is error and confusion.[48]

Further along, Tillich offered a telling insight with the observation that "Love is the foundation, not the negation, of power."[49]

But all of this comes with a serious caveat. How can being-itself be said to *act*? Agents act. God is no existing Prime Agent. *Symbolically* we may speak of God's loving activity but how is this more than an aspect of human yearning for the assurance of the reliability of the ground of being against the encroaching threat of non-being? An apparent shift from Aristotle's unmoved Mover and the One I have identified in Aquinas as an unchanged Changer now becomes the essential Ground of existence that underlies the human "courage to be" by simply *being*. And if God as essentially Love does not actually *do* anything, how can God meaningfully be endowed with the term "love," even if only symbolically?

Nels F. S. Ferré summed up his critique of Tillich on this point in this way:

> Tillich had only a word for a solution without proper correspondence in truth. *Power works because in some sense it is*. If it is not limited static being, then it must be being in some form of dynamic reality . . . If the power *is* and *works* on and in the world, it must be related, but then according to Tillich it cannot be called unconditional and therefore not transcendent or unconditional. Thus Tillich in fact had no solution. His solution was pseudo-theological. Within his own presuppositions he failed to offer a theological ultimate that could stand the light of full analysis.[50]

GOD AS THE POWER OF THE FUTURE: WOLFHART PANNENBERG

The German Lutheran Wolfhart Pannenberg (1928–2014) was a remarkably young man when he first burst on the scene in the mid-1960s. He spent time in his formative teaching years in the company of Jürgen Moltmann at Wuppertal, where both shared an intense interest in the impact of the future on the present, although they subsequently went their separate ways in determining what that impact means. His work initially became a major stimulus on the tasks of theological construction, though the sense of its importance has more recently been on the wane.

Pannenberg tantalized American readers in 1969 when he announced in *Theology and the Kingdom of God*, in the midst of the debate over the presumed death of God, that, strictly speaking, "God does not yet exist."

> Jesus proclaimed the rule of God as a reality belonging to the future. This is the coming Kingdom. The idea was not new, being a conventional aspect of Jewish expectation. What was new was Jesus' understanding that God's claim on the world is to be viewed exclusively in terms of his coming rule. Thus it is necessary to say that, in a restricted but important sense, God does not yet exist. Since his rule and his being are inseparable, God's being is still in process of coming to be.[51]

This was a tantalizing proposal, at the time. It suggested a certain open-endedness that seemed to undergird human freedom of response to the divine initiative by pushing the fullness of God's being ahead to our ultimate future, in the definitive arrival of the eschatological *basileia tou theou*.

The primacy of the future of God is explicitly a corollary of the primacy of the *power* of the future, which is none other than God in the manifestation of God's Reign. God does not appear as one being among others. God has being explicitly as "the power of the future."[52]

Pannenberg went on, however, to clarify his intentions in a direction that showed this way of resolving the power and freedom dilemma to be only a chimera. From our perspective within history, it appears God is out there ahead of us. But from God's own perspective, the end of history is simply the point at which we encounter the reality that was true all along—that God is indeed eternally and self-consistently God but manifests Godself to history only as its forward flow is terminated. What Pannenberg has done, in fact, is stand Augustine on his side: God timelessly embraces our past, present, and future but now is seen to do so *ahead* of us rather than *above* us.[53]

The key in Pannenberg's formulation is his notion of God as the all-determining power. If he were to mean by this that God finally wraps up all the determinations of meaning that we have brought into existence by our human activity, that would be a proposal worth pursuing. But that falls short of Pannenberg's true position. He has insisted that, in light of the ultimate future ahead of us, it is the case not only that God is the all-determining power but is, in fact, the only true power. Omnipotence means not the highest power over other expressions of power but sole power.[54]

Pannenberg has never been reluctant to acknowledge explicitly that the power of God disclosed in the life and message of Jesus is essentially characterized by love. "However, if this love were powerless, then it would not be God, and if it were only one power among others, then it would not be the one God from whom and to whom are all things and who alone can in all seriousness be called God."[55] But even this awareness is qualified by the insistence that the power of God can be understood as one that "dominates all" and is "master over all,"[56] leading to the realization of "the complete dependence of everything real upon God."[57] The consequence of this understanding is the adopting of a position that I have termed "hard determinism," controlling every element in creation, in contrast to "soft determinism," in which God's final victory gives definitive shape to all that we have provisionally worked out by our own exercise of freedom along the way.[58] It is what finally renders Pannenberg's attempt to defend Augustine by shifting God from Eternal Present to Ultimate Future an unsuccessful effort to resolve the issue of theodicy.

I conclude, once again, that herculean efforts at reconceptualizing theology's quandary over the interrelatedness of God's power and love simply have not brought sufficiently fresh insight to the task. The conundrum concerning how Ultimate Being can manifest both love and power in a fully interconnected and fully realized way persists. The biblical witness to a living God whose power is shown forth precisely as a facet of essential love and not vice versa still remains alien to these and numerous other reworkings of the historic theistic synthesis, the detailing of which would finally prove redundant. One further issue will be addressed in the next chapter, before shifting our attention to the output of those who successfully attacked the inherited tradition and laid the groundwork for a recasting of the pivotal issue at hand.

ENDNOTES

1. *The Random House Dictionary of the English Language* (New York: Random House, 1969).

2. Immanuel Kant, *Critique of Pure Reason*, tr. Norman Kemp Smith (New York: St. Martin's Press, 1965), 22, 25 ft.

3. Friedrich Schleiermacher, *The Christian Faith*, 2nd ed., tr. and. ed. by H. R. MacIntosh and J. S. Stewart (New York: Harper & Row, 1963), 1:12.

4. Ibid., 1:52.

5. Ibid., 1:201f., spelled out in detail in 203–28.

6. Ibid., 1:206.

7. Ibid., 1:211f.

8. Ibid., 1:214.

9. Ibid., 1:228–32.

10. Ibid., 2:727–32.

11. Ibid., 2:731f.

12. Barth and Tillich were the theological giants who dominated the scene in my years of initial theological formation, in the 1960s. That has changed. No giants bestride the current landscape of multicultural particularity and fragmentation of focus. Nor did either generate a school called Barthianism or Tllichianism, although Tillich's influence could be seen in departments of Christian education and church school curricula

in mainline U.S. Protestant congregations for decades. A sense of the long-term importance of both has greatly receded in more recent times, and not so much for formulating the wrong answers as for failing to raise the right questions.

13. Karl Barth, *Church Dogmatics*, tr. and ed. G. W. Bromiley and T. F. Torrance (Edinburgh: T. & T. Clark, 1936–1962), Vol. 2, Part 1, 257, 322, et al. (Henceforth: CD.)

14. Ibid., 2:1, 279f.

15. Ibid., 2:1, 283.

16. In a later volume of his *Church Dogmatics*, Barth, in discussing the humanity of God in Jesus, did go on to affirm that "the statements 'God is' and 'God loves' are synonymous," and that John's assertion that God *is* love is "a genuine equation." (4:2, 755f.) Had he dared to develop the implications of this acknowledgment for his doctrine of God, he could not have been included in this chapter on the sinking of the theistic synthesis.

17. Ibid., 2:1, 332.

18. Ibid., 2:1, 346.

19. Ibid., 2:1, 490–607.

20. Barth, *Dogmatics in Outline*, tr. G. T. Thompson (New York: Harper & Brothers, 1959), 47.

21. Anna Case-Winters, *God's Power: Traditional Understandings and Contemporary Challenges* (Louisville: Westminster/John Knox Press, 1990), 100. See Barth, *CD* 1:2, 674: "Freedom means ability, possibility, power–power in its illimitability or its equality over against other powers."

22. Case-Winters, 100f.

23. Barth, *CD* 2:1, 522.

24. Case-Winters, 97.

25. Barth, *CD* 2:1, 531.

26. Ibid., 2:1, 543.

27. Ibid., 2:1, 524.

28. Sheila Greene Davaney also calls attention to this critical point, to wit, that Barth made the correct *claim*, "that we cannot begin with any

general or universal idea of power and then apply it to God in some super- or preeminent manner," but then failed to execute it. Davaney, *Divine Power: A Study of Karl Barth and Charles Hartshorne* (Philadelphia: Fortress Press, 1986), 31.

29. Ibid., 2:1, 491.

30. Ibid., 2:1, 552.

31. Ibid., 2:1, 559, emphasis mine.

32. Ibid., 2:1, 607.

33. Ibid., 4:1, 186f., 191f.

34. Davaney, op. cit., 56.

35. Paul Tillich, *Systematic Theology*, 3 vols. (Chicago: The University of Chicago Press, 1951–63), 1:235.

36. Ibid., 1:238.

37. Ibid., 1:236, for both quotes.

38. Ibid., 1:245.

39. Ibid., 1:271.

40. Ibid., 1:273.

41. Ibid.

42. E.g. Tillich, *Systematic* 1:272.

43. Ibid., 1:274.

44. Ibid., 1:279.

45. Ibid., 1:280, emphasis original.

46. Ibid., 1:283 (both quotes).

47. Tillich, *Love, Power, and Justice* (New York: Oxford University Press, 1954), 8.

48. Ibid., 11.

49. Ibid., 49.

50. Nels F. S. Ferré, "Tillich and the Nature of Transcendence," in *Paul Tillich: Retrospect and Future* (Nashville: Abingdon Press, 1966), 15, emphases original.

51. Wolfhart Pannenberg, *Theology and the Kingdom of God* (Philadelphia:

The Westminster Press, 1969), 56.

52. Pannenberg, *Basic Questions in Theology, Vol. II*, tr. George H. Kehm (Philadelphia: Fortress Press, 1971), 242.

53. See my extended analysis of this position in my *On the Way to God: An Exploration into the Theology of Wolfhart Pannenberg* (Lanham, Maryland: University Press of America, 1989), 249–70.

54. Ibid., 270–80. See also my "The All-Determining God and the Peril of Determinism," in Carl E. Braaten and Philip Clayton, eds., *The Theology of Wolfhart Pannenberg* (Minneapolis: Augsburg Publishing House, 1988), 152–68.

55. Pannenberg, "Response to the Discussion," in James M. Robinson and John B. Cobb, Jr., eds., *Theology as History* (New York: Harper & Row, 1967), 232, ft. 10.

56. Pannenberg, *Theology and the Kingdom of God*, 55.

57. Pannenberg and Lewis Ford, "A Dialog about Process Philosophy," *Encounter* 38, 1977, 320.

58. See my "The All-Determining God and the Peril of Determinism," 160–62.

7

The Victory of a Stoic God

The debate has long been waged as to which Greek philosophical system most extensively underlies the development of Christian thought in the West: the Platonism and neo-Platonism appropriated by Augustine or the Aristotelianism reshaped by Thomas Aquinas. With regard to an understanding of the power and love of God, I contend that neither was victorious. The actual philosophical model that became dominant in this particular respect was, in fact, *Stoicism*.

THE PHILOSOPHY OF STOICISM

The title of this philosophical movement comes from the Greek philosopher Zeno's habit of lecturing formally on the *Stoa Poikile*, the "Painted Porch," in Athens around 300 BCE. The "late Stoics" are represented in Rome by the ex-slave Epictetus (*ca.* 50–138 CE) and the emperor Marcus Aurelius (121–180).

It is not the Stoics' doctrine of God itself so much as the *ethic* of stoicism imposed upon the divine that has been utilized: to be utterly tranquil, unaffected by external exigencies, nonattached, disinterested—in short, apathetic (*apatheia*).

Live according to the benevolence and orderliness of the universe. The consequence of such a life is *apatheia*, or *euthymia*, spiritual peace and well-being ... Having achieved this ultimate goal, one's life is as autonomous, as uniform, and as benevolent as God himself.[1]

In underscoring the inclusion of pathos as a valid aspect of the witness of the biblical prophets, Abraham Heschel traced the avoidance of this concession back to the influence of the fundamental Stoic stance:

> The Stoics regarded passion, impulse, desire—the emotions in the widest sense—as unreasonable, unnatural, and the source of evil. To live rightly was to dominate the emotional life by reason, and so to act by will. Pathos was considered to be the chief danger to the self-determination of man, whereas "apathy"—the subduing of the emotions—was believed to be the supreme moral task.[2]

Heschel quotes Zeno as having defined pathos as "a movement in the soul contrary to reason to the soul's very nature."[3]

Marcus Aurelius observed in his *Meditations* (170–80) the importance of "keeping the divinity within us free from violence and unharmed, superior to pain and pleasure ... not feeling the need of another's doing or not doing something; and, furthermore, accepting all that happens and all that is allotted us, as coming from the source, wherever it is, whence it itself came."[4] There is here, of course, a definite touch of determinism, of simply "going with the flow": "Love only that which happens to you and is woven with the thread of your destiny."[5] But the relevancy of these observations is the notion of not becoming attached to anything outside oneself, so that Aurelius can finally propose: "Wipe out fancy; check desire; extinguish appetite; keep your ruling faculty in control."[6] In short, achieve an attitude of sublime *indifference* toward everything outside your own being.[7] Be benevolent toward others, certainly, but without any expectation of your benevolence making any difference in the flow of the universe.

A STOIC THEOLOGY

I am by no means the first to observe this dominant role of the Stoic ethic in how the theistic synthesis came to be expressed in the theologians I have been analyzing up to this point. Well over half a century ago, Charles Hartshorne offered this observation:

> Just as the Stoics said the ideal was to have good will toward all but not in such fashion as to depend in any degree for happiness upon their fortunes or misfortunes, so Christian theologians, who scarcely accepted this idea in their ethics, nevertheless adhered to it in characterizing God.[8]

And more recently, on this same point, Nicholas Wolterstorff concluded:

> the Augustinian God turns out to be remarkably like the Stoic sage: devoid of passions, unfamiliar with longing, foreign to suffering, dwelling in steady bliss, exhibiting to others only benevolence. Augustine fought free of the Stoic (and neo-Platonic) vision when it came to humanity; when it came to God, he succumbed.[9]

Jürgen Moltmann appears to be the one who has devoted the greatest amount of attention to this matter. His overall contribution to our subject will be examined in a later chapter, but it is pertinent here to lift up his evaluation of the role Stoic ideas played in the established view on God's love and power.

In *The Crucified God* (originally, 1972), an intentionally provocative title, Moltmann saw clearly that traditional Christian thought tried to resolve the tension between God's love and God's self-contained immutability by championing the Stoic elevation of *apatheia* as a way of characterizing a divine love that is no in way affected by the recipient of that love. *Agape* was translated into apathetic love:

> What Christianity proclaimed as the *agape* of God and the believer was rarely translated as *pathos*. Because true *agape* derives from liberation from the inward and outward fetters of the flesh (*sarx*), and loves without self-seeking and anxiety . . . apatheia could be taken up as an enabling ground for this love and be

filled with it. Love arises from the spirit and from freedom, not from desire or anxiety. The apathic God could therefore be understood as the free God who freed others for himself. The negation of need, desire and compulsion expressed by apatheia was taken up and filled with a new positive content.[10]

Clearly the elevation of non-pathos was not limited to Stoic writings; it permeates much of ancient Greek philosophy in general. But it is so explicitly at the heart of Stoicism that I claim justification for the thesis of this chapter. This comes with the strong conviction that the process of undoing the bondage of biblical witness to unhelpful philosophical categories will necessarily include this reversal as a key component of challenge and reconstruction. Apathetic love is not biblical love. A more satisfactory way of comprehending divine love may well pave the way to a more viable way of reconceiving divine power.

MOVING FORWARD BY GOING BACK

Gordon Kaufman (1925–2011) has called attention to an overemphasis on "God's tyrannical omnipotence" that offended many sensitive and thoughtful humanists who found it impossible to worship or believe in such a deity.

> The horrendous evils in human society, especially as these have come clearly into view in the twentieth century, suggest that only a terrible monster-God could have been responsible for our world. If God is indeed omnipotent, the one whose will is being realized in our history, God is not one whom we should serve but rather one whom we should loathe and despise and against whom we should struggle with all our strength. Worship of such a being could, in fact, evoke from devotees harsh and authoritarian attitudes and actions similar to those attributed to God.[11]

It seems hardly coincidental that the term in English for those who reject the reality of God is "atheism." That becomes understandable, to me, specifically as *a-theism*, much more the rejection of *theism's God* than of a God more accurately conceived. Atheism is never the denial of God in general. It always takes the shape of the denial of a particular way of conceiving of God.[12] The Stoic God of classical Christian theism has become a problem to be resolved.

How do we move beyond the impasse? Many voices have not been heard up to now. The voices to which I wish to pay extensive attention are those that might be called "counter-testimonies."[13] Challenges to the Augustinian synthesis can be found as far back as the Middle Ages themselves, but they become stronger and more widespread only in more recent times, continuing emphatically into the present. The variety of concerns and issues finding expression in these counter-testimonies contributes each in its own way to chipping away at a crumbling and increasingly uninhabitable edifice, suggesting valuable alternatives that merit consideration as attempts at a new resolution are explored. To these we now turn.

ENDNOTES

1. Philip P. Hallie, "Stoicism," in Paul Edwards, ed., *The Encyclopedia of Philosophy* (New York: Macmillan Publishing Co., 1967), 8:21.

2. Abraham J. Heschel *The Prophets* (New York: Harper & Row, 1962), 2:32.

3. Ibid., 2:33.

4. Marcus Aurelius, *Meditations* 2:17, tr. Charles Long, rev., in *Marcus Aurelius and His Times* (Roslyn, New York: Walter J. Black, Inc., 1945), 25.

5. Ibid., 7:57 (Long, 76).

6. Ibid., 9:7 (Long, 93). See also 3:6 (Long, 29).

7. See, e.g., ibid., 11:16 (Long, 119).

8. Charles Hartshorne, *Man's Vision of God* (New York: Harper & Brothers, 1941), 116.

9. Nicholas Wolterstorff, "Suffering Love," in Thomas V. Morris, ed., *Philosophy and the Christian Faith* (Notre Dame: University of Notre Dame Press, 1988), 210.

10. Jürgen Moltmann, *The Crucified God: The Cross of Christ as the*

Foundation and Criticism of Christian Theology, tr. R. A. Wilson and John Bowden (New York: Harper & Row, 1974), 269f. See 267–78 for his full discussion of the topic, particularly as it applies to Jewish tradition and responses to the Holocaust.

11. Gordon D. Kaufman, *The Theological Imagination: Constructing the Concept of God* (Philadelphia: The Westminster Press, 1981), 42.

12. As a quick illustration of this point, consider the frequent remarks of Bill Maher on his HBO weekly television show.

13. I am indebted to Walter Brueggemann for this term, in the title of Part II of his *Theology of the Old Testament* (Minneapolis: Fortress Press, 1997), 315.

Part III

The Eventual Collapse of the Untenable

8

Musings on the Mystics' God

The prevailing understanding of the subordination of Love under the dominant role of divine Power that we have been encountering in the history of western Christian thought not only failed to resolve what the philosopher Leibniz termed the "theodicy" problem but, in fact, explicitly gave rise to it. It is precisely in the context of a God whose power is omnipotent and is uninfluenced by any factors outside Godself that the conflict between the reality of God and the sometimes horrific suffering that occurs within God's creation becomes a barrier to belief, a conflict succinctly captured in Archibald MacLeish's *J.B.*:

> I heard upon his dry dung heap
> That man cry out who cannot sleep:
> "If God is God He is not good,
> If God is good He is not God;
> Take the even, take the odd,
> I would not sleep here if I could."[1]

The allusion to the biblical Job can easily be recast thus: *If God is Power, God is Not Love; if God is Love, God is not Power.* That is the dilemma with which twenty centuries of predominant theological construction has left us.

What follows here are a number of investigations into deconstructive activity that varyingly challenge the inherited consensus with what I am calling the church's counter-testimony. Only after that survey has been accomplished are we in a position to visualize an alternative synthesis that returns to the central theme of the biblical witness, of a living God whose love is preeminently powerful *as love*, not an overpowering God whose love is one divine attribute among others and often in contradistinction to that power.

Structurally, **Parts I and II have** proceeded according to historical chronology. **Part III** departs from this orientation, proceeding topically but with some degree of chronology also present, while attempting to surface the varying challenges with attention to when they first arose.

I begin with luminaries in the arena of Christian mysticism—both male and, especially, female.

THE PRIMACY OF LOVE: DIONYSIUS AND BONAVENTURE

DIONYSIUS, EARLY SIXTH CENTURY

The written work of Dionysius "the Areopagite" became the primary source behind almost the whole of Christian mysticism for centuries. Originating early in the sixth century,[2] and now often referred to as "pseudo"-Dionysius to distinguish it from any earlier period, the writings convey a "Godhead" that is, strictly speaking, absolutely beyond all possible distinctions. Dionysius' Godhead, in bringing the world into being, participates in an "emptying process of Differentiation."[3] The Supreme Godhead "is One in an unchangeable and super-essential manner, being neither a unit in the multiplicity of things nor yet the sum total of such units."[4] The Godhead embraces and maintains all unity and plurality, yet in itself is beyond that distinction—as, of course, beyond any other.

Dionysius the mystic wished to limit all perceptions of God to the fundamental conviction about God as undifferentiated. Dionysius the rational thinker was not bound by that. He proceeded to talk indeed about God as differentiated—Trinity, divine attributes, creativity, etc. The value of unpacking "divine names" is that they variously inform our feeble efforts to stumble toward the all-encompassing Ineffable.

Although never genuinely true in any explicit sense, they nevertheless point us in helpful directions.

In that spirit, then, Dionysius could affirm that *love*, as applied to the Godhead, "means a faculty of unifying and conjoining and of producing a special commingling together in the Beautiful and Good . . . and holds together things of the same order by a mutual connection, and moves the highest to take thought for those below and fixes the inferior in a state which seeks the higher."[5]

> [God] moves and leads onward Himself unto Himself. Therefore on the one hand they call Him the Object of Love and Yearning as being Beautiful and Good, and on the other they call Him Yearning and Love as being a Motive-Power leading all things to Himself, Who is the only ultimate Beautiful and Good—yea, as being His own Self-Revelation and the Bounteous Emanation of His own Transcendent Unity, a Motion of Yearning simple, self-moved, self-acting, pre-existent in the Good, and overflowing from the Good into creation, and once again returning to the Good.[6]

So God moves creation not through any direct or conscious activity on God's part but by the power of attraction that Love actualizes.

As we have encountered elsewhere, evil is identified here as the absence of the Good, having no existence in and of itself.[7] Dionysius enthusiastically surpassed Augustine in his attack on evil's substantiality:

> Unto evil we can attribute but an accidental kind of existence. It exists for the sake of something else, and is not self-originating . . . Thus evil is contrary to progress, purpose, nature, cause, principle, end, law, will and being. Evil is, then, a lack, a deficiency, a weakness, a disproportion, an error, purposeless, unlovely, lifeless, unwise, unreasonable, imperfect, unreal, causeless, indeterminate, sterile, inert, powerless, disordered, incongruous, indefinite, dark, unsubstantial, and never in itself possessed of any existence whatsoever.[8]

Dionysius elevated the centrality of love for God without really integrating this in some way with God's power, though he did offer reflections in that direction. The Godhead "transcends and exceeds every mode of Power however conceived."⁹ How that is so, he did not elucidate, beyond the following observation:

> God is Power because in His own Self He contains all power beforehand and exceeds it, and because He is the Cause of all power and produces all things by a power which may not be thwarted nor circumscribed, and because He is the Cause wherefrom Power exists whether in the whole system of the world or in any particular part. Yea, He is Infinitely Powerful not only in that all Power comes from Him, but also because He is above all power and is Very Power, and possesses that excess of Power which produces in infinite ways an infinite number of other existent powers.[10]

Dionysius did comment at one point about something he called "the omnipotent goodness of the Divine weakness,"[11] but he did not elaborate on the implications of this insight.

All in all, his provocative notion of love as a power of attraction, engendering in that which emanates from God (or is created by God) a desire for reunification—the mystic's goal—is intriguing but insufficiently fulfilling. Love is no purposive activity on the part of a God who is beyond all entanglements of interrelationship.

BONAVENTURE, 1221–1274

Dionysius was one of the major influences on Bonaventure of Bagnoregio, as was Richard of St. Victor whom we met earlier. Denis Edwards credits Bonaventure with having developed a trinitarian theology that is fully dynamic and relational—both within the Trinity and toward creation.[12] He was the first to speak of a *circumincessio*, a "mov[ing] around one another" that brings to mind the image of a "divine dance . . . of unthinkable intimacy and mutual love" that overflows into the universe.[13] More recently, he has become a major focus in the writings of the Franciscan theologian Ilia Delio, whose interpretive work aids the summary undertaken here.

Bonaventure could use "love" as the name for the third person of the Trinity,[14] Pairing this with God's essential goodness, he saw God and God's love to be "self-diffusive," a key concept; God *diffuses* Godself throughout creation: "The pure actualization of the principle of Charity" pours forth "free and due love, and both mingled together, which is the fullest diffusion according to nature and will."[15]

This understanding starts in the interrelationships of the persons of the Trinity but then constitutively flows out from there. As Ilia Delio has expressed it:

> Love cannot exist in isolation or autonomously because love shares itself with another. Love requires a lover and a beloved, a giver and a receiver. It is the receptivity of love that makes it a gift. The Father who is the fountain fullness of love is always moving toward the Son in the sharing of love, and this sharing of love is the Spirit . . . If we really believe that God is love and this love is the love of the Father for the Son united in the Spirit, then we must also believe that we are part of this wonderful, awesome, incredible relationship of love.[16]

This diffusion of love is powerfully expressed in Bonaventure's second "Sermon on the Nativity of the Lord": "'The Word was made flesh' [John 1:14]. These words give expression to that heavenly mystery . . . that *the eternal God has humbly bent down* and lifted the dust of our nature into unity with his own person." Because we are finite creatures, God "bends over in love to embrace us."[17] The God who is "Most High" is the God who is "most intimately related to us."[18] Delio concludes:

> What Bonaventure points out is that the cross reveals the mystery of God's *overflowing* love. Unlike finite human love that draws up conditions for its wants and needs, God's love is unconditional and totally self-giving . . . In Bonaventure's view, the mystery of cruciform love leads us into the very heart of the mystery of God."[19]

What we have encountered here, in both Dionysius and Bonaventure, is a turning away from God the powerful to God the loving, without actually attempting any fresh explanation of the relationship between these two facets of God's being. But it is an important step in the right direction, correcting the prevailing overemphasis on power and introducing us to an alternative begging to be explored further.

REPRESSED VOICES: THE CONTRIBUTIONS OF WOMEN MYSTICS

Had male theologians paid serious attention to the recorded visions and voices of the women mystics of the High Middle Ages, Augustine's folly might well have been overturned centuries ago. Their writings were never systematic in nature, so that hints and allusions without conceptual integration abound. For today, that remains both their tantalizing charm and their incompleteness. There are six who merit inclusion here.

HILDEGARD OF BINGEN, 1098–1179

Hildegard was a visionary prophetess and not so much a mystic per se. Serving as a prophet was a safe way for a woman of that time to share her theological insights out loud. Barbara Newman writes in her introduction to Hildegard's *Scivias* (1141–51), "If Hildegard had been a male theologian, her *Scivias* would undoubtedly have been considered one of the most important early medieval summas . . . it is a prophetic proclamation, a book of allegorical visions, an exegetical study, a theological summa."[20]

For the most part, Hildegard was quite traditional. In every cosmic development "God continues immovable, without any change of any mutability in His power."[21] God is "Omnipotent God."[22] "No weak, mortal sinner can understand the serenity and beauty of the power of God or attain a likeness to it, for God's power is unfailing."[23] God's omnipotent power is "incomprehensible."[24]

In contrast to this traditional supremacy of God's immutable power, Hildegard went on to take a sharp right turn. In *The Book of Divine Works* (*De operatione Dei*, 1163–73), at the very end of her commentary on her second vision, of the cosmic wheel, she entitled section 46: "On love as the vital power of the universe."[25] The first of three figures in Vision 8 is "Love, the splendor of the living God."[26] Love speaks of the second figure, Wisdom, as one whom "nothing can resist . . . Out of her own being and by herself she has formed all things in love and tenderness."[27] "The bubbling source of the living God is the purity in which God's splendor is revealed."[28] "Everything God has made has been made in love, humility, and peace."[29]

There is, alas, no real wrestling with any conceptual integration of divine love and power here. God the Almighty is still comprehended in traditional terms of omnipotence and total foreknowledge. Love and wisdom are seen as significant female attributes of a God who remains, in the final analysis, decidedly male. Hildegard represents but a beginning in a retrieval of the theme of love as central to the being of God. Deeper insights were to follow.

HADEWIJCH OF ANTWERP, ACTIVE 1220–1240

Very little is known about the life of Hadewijch. She lived in the Netherlands and wrote in Flemish. She was a beguine, a member of a woman's religious community but without taking a nun's vows. A contemporary of Aquinas, she was very committed to the works of Augustine.

Hadewijch was a poetic mystic. According to Bernard Brady, she was "consumed by love."[30] The word she used for love was *minne*, "the dynamic love of a person for God,"[31] giving one the impression that Hadewijch took the medieval tradition of *courtly love* and spiritualized it.

In her *Letters*, Hadewijch wrote of "omnipotent Love."[32] God orders the world properly, from the indigent to the commoner to the noble knight to the peer of the realm. God is "powerful and sovereign above all power."[33] Love is "God himself by Nature."[34]

Hadewijch continued, in her poetry, to juxtapose without integration or explanation the themes of love and power in God.

> For Love's rich power
> Is new and indeed friendly.[35]
> Love "renews itself in all."[36]
> Oh, Love is ever new,
> And she revives every day![37]
>
> Were anyone ready in Love's service,
> He would receive from her a reward:
> New consolation and new power;
> And if he loved Love with the power of love,
> He would speedily become love with Love.[38]

> "Love's nature . . . conquers all powers . . .
> Love's nature is . . . powerful in its activity . . .
> In it is all the power of God."[39]

The phrases are tantalizing and provocative. Even in their lack of full integration they dance in the mind with promises of possible conjunctions not hitherto observed. They leave the reader with the question, "Yes—but how so?" It is precisely the question of *how* love is powerful in God, in contrast to traditional understandings of the nature of divine power, that continues to whet the theological appetite.

GERTRUDE OF HELFTA, *THE HERALD OF DIVINE LOVE*, 1289–1302

Gertrude of Helfta was a German Benedictine nun who wrote, mostly for the benefit of her younger monastic sisters, as the result of the experiencing of numerous visions. Of the five books of the surviving *The Herald of Divine Love*, only Book Two was actually written by her.

God, for Gertrude, is love above all else. Indeed, her visions often took the form of a spousal mystical union with the Son in the Trinity, as Bride of Christ. And this love is characterized, once again, as qualifying the nature of God's power: "Not that you, Divine Omnipotence and Eternal Wisdom, gave unwillingly, as though compelled by some sort of necessity, but rather that you freely bestowed your love, out of the boundless flood of your loving generosity, upon an unworthy and ungrateful creature."[40] In an earlier paragraph she recited her inference of what God had disclosed to her:

> How would my infinite power be extolled if I did not reserve to myself the power, in whatever place I might be, of keeping myself to myself, so that I might make myself felt or seen only in the way that is most fitting according to places, times, and persons? For from the beginning of the creation of heaven and earth, and in the whole work of the Redemption, I have employed wisdom and goodness rather than power and majesty. And the goodness of this wisdom shines forth best in my bearing with imperfect creatures till I draw them, of their own free will, into the way of perfection.[41]

Love, then, as we have observed previously, appears to be an "attractive" power, drawing God's creatures godward of their own free will. But so much remained undeveloped that we can only thank Gertrude of Helfta for her visionary insights and probe further into their underlying implications.

CATHERINE OF SIENA, 1347–80

Catherine was the second woman to be named by the pope a doctor of the church, in 1970, though she was earlier than the first, Teresa of Avila. Refusing marriage but not becoming a nun, she lived an active, engaged life outside a convent's walls as a Dominican laywoman, even interceding on Pope Gregory XI's behalf to end his exile in Avignon and return to Rome. She was said to have had her first vision of God at age six. She had no formal education in matters theological and, in fact, did not learn to write until late in life, even then writing in her own Sienese dialect and not in the Latin of the church's scholars.

Other than her collected letters and prayers, Catherine's body of work consists of a running conversation between her and God, simply entitled *The Dialogue* (1377–78). Very often the "I" as well as the "you" of the text is understood to be the God Catherine is "hearing" in her meditating. And the central theme that runs all through this recorded experience is none other than *love*. It puts in an appearance on almost every page, whereas *power* appears hardly at all.

Catherine's notions about divine power break no new ground. But she waxed enthusiastic, with vivid imagery, about the centrality of love in God's way with us. God can be said to be "drunk with love,"[42] "madly in love" with us.[43] It is an "immeasurable" love,[44] a "gratuitous" love,[45] an "unimaginable" love. It constitutes the "why" behind God's act of creation: "With unimaginable love you looked upon your creatures within your very self, and you fell in love with us. So it was love that made you create us and give us being just so that we might taste your supreme eternal good."[46]

The work of Catherine of Siena contains little of interest to add to our discussion with the singular and very important exception that she is in that select number of early voices to counsel the church to consider, in its theology, what it means to take seriously the biblical notion that God *is* love. It has taken a long time for that counsel to bear fruit, but the bestowing of her "doctor of the church" status gives added ecclesiastical weight to her contribution.

JULIAN OF NORWICH, *REVELATIONS OF DIVINE LOVE*, 1373–74

Julian was an English anchoress who, at the age of thirty and before entering a convent, suffered a nearly fatal illness. While apparently on her deathbed she experienced sixteen intense visions of Jesus Christ, and wrote down her recollection of them immediately after her recovery. That initial transcription is known as the "Short Text" and is the earliest surviving instance of a woman writing in the English language. The "Long Text," not used here, was completed twenty years later with further reflections on the initial visions.

Once again we encounter emphases on the pivotal role of love in God's relations with us. God is "the maker, lover, and keeper."[47] God is "almighty, all wise, and all loving . . . every created thing has been made for love, and is sustained by that same love."[48]

But this understanding of love is extremely complex. There is in Julian a touch of spiritual masochism, in her mystical union with Christ in his sufferings. "God freely gives pleasure when he chooses, and other times he leaves us in pain. Both are done for love."[49]

Why does the good God allow sin to occur? It is to manifest to human beings the great love of God, poured out for us in the passion of the Christ, so that we will be led to love God in return and not take God's love for granted.[50] Jesus tells her in her visions, "I shall make all things well . . . All shall be well."[51] In other words, the power of God's love is manifest in the saving, for the bliss of eternity, of all those souls whose "natural will" never actually "assented to sin."[52] "When it comes to our salvation, God is as eager as he is powerful and wise . . . Thus we can see that *he is love itself.*"[53] "The love of God is so great that he considers us to be partners in his good deed."[54] God takes pleasure in our willing (in prayer, especially) what God already desires and intends.

This overarching focus on divine love has not entered, thus far, into any inquiry into how this relates to divine power. But Julian had one final surprise in store for her readers. As she reflected on her visions, at the very end, she had this to say:

> Many men and women believe that God is all mighty and may do all, and that he is all wisdom and can do all; *but that he is all love and will do all—there they stop* . . . Of all the properties of the blessed trinity, God wants us to feel the *greatest confidence and pleasure in love, for love makes power and wisdom humble before us.*[55]

This is a very strong statement. For love to make power humble is a bold assertion indeed. But it requires further unpacking if it is to be helpful.

Sheila Upjohn summarized her perceptive study of Julian in these words:

> But the fact that Christ became man, so that God could know evil by experience, and not only intelligence, means that every sorrow, every grief, every agony has been experienced by God himself—and that there is no place so dark and painful that God has not been there before us and stays there with us. And the fact of the resurrection means that there is no evil so bad that he cannot turn it into good.[56]

Upjohn goes on to say: "the God who can lack nothing—who has everything, is in everything, does everything—is shown to be the God made needy by love."[57] Reasons for the recovery of the importance of Julian of Norwich for contemporary theology are obvious, given the powerful direction in which her interpretation of her visions pointed.

TERESA OF AVILA, 1515–82

Teresa appeared on the historical scene two centuries later in Spain, in the midst of the sometimes bloody and repressive Catholic Counterreformation that included the Inquisition. Her own work unquestioningly accepted the absolute omnipotence of God: God is "all-powerful" and can do whatever God wills to do.[58] The final chapter in *The Book of Her Life* includes reflections on God's "majesty and power"[59] as "all-powerful Lord."[60] And in the *Soliloquies*, she expressed to God: "O Lord, I confess Your great power. If You are powerful, as

You are, what is impossible for You who can do everything? . . . I firmly believe You can do what You desire."⁶¹

Her focus on God's love is present though less developed. It is also hardly benign. "Oh, *powerful love of God*, how different are your effects from those of the world's love!"⁶² The great love of God comes to undeserving sinners in a transforming way that is piercingly painful as well as spiritually soothing. In one instance she shared a vision in which an angel is holding "a large golden dart" with a fire blazing at the end of the iron tip. "It seemed to me this angel plunged the dart several times into my heart and that it reached deep within me. When he drew it out, I thought he was carrying off with him the deepest part of me; and he left me all on fire with great love of God."⁶³

The six women mystics reviewed in this section punctured the prevailing limitations on the full nature of divine love, although there does not appear to have been any concomitant focus on how this might help redefine divine power. A major facet of the contributions of the medieval women mystics is their daring to lift up aspects of the being of God that are unabashedly characterized as more feminine than masculine in character, a direction that will be pursued heartily in the fresh voices of women theologians in the twentieth century and on into the twenty-first. The initial lack of fulfillment of that "opening up" of the being of God is seen in not taking the further step, of reclothing male virtues of power and control and implacability in new alternative understandings.

ENDNOTES

1. Archibald MacLeish, *J.B.* (Cambridge, Massachusetts: The Riverside Press, 1956), Prologue, 11. The words are spoken by the character Nickles, representing Satan.

2. The first recorded reference to Dionysius is from the Council of Constantinople of 533 CE.

3. Dionysius the Areopagite, *On the Divine Names*, 2.11, tr. CE. Rolt (Berwick, Maine: Ibis Press, 2004; orig. pub. 1920), 79. The translator is the same Clarence Edwin Rolt whom we will encounter later in the chapter on "Breakthroughs to a Loving God." Rolt's footnote to this topic a bit further on is apropos: God "creates the world as being the

Object of its desire. He attracts it into existence." (Rolt, 87, ft. 1.)

4. Ibid., 2.11 (Rolt, 79).

5. Ibid., 4.12 (Rolt, 105.) In an earlier footnote regarding this subject, Rolt wrote that, for Dionysius, "Love is the most perfect manifestation of God. Yet God is in a sense beyond even love as we know it. For love, as we know it, implies the distinction between 'me' and 'thee', and God is ultimately beyond such distinction." (Rolt, 57, ft. 2.)

6. Ibid., 4.14 (Rolt, 107).

7. Ibid., 4.19-20 (Rolt, 111–17).

8. Ibid., 4.32 (Rolt, 127).

9. Ibid., 8.1 (Rolt, 155).

10. Ibid., 8.2 (Rolt, 155).

11. Ibid., 3.2 (Rolt, 84).

12. Denis Edwards, "The Discovery of Chaos and the Retrieval of the Trinity," in Robert John Russell, Nancey Murphy, and Arthur R. Peacocke, eds., *Chaos and Complexity: Scientific Perspectives on Divine Action* (Berkeley: The Center for Theology and the Natural Sciences, 1995), 160.

13. Ibid., 161.

14. Bonaventure, *Journey of the Mind into God*, 3.5. Online: www.crossroadsinitiative.com /library_article/666/journey_of_the_Mind_into_God_St._Bonaventure.html

15. Ibid., 6.2.

16. Ilia Delio, *The Humility of God: a Franciscan Perspective* (Cincinnati: Franciscan Media, 2005), 41, 44.

17. Ibid., 51, emphasis Delio's, quoting from *What Manner of Man? Sermons on Christ by St. Bonaventure*, tr. Zachary Hayes (Chicago: Franciscan Herald Press, 1989), 57.

18. Ibid., 52.

19. Ibid., 54.

20. Barbara J. Newman, "Introduction," in Hildegard of Bingen, *Scivias*, tr. Columba Hart and Jane Bishop (New York: Paulist Press, 1990), 23, 25.

21. Hildegard, *Scivias*, Book I, Vision 2, Para. 1 (73 in Paulist Press ed.).

22. Ibid., I.3.2 (94).

23. Ibid., I.6.5 (141).

24. Ibid., II.1.1,6, (150, 152). See also III.1.11 (316f.).

25. Hildegard of Bingen, *Book of Divine Works*, ed. Matthew Fox, tr. Robert Cunningham (Santa Fe, NM: Bear & Co., 1987), Appendix, 395.

26. Ibid., 8.2 (204).

27. Ibid., 8.2 (206).

28. Ibid., 8.2 (207).

29. Ibid., 8.3 (208).

30. Bernard V. Brady, *Christian Love* (Washington, D.C.: Georgetown University Press, 2003), 141.

31. Ibid., 141.

32. Hadewijch, *Letters*, 1, 18, in *The Complete Works*, tr. Columba Hart (New York:Paulist Press, 1980), 48, 87.

33. Ibid., L18 (85).

34. Ibid., L19 (89).

35. Hadewijch, *Poems in Stanzas*, 7.1, in *The Complete Works*, 144. This novelty is asserted in striking contradiction to God's essential immutability.

36. Ibid., 7.2 (145).

37. Ibid., 7.3 (145).

38. Ibid., 8.1 (147). This renders poetically an understanding in process theology, in the twentieth century, of how our openness to God's initial aim for us moment by moment empowers us for further and greater responses to even higher aims. This will be pursued in later chapters.

39. Hadewijch, *Poems in Couplets*, P10, in *The Complete Works*, 336f.

40. Gertrude of Helfta, *The Herald of Divine Love*, 2.19, tr. and ed. Margaret Winkworth (New York:Paulist Press, 1993), 120.

41. Ibid., 2.17 (118).

42. Catherine of Siena, *The Dialogue*, ch. 17, tr. Suzanne Noffke (New York: Paulist Press, 1980), 55.

43. Ibid., ch. 25 (63).

44. Ibid., ch. 4 (31).

45. Ibid., ch. 64 (121).

46. Ibid., ch. 13 (49).

47. Julian of Norwich, *Revelations of Divine Love*, ch. 4, tr. Frances Beer (Rochester, New York: D.S. Brewer, 1998), 30.

48. Ibid., ch. 5 (Beer, 31).

49. Ibid., ch. 9 (Beer, 37).

50. Ibid., chs. 13–18 (Beer, 43–50).

51. Ibid., chs. 15–16 (Beer, 45f.).

52. Ibid., ch. 17 (Beer, 47).

53. Ibid., ch. 18 (Beer, 50), emphasis mine.

54. Ibid., ch. 19 (Beer, 52).

55. Ibid., ch. 25 (Beer, 58f.), emphases mine.

56. Sheila Upjohn, *Why Julian Now? A Voyage of Discovery* (Grand Rapids: Wm. B. Eerdmans, 1997), 93.

57. Ibid., 94f.

58. Teresa of Avila, *Spiritual Testimonies*, 29, in *The Collected Works of St. Teresa of Avila*, tr. Kieran Kavanaugh and Otilio Rodriquez (Washington, D.C.: ICS Publications; Vol. 1, 2nd ed. rev., 1987; Vol. 2, 1980), 1:401.

59. Teresa of Avila, *The Book of Her Life*, 40.3, in *The Collected Works*, 1:355.

60. Ibid., 40.4 (1:356).

61. Teresa of Avila, *Soliloquies* 4.2, in *The Collected Works*, 1:447.

62. Ibid., 2.1 (1:444), emphasis mine. Were it not for this remark, Teresa would probably not appear at all in this chapter.

63. Teresa of Avila, *The Book of Her Life*, 29.13 (1:252).

9

Challenges to an Unchanging God

J. K. MOZLEY'S SURPRISING DISCOVERY

The earliest direct attack on the Augustinian synthesis of Christian theism is to be found in those bold individuals who dared to question the doctrine of divine immutability. That underlies pretty much everything else that followed. In the early 1920s, leaders in the Church of England asked one of their own, John Kenneth Mozley, to prepare a report on how theologians were dealing with the doctrine, particularly as the British were coming to grips with the implications of massive human waste in the World War just concluded. His discoveries, published in his *The Impassibility of God* (1926), were surprising. The questioning had already been underway for quite some time. Mozley's summary was that a fresh emphasis on God as Love was the motivation for calling into question the traditional doctrine of God's impassibility. And the cross pointed inward into the very heart of God.[1]

Mozley found his earliest kindred spirit in the American Horace Bushnell, whose *The Vicarious Sacrifice* was first published in London in 1866. Bushnell recognized the importance of love as a key aspect of God's reality and affirmed that "love is a principle essentially vicarious in nature."[2] And this love that is God's is distinctly seen in the event of Jesus' crucifixion: "There is a Gethsemane hid in all love."[3]

For Bushnell, this holds far-reaching implications for how we make sense of God's reality.

> It is as if there were a cross unseen, standing on its undiscovered hill, far back in the ages, out of which were sounding always, just the same deep voice of suffering love and patience, that was heard by mortal ears from the sacred hill of Calvary.[4]

In his vicarious sacrifice, Jesus "was God, fulfilling the obligations of God . . . There is an eternal cross in his [God's] virtue itself, and the cross that he endures in Christ only reveals what is in those common standards of good, which are also eternally his."[5]

The whole point of Bushnell's bold presentation is that "vicarious sacrifice" is eternally at the very heart of God, not just by happenstance or uniquely in Jesus' earthly fate: "there is a cross in God before the wood is seen upon Calvary."[6] For Bushnell essentially to adopt the historic heresy known as *patripassionism*—namely, that the Father in the Trinity also suffered when Christ was crucified—opened the way to a fresh understanding of what a new orthodoxy might be able to embrace. And it knocked the props out from under the inviolability of God's transcendent immutability.

Simultaneously in Denmark, Hans Martensen, the Lutheran bishop of Seeland, was moving on a parallel track. In his *Christian Dogmatics*, also first published in 1866, in German, he continued to swear allegiance to God's omnipotence[7] but offered hints of a challenge to it. In discussing God's love Martensen recognized that God's "blessedness must be conceived of as conditional upon the perfecting of His kingdom; because divine love can satisfy itself only as it is bliss-giving." This is seen as a "contradiction," which he resolved by presenting the notion that "God has a twofold life—a life in himself of unclouded peace and self-satisfaction, and a life in and with His creation, in which He not only submits to the conditions of finitude, but even *allows His power to be limited* by the sinful will of man."[8]

Among several writers in the pre-war era whom Mozley identified, the Scottish scholar A. M. Fairbairn stands out. In lifting up the centrality of the statement that "God is love,"[9] he explicitly proclaimed: "Theology has no falser idea than that of the impassibility of God."[10] In 1906, Charles Allen Dinsmore introduced Bushnell's vision to the British isles, mirroring him in the claim: "There was a cross in the heart of God before there was one planted on the green hill outside of Jerusalem."[11] He went on to say that "the Christian doctrine of God would be inferior to that of the Greeks, did it not supplement this teaching of the *infinite passibility of God* with the assertion that the Almighty abides in perfect felicity,"[12] whereupon "the revelation of the cross is the *persuasive power* which brings all men to God."[13]

The most powerful voice wrestling with the question of, if God be God, how in the name of all that is holy can "the War" be comprehended, I find to be that of Geoffrey Anketell Studdert-Kennedy. A scholarly man and a chaplain in the trenches, he agonized over just that issue, insisting that God had to "bind Himself with chains and pierce Himself with nails, and take upon Himself the travail pangs of creation."[14] "The true God is naked, bloody, wounded, and crowned with thorns, tortured, but triumphant in His love."[15] The denial of immutability leads immediately to the denial of impassibility, the direct consequence, though sometimes that runs in exactly the opposite direction to the same result. These indicators are but a foretaste of a lengthier encounter with Studdert-Kennedy when we turn later to the subject of God and suffering.

JÜRGEN MOLTMANN'S CRUCIFIED GOD

The German "theologian of hope" Jürgen Moltmann, many decades later, gave grudging recognition of his dependence on these early pioneers, developing his pivotal *The Crucified God* (orig., 1972) without explicit indication of the derivative quality of many of his key insights, and only acknowledging his quoting of Horace Bushnell, in his later *The Trinity and the Kingdom* (orig, 1980), in footnotes. His other major sources for challenging God's immutability and *apatheia* were G. A. Studdert-Kennedy and the Jewish biblical scholar Abraham Heschel.[16] Even so, he significantly advanced the discussion.

God (himself) suffered in Jesus, God himself died in Jesus for us. God is on the cross of Jesus "for us," and through that becomes God and Father of the godless and the godforsaken . . . God became the crucified God so that we might become free sons of God . . . The cross of Jesus, understood as the cross of the Son of God, therefore reveals *a change in God*, a *stasis* within the Godhead: "God is other." And this event in God is the event on the cross. It takes on Christian form in the simple formula which contradicts all possible metaphysical and historical ideas of God: "God *is* love."[17]

Accordingly, Moltmann fully rejected classical theism because of its insistence on divine dispassionate immutability.[18] He understood atheism to be, in fact, a rejection of and protest against *theism's* doctrine of a God aloof from, and yet somehow responsible for, suffering.[19]

This, then, spilled over into Moltmann's rejection of the traditional doctrine of God's omnipotence: "a God who is only omnipotent is in himself an incomplete being, for he cannot experience helplessness and powerlessness."[20] So, in regard to another challenge to the conventional that we will visit later, he could write: "Without liberation of the crucified God from the idols of power, there is no liberating theology!"[21]

Without fully developing the correlation between God's real power and God's identity as love, Moltmann nevertheless did champion 1 John 4:8, 16. "God is unconditional love." Love's "might is powerful in weakness and gains power over its enemies in grief, because it gives life even to its enemies and opens up the future to change."[22]

Both divine love and divine power assure, for Moltmann, the eventual, eschatological consummation of God's intentions for God's creation. "*God is* present in the way in which his future *takes control over the present* in real anticipations and prefigurations. *But God is not as yet* present in the form of his eternal presence. The dialectic between his being and his being-not-yet is the pain and power of history.[23]" The future that is God's is "a power which already qualifies the present—through promise and hope, through liberation and the creation of new possibilities. As this *power of the future*, God reaches into the present."[24]

There is a very real sense here that Moltmann, like his contemporary Wolfhart Pannenberg, varied essentially from Augustine's stance on God as Eternal Present, beyond temporality, in shifting the locus of God's eternity—from our perspective, as it were—from Eternal Present to Eternal, or Ultimate, Future. The future of the *novum ultimum* is the point at which the creation encounters God in God's powerful fullness. In this eschatological assurance, it is clear that Moltmann has not truly qualified the ultimate nature of God's omnipotence. As was clear in the previous paragraph, God always retains the capacity to "take control" over creation's destiny, when and as God chooses. In this respect, he retains the same dilemma that we saw in Pannenberg, although Moltmann did succeed in pushing the envelope on God's mutability and pathos, and the identifying of God with essential love.

ENDNOTES

1. John Kenneth Mozley, *The Impassibility of God: A Survey of Christian Thought* (London: Cambridge University Press, 1926), 175–77.

2. Horace Bushnell, *The Vicarious Sacrifice*, vol. 1 (New York: Charles Scribner's Sons, 1883), 42. See, also, 46, 51-53, 59, 68.

3. Ibid., 47.

4. Ibid., 69.

5. Ibid., 58.

6. Ibid., 73. See the whole discussion, 69-73. Some of Bushnell's phrases anticipate what will later be encountered in the work of the German "theologian of hope" Jürgen Moltmann, to be investigated below, but Moltmann was vividly aware of that, even quoting Bushnell explicitly as we will see.

7. Hans Martensen, *Christian Dogmatics*, tr. William Urwick (Edinburgh: T. & T. Clark, 1878), 95f.

8. Ibid., 101, both quotes. Emphasis mine.

9. Andrew Martin Fairbairn, *The Place of Christ in Modern Theology* (New York: Charles Scribner's Sons, 1903), 394. We will visit Fairbairn more extensively in the chapter on "Breakthroughs to a Loving God."

10. Ibid., 483.

11. Charles Allen Dinsmore, *Atonement in Literature and Life* (London:

Archibald Constable & Co., 1906), 232.

12. Ibid., 233, emphasis mine.

13. Ibid., 234, emphasis mine.

14. Studdert-Kennedy, Geoffrey Anketell, *The Hardest Part* (New York: George H. Doran Co., 1918; 2nd ed., 1925), 24.

15. Ibid., 67.

16. See Jürgen Moltmann, *The Trinity and the Kingdom*, tr. Margaret Kohl (San Francisco: Harper & Row, 1981), 25–36.

17. Moltmann, *The Crucified God: The Cross of Christ as the Foundation and Criticism of Christian Theology*, tr. R. A. Wilson and John Bowden (New York: Harper & Row, 1974), 192f., first emphasis mine, second emphasis original.

18. Ibid., 214f.

19. Ibid., 220–22.

20. Ibid., 223.

21. Moltmann, *The Experiment Hope*, tr. M. Douglas Meeks (Philadelphia: Fortress Press, 1975), 83, from ch. 6, "The Crucified God and the Apathetic Man," first appearing in *Theology Today*, April, 1974. On the last phrase, see the chapter on "Hunger for a Liberating God."

22. Moltmann, *The Crucified God*, 248f.

23. Moltmann, *Religion, Revolution, and the Future*, tr. M. Douglas Meeks (New York: Charles Scribner's Sons, 1969), 209; essays from 1967-68 in the USA. First and third emphases original; second emphasis, "takes control over the present," mine.

24. Ibid., emphasis mine.

10

Odes to a Suffering God

God's immutability and God's impassibility as *apatheia* are two sides of one coin. If God is beyond change, then it is not possible for God to be affected by what is other than God, wherefore God can be said to be "apathetic." True, God could change in some ways and still be beyond affectations. But the notion that began to gain traction, in the midst of the twentieth century's horrors piled one on top of another, that God truly *suffers*, becomes possible only when the illusion of divine immutability is shed. Therefore I turn immediately to this topic before pursuing others than may have initially arisen in history at an earlier date.

THE "HARDEST PART": G. A. STUDDERT-KENNEDY

We have already met Geoffrey Anketell Studdert-Kennedy. Of Irish extraction, he was an Anglican vicar of a very poor parish in Worcester at the beginning of the war, then became a chaplain to the British forces in 1915.

> He went through a good deal of fighting, and the brutal realities of war brought him face to face with the problem of reconciling belief in the love of God with the omnipotence of the

Deity . . . These pages express the thoughts which came to the writer amid the hardships of the trenches and the brutalities of war. It is literally theology hammered out on the field of battle.[1]

Studdert-Kennedy spelled out the nature of his situation vividly in his own Preface to the 1925 second edition:

> If the doctrine of the sovereign Kaiser-God was impossible to hold on the battle-fields of Flanders and of France, it is even more impossible in the Europe of to-day. That God is dead, as dead as cold mutton, and even deader, because He can be no longer used as food even for the poor, Even the most poverty-stricken in mind and spirit have in these days learned to spew out any teaching about God which makes Him less good than Jesus.[2]

With irony dripping from his pen, he went on to concede: "Of course the book won't satisfy theologians, but then it's not written for them to read but for the man who has to earn his bread in the sweat of his brow."[3]

Studdert-Kennedy's writing is colorful, vivid, and highly contextualized (right in the middle of the blazing guns). "One needs a Father, and a Father must suffer in His children's suffering. I could not worship the passionless potentate."[4] His agonized bluntness is embodied in the poem he wrote for the title page of the book, from which its title was taken:

> The sorrows of God mun be 'ard to bear,
> If 'e really 'as Love in 'is 'eart,
> And the 'ardest part i' the world to play
> Mun surely be God's Part.[5]

His dissatisfaction with the inherited notion of a God-in-charge, a God ultimately over everything and in control of everything, fairly screams from the printed page. "I don't know or love the Almighty potentate—my only real God is the suffering Father revealed in the sorrow of Christ."[6]

> Nothing makes much odds. God Himself seems non-existent—the Almighty Ruler Whom all things obey. He seems to have

gone to sleep and allowed things to run amuck. I don't believe there is an absolute Almighty Ruler. I don't see how anyone can believe it. If it were a choice between that God and no God, I would be an atheist.[7]

And so he proclaimed rather "God, not Almighty, but God the Father, with a Father's sorrow and a Father's weakness, which is the strength of love; God splendid, suffering, crucified."[8]

Behind the vast history of effort he could see "a will" but "not an absolutely omnipotent will that knows no failure and no strain."[9] Either "God is helpless to prevent war, or else He wills it and approves of it."[10] Christians in the past have affirmed the latter. If God is indeed omnipotent, we are inevitably "driven to the conclusion that war is the will of the Almighty God. If it is true, I go morally mad."[11] Therefore Studdert-Kennedy concluded: "God, the Father God of Love, is everywhere in history, but nowhere is He Almighty."[12] "If the Christian religion means anything, it means *that God is Suffering Love*, and that all real progress is caused by the working of Suffering Love in the world."[13]

> War is the crucifixion of God, not the working of His will. The cross is not past, but present. Ever and always I can see set up above this world of ours a huge and towering Cross, with great arms stretched out east and west from the rising to the setting sun, and on that Cross my God still hangs and calls on all brave men to come out and fight with evil, and by their sufferings endured with Him help to lift the world from darkness into light.[14]

What was then known simply as "the War" challenged theology to give up time-worn declarations of the sublime power of God. J. K. Mozley observed, after reviewing Studdert-Kennedy's contributions: "as the War sounded the doom of absolute monarchy upon earth, so we must abandon the idea of such power as vested in God."[15] Clearly, the collapse of an apathetic God untouched by human suffering is a fierce blow to the traditional doctrine of divine omnipotence, leaving open the question of just what kind of power could be attributed to God at all.

TRAGEDY IN GOD: NICOLAS BERDYAEV

Nicolas Berdyaev, born in Kiev, Russia, in 1874, was a Marxist who was also a Christian and an anti-totalitarian who was expelled from his homeland in 1922 because of his opposition to the Communist regime. He eventually settled in Paris where most of his important books were written prior to his death in 1948. His religious writings occupy the boundary of theology with philosophy.

Berdyaev identified *freedom* as the essential will of God for God's creation. "Freedom is not created because it is not a part of nature; it is prior to the world and has its origin in the primal void. God is All-Powerful in relation to being but not in relation to nothingness and to freedom."[16] So freedom is a given for God, leading to an understanding of a self-chosen *tragedy* in God: God's love of what God has created, and especially the other dearest to God, the one bearing God's image—i.e., humans—is the origin of God's *suffering*. God *expects* freedom from us; God waits for our free response to the divine call. And this response cannot be compelled. Compulsion and constraint mark the absence of freedom.[17]

If the destiny of freedom's availability is tragic, in its misuse, how is that fate overcome?

> How, in a word, can freedom be separated from the evil it brings in its train except by the destruction of freedom itself? To this universal problem there is no solution save in the coming of Christ . . . The grace of Christ is the inner illumination of freedom without any outward restraint or coercion . . . The mystery of Christianity, the religion of God made man, is above all the mystery of liberty.[18]

The mystery of the cross conveys, once again, the mystery of "a crucified God,"[19] wherefore the topic of love enters the discussion.

> Truth crucified possesses no logical nor juridical power of compulsion and it made its appearance in the world as infinite love, and love does not compel; rather it makes man infinitely free . . . In the suffering of the God-Man willingly endured, which sets men free, there lies hidden the mystery of Christian love.[20]

"God is infinite Love, and Love cannot rest shut up within itself; it is always moving out to others."[21] The third person of the Trinity is "the Spirit Who is Love realized. The kingdom of Love in freedom is the kingdom of the Trinity."[22] Again, the reign of God cannot be built "by force; it can only be created in freedom."[23] In that coming realm, "all power and all autocracy, whether individual or collective, are limited, for there only the power of truth and justice are recognized . . . God will be all in all and freedom will triumph over force."[24] Of course, the obvious question remains: How? What is the nature of the power-in-freedom that prevails over compulsion?

Redemption, we are led to see, is understood as a divine "work of love," which is no less than a suffering love: "the sacrifice of a divine and infinite love, not a propitiatory sacrifice . . . *God himself longs to suffer with the world.*"[25] In the passion enacted on Calvary, "freedom becomes *the power of divine love.*"[26] All of this leads Berdyaev to conclude that Christianity is no less than "*the religion of the suffering God.*"[27] This isn't patripassianism, Berdyaev insisted. The interpenetration of the three persons of the Trinity causes Berdyaev to say that *God*, not just the human aspect of Jesus on the cross, suffers. Aquinas was wrong, Berdyaev contended: God is not a static constant. The cross discloses to us "*a process in God*, a divine tragedy."[28]

The phrases are provocative. Human freedom is not cancelled out because God exercises power as love that leads but does not compel. Rather than curtailing our exercise of freedom, God enters into our tragic condition of self-inflicted suffering that has arisen through freedom's abuse. The concession to divine suffering is an empowering acknowledgment. It does not, by itself, however, solve the riddle of how power that is defined by love is to be understood, in contrast to traditional understandings of power.

VOICES FROM EAST ASIA: KAZOH KITAMORI AND JUNG YOUNG LEE

Born in 1916, Kazoh Kitamori was a pastor and professor in his native Japan through the devastating years of World War II. His book on

Theology of the Pain of God was first published in the year after the war ended, and translated into English in 1958 after going through five editions. Ironies abound. This is one of the earliest examples of nonWestern theology but almost all the dialogue is with the West; the Japanese tradition of tragedy comes into the discussion only on a few pages.[29] It was written during World War II and published a year after Hiroshima and Nagasaki, yet seems blissfully unaware of any of this context. The author champions the "pain of God" yet distances himself, unconvincingly, from patripassianism—unconvincing because, e.g., "the pain of God is neither merely the pain of God the Son, nor merely the pain of God the Father, but the pain of the two persons who are essentially one."[30]

The title phrase was triggered by Kitamori's reflection on Jeremiah 31:20 ("I am deeply moved for him [i.e., Ephraim]," NRSV; "my heart yearns for him," NIV). Kitamori understood the Hebrew verb (*hamah*) to mean "to be in pain."[31]

> The theology of the pain of God does not mean that pain exists in God as *substance*. The pain of God is not a '"concept of substance"—it is a "concept of relation," a nature of "God's love."[32]

In God, there is a unity of "love rooted in pain."[33] Jesus "is the very pain of God."[34] Kitamori was finally led to conclude: "The concept 'love rooted in the pain of God' expresses the whole of God's love."[35]

In 1974, Jung Young Lee published *God Suffers for Us* at a publishing house in the Netherlands. A Korean who studied and taught in the USA, his work has been pretty much ignored in scholarly dialogue. That is unfortunate. The heart of his position is encapsulated in the following passage.

> The *Agape* of the Cross implies the inclusive unity of both the depth of divine love and that of divine possibility. Thus, it is neither the depth of divine love alone nor the divine possibility alone, but combination of the two which manifests itself as the depth of divine empathy to participate in the world. . . . the redemptive love is always love with suffering. Neither love without suffering nor suffering without love is redemptive. . . . If love is really to be redemptive, it must be a suffering love, that

is, the *Agape* of the Cross. *Agape* is not redemptive unless it is also suffering. To deny the suffering of God is to deny the redemptive work of God."[36]

Empathy was a central tenet for Lee: "in the empathy of God, God fully participates in us" without losing God's godness (my word) and without our losing our essential humanness.[37] "Love directs the course of divine movement."[38] In that regard, Lee posited God's *self*-limitation, deriving from the divine empathy, as the reason for God's non-omnipotence.[39]

THE GOD WHO SUFFERS WITH THE SUFFERING: DOROTHEE SÖLLE

Dorothee Sölle (1929–2003) was a German theologian who wound up spending much of her teaching career at Union Theological Seminary in New York City. She unflinchingly blasted "the omnipotence of a heavenly being who decrees suffering"[40] as a manifestation of either "Christian masochism" (the calamities we accept as somehow God's will) or "Christian sadism" (the calamities we inflict on others in God's name), or both.[41] There is "no way to combine omnipotence with love."[42] Christian sadism took an extreme form in Calvin:[43] "There is little doubt that the Reformation strengthened theology's sadistic accents."[44]

The key section of Sölle's attack is found in ch. 2 of *Suffering* (1975), on "The Christians' Apathetic God." "*Apatheia* is a Greek word that literally means nonsuffering, freedom from suffering, a creature's inability to suffer."[45] The "apathetic" God "fulfills the ideal of one who is physically beyond the reach of external influences and psychologically anaesthetized—like things that are dead . . . This apathetic God became the God of the Christians, although he was a contradiction to the biblical God, with his emotions and suffering."[46] This leads to the realization that "the stoic concept of suffering triumphs over a Christian concept" of the divine.[47]

> The almighty Lord, who ordains suffering or frees one from it has . . . lost his all-surpassing significance. Whoever grounds suffering in an almighty, alien One who ordains everything has to face the question of the justice of this God—and he must be

shattered by it. Then all that remains is either total submission to God's omnipotence, together with a renunciation of the question about his justice, as Job did at the last, or else rebellion against this God and the awaiting of another deliverer.[48]

Wherever we are confronted with senseless suffering, "faith in a God who embodies both omnipotence and love has to waver or be destroyed."[49]

So what is the alternative, to the extent that Sölle presents one? Is God now simply Love, bereft of all Power? To wit: "Our oneness with love is indissoluble. To learn to suffer without becoming the devil's martyrs means to live conscious of our oneness with the whole of life. Those who suffer in this way are indestructible. Nothing can separate them from the love of God."[50] Certainly God is not the one who brings the suffering but the one who sides with us in our suffering, who remains with us.

Sölle took Elie Wiesel's story of a boy's lingering death on the gallows[51] and christianized it.

> The decisive phrase, that God is hanging "here on this gallows," has two meanings. First it is an assertion about God. God is no executioner—and no almighty spectator (which would amount to the same thing). God is not the mighty tyrant. Between the sufferer and the one who causes the suffering, between the victim and the executioner, God, whatever people make of this word, is on the side of the sufferer. God is on the side of the victim, he is hanged.[52]

She then went on to conclude: "God is not in heaven; he is hanging on the cross. Love is not an otherworldly, intruding, self-asserting power—and to meditate on the cross can mean to take leave of that dream."[53]

So what Sölle finally dared to do was take Jesus' statement in John 10:30 that "I and the Father are one" and, essentially, reverse it: "The essence of Jesus' passion history is the assertion that this one whom God forsook himself becomes God."[54] The cross is "neither a symbol expressing the relationship between God the Father and his Son nor a symbol of masochism which needs suffering in order to convince itself of love. It is above all a symbol of reality. Love does not 'require' the cross, but *de facto* it ends up on the cross."[55]

Sölle then went on to quote the Russian poet Konstantin Simonov: "There is no alien sorrow, we are all a part of it, we share in it."[56] So in the final analysis she came to regard God not "as an alien superior power but as that which occurs between people" in their living through, and not only enduring, but sometimes even triumphing over, a suffering that can only be fully shared.[57]

This is the most thoroughgoing analysis I have encountered of the difficulties that emerge when God is identified as being on the side of those who cause suffering rather than its victims. Sölle was scathing in her attacks on theological masochism/sadism. But to understand God to be truly on the side of those of suffer, to the extent of being able to proclaim God's own co-suffering, only pointed up the problem, without resolving at all how a God of pathos and suffering love remains with any meaningful power at all.[58] That is yet to be uncovered.

ENDNOTES

1. Geoffrey Anketell Studdert-Kennedy, *The Hardest Part* (New York: George H. Doran Co., 1918; 2nd ed., 1925), from the Preface by W. Moore Ede, xiif.

2. Ibid., ix.

3. Ibid.

4. Ibid., 9.

5. Ibid., iii.

6. Ibid., 10.

7. Ibid., 11.

8. Ibid., 13.

9. Ibid., 23.

10. Ibid., 32.

11. Ibid., 33.

12. Ibid., 39.

13. Ibid., 41, emphasis mine.

14. Ibid., 42.

15. J. K. Mozley, *The Impassibility of God*, 159.

16. Nicolas Berdyaev, *Freedom and the Spirit*, tr. Oliver Fielding Clarke (London: Geoffrey Bles: The Centenary Press, 1935), 160.

17. Ibid., 126f.

18. Ibid., 135.

19. Ibid., 140.

20. Ibid., 141.

21. Ibid., 138.

22. Ibid., 139.

23. Ibid., 154.

24. Ibid., 157.

25. Ibid., 174, emphasis mine.

26. Ibid., 178, emphasis mine.

27. Ibid., 192, emphasis mine.

28. Ibid., 193, emphasis mine.

29. Kazoh Kitamori, *Theology of the Pain of God* (Richmond, Virginia: John Knox Press, 1958), 134-36.

30. Ibid., 115.

31. Ibid., Appendix, 152–53.

32. Ibid., Preface to the Fifth Edition, 16.

33. Ibid., 39.

34. Ibid., 34.

35. Ibid., 117.

36. Jung Young Lee, *God Suffers for Us: A Systematic Inquiry into a Concept of Divine Possibility* (The Hague: Martinus Nijhoff, 1974), 60.

37. Ibid., 13.

38. Ibid., 19.

39. Ibid., 43f.

40. Dorothee Sölle, *Suffering*, tr. Everett R. Kalin (Philadelphia: Fortress Press, 1975), 25.

41. Ibid., ch. 1, 9–32.

42. Ibid., 25.

43. Ibid., 23, 26.

44. Ibid., 22. Sölle critiqued Moltmann in *The Crucified God* for not going far enough in his attempt to move beyond this tradition. (26f.)

45. Ibid., 36.

46. Ibid., 42.

47. Ibid., 43. Cf. above, ch. 6.

48. Ibid., 134.

49. Ibid., 142.

50. Ibid., 141.

51. Elie Wiesel, *Night,* tr. Stella Rodway (New York: Hill & Wang, 1960), 70f.

52. Sölle, *Suffering,* 148.

53. Ibid.

54. Ibid., 147.

55. Ibid., 163.

56. Ibid., 172f., the last phrase being Sölle's.

57. Ibid., 173.

58. See my subsequent chapter on "Inklings of an Impotent God," where Sölle's contributions might also be seen to belong. Other voices that merit attention here include Paul Fiddes, *The Creative Suffering of God* (Oxford: Clarendon Press, 1988), and Wendy Farley, *Tragic Vision and Divine Compassion: A Contemporary Theodicy* (Louisville: Westminster/John Knox Press, 1990). Farley's work will be reviewed instead in the chapter on "Breakthroughs to a Loving God."

11

Mourning over a Dead God

Let us now turn back the pages of time and visit another kind of challenge to the theistic consensus that has accompanied what we have just been observing, as a concomitant undercurrent—namely, that the God of unqualified and opposable omnipotence is, in fact, not the *living* God of scripture at all but is, for all intents and purposes, no less than *dead*. It is one thing to assert that such a God never had true being in the first place. It is altogether another to recognize that such a God had tremendous power over the minds and faith of Christians for two millennia but has now ceased to wield such clout. Mourners of this celebrated demise have not exactly been clothed in black. Might one rather say, "*rejoicing* over a dead God"?

We begin in the nineteenth century with two influential philosophers and a Russian novelist, then move forward to the "radical" decade of the 1960s and the rewriting of theology in the light of the Holocaust.

A PROJECTION OF HUMAN WISHING: LUDWIG FEUERBACH

Ludwig Feuerbach (1804–72) adopted G. W. F. Hegel's understanding that the cosmos is the "objectification" of Absolute Spirit and took it one step further: God became for him the objectification of the *human spirit* writ large. In his groundbreaking *The Essence of Christianity* (1841), Feurbach observed that Christianity (and religion in general) represents the projecting of humankind's most desirable attributes onto an Other, named "God."[1]

The fundamental claim that Feuerbach made is that "the qualities of God are nothing else than the essential qualities of man himself."[2] Specifically, they are projected onto an externalized God by the desires of humans for the image of perfection: "Man—this is the mystery of religion—projects his being into objectivity, and then again makes himself an object to this projected image of himself thus converted into a subject."[3] Therefore, in God, we have only ourselves and our own activity as an object;[4] in religion, we contemplate our "own latent nature."[5]

What I find truly fascinating is that Feuerbach concentrated a great deal of energy on *love*, not on *power*, as being at the heart of this projective activity. He discussed *omniptence* in the contexts of God's providence and of prayer,[6] and then later in the sections in Part II on the false, or "theological," essence of religion. But I have found him minimally making what seems the obvious statement to be explored, namely, that the doctrine of *omnipotence* is the projection onto God of *the wish for absolute, controlling power* among human beings. A passage from his *The Essence of Faith According to Luther* (1844) must suffice: "Omnipotence confirms the divine promises." It is based not on specific wishes but rather "on the unspecific over-all wish that there be in general no natural necessity, no limitations, no opposition to the human being and to human wishes; it is based on the wish that everything be only for men and nothing against men."[7]

One relevant assertion maintains: "Creation out of nothing is the highest expression of omnipotence; but omnipotence is nothing else than subjectivity exempting itself from all objective conditions and limitations, and consecrating this exemption as the highest power and reality."[8]

Love, on the other hand, occupies the very center of Feuerbach's thesis.

> Love is God himself, and apart from it there is no God. Love makes man God and God man . . . What the old mystics said

of God, that he is the highest and yet the commonest being, applies in truth to love, and that not a visionary, imaginary love—no! a real love, a love which has flesh and blood, which vibrates as an almighty force through all living.[9]

"God is love" means essentially, for Feuerbach, that love is God for us.[10] The divine love "is only human love made objective, affirming itself."[11] This image of love becomes perverted when

> God appears to me in another form besides that of love; in the form of *omnipotence*, of a severe power not bound by love ... So long as love is not exalted into ... an essence, so long there lurks in the background of love a subject who even without love is something by himself, an unloving monster, a diabolical being, whose personality, separable and actually separated from love, delights in the blood of heretics and unbelievers,—the phantom of religious fanaticism."[12]

It is a chilling reminder of just why Feuerbach as well as others could come to regard this understanding of God as an *enemy* to be done away with.

So, finally, "the imperative of love has infinitely more *power* than that of despotism. Love *does not command* ... The imperative of love works with electro-magnetic power; that of despotism with the mechanical power of a wooden telegraph."[13]

"God is love," Feuerbach avowed, "is the sublimest dictum of Christianity."[14] The death of a controlling deity external to human projections provides a basis for Feuerbach's intriguing reversal of 1 John 4:8,16, whereby it became possible for him to proclaim the obverse, that love, in fact, *is God*: "Love is not holy because it is a predicate of God, but it is a predicate of God because it is in itself divine."[15]

Eberhard Jüngel raised the telling question: "Is not Feuerbach right when he fears that theology is more interested in the 'absolute power of God' and in the 'hidden God' *(potentia dei absoluta, deus absconditus)* than it is in the truth that God *is* love?"[16] But the direction in which Feuerbach took his challenge to the conventional notion of God is finally not all that helpful, given that the projections are toward those of an Ideal Human who has no real existence. We are left with a void, after all is said and done.

"RETURNING THE TICKET": FYODOR DOSTOYEVSKY

I interrupt this parade of Christian theologians (and a philosopher) to take a brief detour sideways to the insight of a Russian novelist of note, Fyodor Dostoyevsky (1821–81). In *The Brothers Karamazov* (1880), in the section immediately preceding his powerful narration of the Grand Inquisitor and the returned Jesus, Dostoyevsky has Ivan Karamazov relate to his brother Alyosha a number of incidents involving the utterly unimaginable suffering visited upon innocent children, and then states, in regard to the promise of eternal bliss:

> I can't accept that [eternal] harmony . . . I renounce the higher harmony altogether. It's not worth the tears of that one tormented child who beat itself on the breast with its little fist and prayed in its stinking outhouse, with its unexpiated tears to "dear, kind God!" It's not worth it, because those tears are unatoned for. They must be atoned for, or there can be no harmony. But how? How are you going to atone for them? . . . I don't want harmony. From love for humanity I don't want it. I would rather be left with the unavenged suffering. I would rather remain with my unavenged suffering and unsatisfied indignation, *even if I were wrong*. Besides, too high a price is asked for harmony; it's beyond our means to pay so much to enter on it. And so I hasten to give back my entrance ticket, and if I am an honest man I am bound to give it back as soon as possible. And that I am doing. It's not God that I don't accept, Alyosha, only I most respectfully return Him the ticket.[17]

The theme of truth masked in fiction is not so much that God is dead but that God has become the enemy, the One to be rejected—a theme we have previously noticed. If such a God as tradition champions reigns in eternal bliss, then give my ticket to Heaven to someone else, Ivan pleads.

That vision of an inimical god had been cryptically presented nearly a century earlier in the apocalyptic poetry of William Blake in his *Jerusalem* (1804):

Satan: Worshipd as God by the Mighty Ones of the Earth . . .
such is the way of the Devouring Power.[18]

Blake's vision of omnipotence turned evil was strongly highlighted by another scholar to be encountered shortly in this chapter, Thomas Altizer.[19] But first, the wish was strong to rid humankind of a deity whose unchecked power wreaked havoc on the lives of the innocent, and this option was seized exuberantly by our next challenger.

"WE HAVE KILLED GOD": FRIEDRICH NIETZSCHE

The German scholar Friedrich Nietzsche (1844–1900) was an intellectual prodigy whose career in teaching and writing was foreshortened by the severe onset of mental illness, the cause of which has been debated ever since. Even though his writings were characterized by often bewildering flights of the imagination, I find no justification for regarding them as inflicted with mental disability. His was simply a genius difficult to categorize.

The most well-known of Nietzsche's imaginings is encapsulated in his tale of the madman who went about the marketplace loudly proclaiming that God had died and that we, God's minions, have performed the fatal deed. Even given its familiarity, I believe it merits citing here at length.

> Have you not heard of that madman who lit a lantern in the bright morning hours, ran to the market place, and cried incessantly: "I seek God! I seek God!"—As many of those who did not believe in God were standing around just then, he provoked much laughter. Have he got lost? asked one. Did he lose his way like a child? asked another. Or is he hiding? Is he afraid of us? Has he gone on a voyage? emigrated?—Thus they yelled and laughed.
>
> The madman sprang into their midst and pierced them with his eyes. "Whither is God?" he cried; "I will tell you. *We have killed him*—you and I. All of us are his murderers. But how did we do this? How could we drink up the sea? Who gave us the sponge to wipe away the entire horizon? What were we

doing when we unchained this earth from its sun? Whither is it moving now? Whither are we moving now? Away from all suns? Are we not plunging continually? Backward, sideward, forward, in all directions? Is there still any up or down? Are we not straying as through an infinite nothing? Do we not feel the breath of empty space? Has it not become colder? Is not night continually closing in on us? Do we not need to light lanterns in the morning? Do we hear nothing yet of the noise of the gravediggers who are burying God? Do we smell nothing yet of the divine decomposition? Gods, too, decompose. God is dead. God remains dead. And we have killed him.

"How shall we comfort ourselves, the murderers of all murderers? What was the holiest and mightiest of all that the world has yet owned has bled to death under our knives: who will wipe this blood off us? What water is there for us to clean ourselves? What festivals of atonement, what sacred games shall we have to invent? Is not the greatness of this deed too great for us? Must we ourselves not become gods simply to appear worthy of it? There has never been a greater deed; and whoever is born after us—for the sake of this deed he will belong to a higher history than all history hitherto."

Here the madman fell silent and looked again at his listeners; and they, too, were silent and stared at him in astonishment. At last he threw his lantern to the ground, and it broke into pieces and went out. "I have come too early," he said then; "my time is not yet. This tremendous event is still on its way, still wandering; it has not yet reached the ears of men. Lightning and thunder require time; the light of the stars requires time; deeds, though done, still require time to be seen and heard. This deed is still more distant from them than the distant stars— *and yet they have done it themselves.*"

It has been further related that on that same day the madman forced his way into several churches and there struck up his *requiem aeternam deo*. Led out and called to account, he is said always to have replied nothing but: "What after all are all these churches now if they are not the tombs and sepulchers of God?"[20]

Nietzsche penned the paradigmatic obituary for the classic conception of God as essentially omnipotent over all. He wrote in *The Antichrist* (1888):

> That we find no God—either in history or in nature or behind nature—is not what differentiates *us*, but that we experience what has been revered as God, not as 'godlike' but as miserable, as absurd, as harmful, not merely as an error but as a *crime against life*. We deny God as God. If one were to *prove* this God of the Christians to us, we should be even less able to believe in him.[21]

For Nietzsche, God has to die in order for *Übermensch*, "overhuman," to be born. That is the essential direction in which his provocative project of thought ran. Overhuman is not some projected aspect of contemporary humanness at its most actualized. Rather, the human race itself is merely a bridge between apes and overhuman,[22] who is the only alternative for Nietzsche to nihilism. If value is not received from the divine, it must be self-created. We in our present state are not equipped to achieve that. So the transvaluation of values awaits the coming of the overhuman for its full accomplishment.

In *Thus Spake Zarathustra* (1883–85), Nietzsche repeated his proclamation that God is dead[23] and proceeded immediately to follow that with the proposal, "*I teach you the Superman*. Man is something that is to be surpassed."[24] The death of God has freed humankind to reach forward toward its own true destiny. It is therefore a *liberating* death, freeing humans (the overhuman) to take on the responsibility of defining good and evil, right and wrong.

In this respect, Nietzsche seemed to take no interest in Feuerbach's elevation of *love* as the most important aspect of our projection of ultimate perfection. Quite to the contrary, his passion was for an unchecked "will to *power*," the title of his published notebooks edited after his death by his devoted sister Elisabeth.[25] One can readily read out of this objective the sense of a power struggle that Nietzsche's madman and prophet gave voice to: a power struggle between God and humankind. And for him, God's death is the necessary outcome of that struggle.

Certainly the later Nazi obsession with an *Über*-race that stood conventional notions of morality on their head and brought about massive human destruction can be characterized as a perversion of Nietzsche's *Übermensch*. But the very fact that overman is something toward which we are moving, rather than an aspect of the present human scene, is an indication of how perilous the negative potential in Nietzsche's vision is. The will to power among mere mortals who are not overman can be devastating to the point of demonic. The outcome here, alas, is that power has won out over love even as the God of absolute omnipotence has been seen to have expired.

GOD'S SELF-ANNIHILATION: THOMAS J. J. ALTIZER

It was the "cool" thing to be part of the announcing God's demise in the decade of the '60s, the presumed event even gracing the cover of *Time* magazine.[26] For Thomas J. Altizer (b. 1927), the reality driving his intellectual output was anything but a temporary fad. It was *deadly* serious.

Although his work penetrated more deeply into the issue of transcendence over against immanence, Altizer was joined in his quest by other scholars and particularly by the American Jewish educator Richard L. Rubenstein, who maintained that "after Auschwitz," the title of his book on this subject,[27] it was no longer possible to entertain the idea of a Judeo-Christian God presiding over the affairs of humankind. The horrors experienced by some six million Jews and others in the Holocaust simply shattered all conventional claims that God will somehow "make it all right" in the end. Eventual heavenly bliss cannot be seen as a justification for unrelenting suffering on Earth.

> We live in the time of the "death of God." This is more a statement about man and his culture than about God. The death of God is a cultural fact . . . I am, however, a religious existentialist after Nietzsche and after Auschwitz. When I say we live in the time of the death of God, I mean that the thread uniting God and man, heaven and earth, has been broken. We stand in a cold, silent, unfeeling cosmos, unaided by any purposeful power beyond our own resources.[28]

For Rubenstein, "God really died at Auschwitz."[29] For Altizer, however, God really died, first, on Golgotha. He writes in *The Gospel of*

Christian Atheism (1966) that in the crucifixion, but even in the incarnation itself, God ceased to "exist or to be present in his primordial form." God "abandoned or negated his transcendent form."[30] This entails "an understanding of a fully kenotic Christ" with the concomitant "emptying of the power of God," a movement theologians have heretofore been unwilling to acknowledge.[31]

A "metamorphosis of the sacred into the profane . . . negate[s] its original identity, thereby passing through the death of its original form . . . Christianity, and Christianity alone, proclaims the death of the sacred."[32] The Word becoming flesh in Jesus "is only truly and actually real if it effects the death of the original sacred, the death of God himself."[33] But this God whose death Altizer is proclaiming is precisely *theism's* God, the classic God-image that represents the triumph of power over love, a God "known as transcendent and impassive . . . a primordial deity who is unaffected by the processes of time and history."[34] Chapter 4 is entitled "The Self-Annihilation of God," where Altizer states that "to confess the death of God is to speak of an actual and real event . . . a historical and a cosmic event, and, as such, it is a final and irrevocable event."[35]

God's dying into total immanence is not an end in itself but is the necessary precursor to the eventual dawning of an apocalyptic fulfillment of human potentiality. The explanation shows Altizer's affinity for the apocalyptic poetry of William Blake that we observed above.

> When the reality of God is eschatologically identified with his dawning Kingdom, then God can be known only as an active and apocalyptic process that even now is becoming all in all . . . This is precisely the function of a poetic apocalypse. Accordingly, such an apocalypse must be an imaginative disclosure of a universal and kenotic process that moves through an absolute and total negation to reach the epiphany of a divine and human Totality that thereby becomes all in all.[36]

Altizer goes on in *History as Apocalypse* (1985) to interpret Blake's final apocalyptic vision in *Jerusalem* 96 that God, who is love, dies precisely in order that the human being, who is love, may be fully actualized. "The 'Divine Image' dies in Jesus so as to abolish the solitary and transcendent

God who is the source of judgment and bring about an apocalyptic union that is a full coming together of God and man."[37]

Altizer's program is bold and unflinching. It is an attack on divine transcendence that shares with his predecessors a veritable celebration of the death of the traditional God of theism. But is it genuine, and is it necessary? If God is conceived differently than tradition has presented and elevated, if the transcendent God is *simultaneously* the immanent God who is perennially *with* us and not *over against* us, if God's being is first *love*, after which *power* comes to be defined within the implicates of love, then such a God would be one whose death truly would be mourned. The question at the funeral is quite obviously: Which God, whose God, died?

ENDNOTES

1. Ludwig Feuerbach, *The Essence of Christianity*, tr. George Eliot (New York: Harper & Brothers, 1957), 14.

2. Ibid., 19f.

3. Ibid., 29f.

4. Ibid., 30.

5. Ibid., 33.

6. Ibid., chs. 10, 12.

7. Feuerbach, *The Essence of Faith According to Luther*, tr. Melvin Cherno (New York: Harper & Row, 1967), 59 (both quotes).

8. Feuerbach, *The Essence of Christianity*, 101f.

9. Ibid., 48.

10. Ibid., 52f. See ibid., 64, where Feurbach defended the proposition that "Love is God, love is the absolute being."

11. Ibid., 55f.

12. Ibid., 52f., emphasis mine.

13. Ibid., 125f.

14. Ibid., 263.

15. Ibid., 273.

16. Eberhard Jüngel, *God as the Mystery of the World* (Grand Rapids: Eerdmans, 1983), 316.

17. Fyodor Dostoyevsky, *The Brothers Karamazov*, tr. Constance Garnett (New York: Random House, 1950), 290f., emphasis original.

18. William Blake, *Jerusalem*, Plate 29 [33], lines 17–18, 24, in David V. Erdman, ed., *The Complete Poetry and Prose of William Blake*, newly revised edition (New York: Random House, 1988), 175.

19. Altizer notes that Blake understood how our worship of a God of ultimate and absolute power turns God into its obverse, Satan, "the way of the Devouring Power." "The closing pages of *Jerusalem* record a vision of a coming apocalyptic *coincidentia oppositorum*, revealing how the final union of God and man will annihilate the God who alone is God by resurrecting him as 'The Great Humanity Divine'." Altizer, "William Blake and the Role of Myth in the Radical Christian Vision," in Thomas J. J. Altizer and William Hamilton, *Radical Theology and the Death of God* (Indianapolis: The Bobbs-Merrill Company, 1966), 191.

20. Friedrich Nietzsche, *The Gay Science*, Bk. 3, #125, tr. Walter Kaufmann (New York: Random House, 1974), 181f. This was a part of the first edition, published in 1882.

21. Nietzsche, *The Antichrist*, in *The Portable Nietzsche*, ed. and tr. Walter Kaufmann (New York: The Viking Press, 1954), 627, emphases original.

22. "Man is a rope stretched between the animal and the Superman—a rope over an abyss." Nietzsche, *Thus Spake Zarathustra*, Prologue 4, tr. Thomas Common, in *The Philosophy of Nietzsche* (New York: Random House, n.d.), 29

23. Ibid., Prologue 2 (27).

24. Ibid., Prologue 3 (27), emphasis original.

25. Nietzsche, *The Will to Power*, ed. Walter Kaufmann, tr. Walter Kaufmann and R. J. Hollingdale (New York: Random House, 1967).

26. *Time*, April 8, 1966, the cover asking the question, "Is God Dead?"

27. See Richard L. Rubenstein, *After Auschwitz: Radical Theology and Contemporary Judaism* (Indianapolis: The Bobbs-Merrill Company, 1966).

28. Ibid., 151f.

29. Ibid., 224.

30. Thomas J. J. Altizer, *The Gospel of Christian Atheism* (Philadelphia: The Westminster Press, 1966), 44.

31. Ibid., 43.

32. Ibid., 51.

33. Ibid., 54.

34. Ibid., 43.

35. Ibid., 103.

36. Altizer, "William Blake and the Role of Myth," op.cit., 187.

37. Altizer, *History as Apocalypse* (Albany, New York: SUNY Press, 1985), 204.

12

Obituaries for a Patriarchal God

From the 1970s, female scholars began to unveil what should have been obvious all along but had not been: that the champions of traditional theism were males championing a one-sidedly male image of the divine. Genesis 1:27 may have proclaimed that God created humankind in God's own image, and created us "male and female," but somehow the word failed to get around that *both* male and female were created in God's non-gender-specific image. The God who transcends distinctions of gender was nevertheless burdened with characteristics that were predominantly male.[1]

So we move directly from a consideration of the death of God overall to inquiries into the demise of a God of strictly male qualities, whose obituaries point the way forward to a more encompassing grasp of the fullness of Who God Is. A vast body of work has emerged from women theologians, often though not always termed "feminist" thinkers, and reaching far beyond the specific focus of this chapter on supplanting male-dominated understandings of God with more fecund investigations into the divine mystery of power and love. Thus it has been necessary here, in the selection process, to omit many voices perhaps equally deserving of attention.[2]

THE UNMASKING OF PATRIARCHY'S DOMINANT SWAY: MARY DALY

Mary Daly (1928–2010) provided important pioneering work in her *Beyond God the Father* in 1973, calling attention to the fact that indeed the God who had been pronounced dead was precisely God the *Father*.[3]

> The symbol of the Father God, spawned in the human imagination and sustained as plausible by patriarchy, has in turn rendered service to this type of society by making its mechanisms for the oppression of women appear right and fitting. If God in "his" heaven is a father ruling "his" people, then it is in the "nature" of things and according to divine plan and the order of the universe that society be male-dominated.[4]

A tremendous portion of Daly's work was aimed at surfacing the consequences of male-dominated thinking about God for women's day-to-day experience.

> The widespread conception of the "Supreme Being" as an entity distinct from this world but controlling it according to plan and keeping human beings in a state of infantile subjection has been a not too subtle mask of the divine patriarch.[5]

Out of her own experience of diminishment by males, she unflinchingly wrote of "castrating God" and "cutting away the Supreme Phallus"[6] as an important part of the process of transforming the collective imagination.

Daly's counterproposal was to de-objectify God as a being, following Tillich, and render God instead as a "verb":[7] "the God who is power of being acts as a moral power summoning women and men to act out of our deepest hope and to become who we can be."[8] God endlessly unfolds, and develops. God is "a power of being which both is, and is not yet."[9]

The re-creative work that followed Daly essentially assumed the clarion call of the traditional Father's death, so that the rest of this chapter will pursue the work of her female colleagues in developing evocative and propitious insights into the God who rises from the ash-heap of patriarchy. This activity has come to be known collectively as "feminist" theology; it is, of course, so much more than just that. Many of the developments to be addressed here will also be seen in later chapters on love and relationality, since these themes both recur with refreshing frequency. So this is but a foretaste of what lies ahead.

TOWARD A GOD OF MUTUAL RELATIONS: CARTER HEYWARD

Carter Heyward (b. 1945) blazed trails in American Protestant circles equal to those of the initially Roman Catholic Mary Daly. Heyward was one of eleven women whose ordination in 1974 paved the way for the recognition of women priests in the Episcopal Church. Her fundamental challenge to the dominance of patriarchy has been to move the issue of God's relations to others to front and center in reconceiving the being of God. God is identified at the very beginning of Heyward's first book, *The Redemption of God* (1982), as "power in relation" and "the power of relation,"[10]—or, as her subtitle implies, "*the power and intimacy in mutual relation.*"[11] This was actualized, "in-carnated," in Jesus as *dunamis* (power).[12] Jesus' *exousia* (authority) derives from his *dunamis*, not the other way around.[13]

Seven years later, following on the heels of Rita Nakashima Brock's initiating of the theme of "erotic power,"[14] Heyward observed that "to speak of the erotic or of God is to speak of *power in right relation*,"[15] defining "erotic" as "the sacred/godly basis of our capacity to participate in mutually empowering relationships."[16]

> Our power is erotic because it is about embodying relational connections. This power is sacred because it is shared. It is transforming because it is creative. And our power is liberating because it moves the struggle for justice. By this power, in this power, and with this power, we find ourselves-in-relation, breaking out of the isolation imposed by silence and invisibility.[17]

Mutuality is a central focus for Heyward, critiquing the patriarchal God for having mutual relations only internally, in the interactions among the persons of the Trinity. She defines mutuality as "sharing power in such a way that each participant in the relationship is called forth more fully into becoming who she is—a whole person, with integrity."[18]

Two modes of being powerful are contrasted: *power-with*, and *power-over*. "Power-with serves to further empower all persons in a relationship. Power-over serves to further empower a few and disempower others."[19] This is an absolutely vital insight. To discern explicitly how divine power can come to be perceived as divine *empowerment* is absolutely central to the thesis of my exploration.

Heyward wraps up her revisionary understanding with a statement that is refreshing in its insight.

> *God is our relational power—our power in mutual relation.* It is from this God that you and I draw our power to be in life in the first place, and to sustain our lives in relation. In sustaining and becoming ourselves in relation, we are giving birth to more of this same sacred power who needs us, her friends, to bring her to life and help nourish her life on the earth. She is being born among us, and yet she is seldom fully present, fully herself. To that extent, she is not yet but becoming. Where there is brokenness, fear, despair, or violence, the power may not be—yet. But with our help, she is becoming . . . It is a paradox: God is becoming our relational matrix insofar as we are the womb in which God is being born. This may be easier to comprehend *if we substitute the word "love" for "God."*[20]

Switching the pronoun for God from "he" to "she" is liberating. It is part of the process of completing the obituary for the patriarchal God. It is not that God is "she" only, but that God is "she" also, in a way that gets to the very heart of God's true identity. To call attention to the "womb" of God is not to lead us in the direction of a matriarchal replacement; it is rather to challenge us to find all the helpful female symbology for characterizing God that overcomes the previous patriarchal one-sidedness.

EROTIC POWER: RITA NAKASHIMA BROCK

As the latest move in a highly varied and richly textured career of passionate scholarship, Rita Nakashima Brock currently serves as founding co-director of the Soul Repair Center at Brite Divinity School in Texas.

Her award-winning first book, *Journeys by Heart* (1988), essentially blew the work of Anders Nygren on *Agape and Eros* out of the water by reversing the terms: God's love is not agapic, but *erotic*.

Brock identified agape love with the wrong direction of classical (patriarchal) theism in championing "disinterested" love, "dispassionate" love that includes no dynamic interrelationship between Lover and beloved and leaves God utterly unaffected by the creaturely response to God's love.[21] Erotic love, by contrast, "connotes intimacy through the subjective engagement of the whole self in a relationship."[22]

But what Brock really wished to do with this emphasis was to shift how we understand the nature of *power*: God's power is *erotic* power, as the subtitle of her book proclaims. "Erotic power is the power of our primal interrelatedness." It is an ontic category; "all other forms of power emerge from the reality of erotic power."[23] She went on to say: "Erotic power is the fundamental power of existence-as-a-relational-process . . . Connection is the basic power of all existence, the root of life. The power of being/becoming is erotic power."[24] This does not aim toward control, but connectedness. In fact, "erotic power denied and crushed" is precisely what generates dominance and control,[25] as power perverted.

SHE WHO IS: ELIZABETH JOHNSON

The day after Elizabeth Johnson was born in 1941, Pearl Harbor was bombed. Perhaps that was something of an omen in the work of a Roman Catholic woman theologian who challenged the priorities and perspectives of a male-dominated world of achievement by force and "might makes right." In her trailblazing *She Who Is* (1992), the title boldly confronting the reader like a 100-point headline on the front page of a newspaper, Johnson identified the death of patriarchy's God emphatically.

> Classical theism emphasizes in a one-sided way the absolute transcendence of God over the world, God's untouchability by human history and suffering, and the all-pervasiveness of God's dominating power to which human beings owe submission and

awe. Is this idea of God not the reflection of patriarchal imagination, which prizes nothing more than unopposed power-over and unquestioned loyalty? Is not the transcendent, omnipotent, impassible symbol of God the quintessential embodiment of the solitary ruling male ego, above the fray, perfectly happy in himself, filled with power in the face of the obstreperousness of others? Is this not "man" according to the patriarchal ideal?[26]

Johnson's insights overflow extensively into other aspects of divine reality being explored throughout Part III. Her supplanting of masculine ways of thinking about God delve quite consequentially into the issues of divine suffering, the importance of relationality over against self-sufficiency, and the centrality of divine love.

From a feminist perspective the denial of divine relation to the world codified in the highly specialized scholastic language reflects the disparagement of reciprocal relation characteristic of patriarchy in its social and intellectual expressions. If the ideal is the potent, all-sufficient ego in charge of events and independent of the need for others, then to be connected in mutuality with others introduces "deficiency" in the form of interdependence, vulnerability, and risk. Genuine mutuality threatens any form of domination, including the paternalistic ordering of things. Thus it is not accidental that classical theism insists on a concept of God with no real relation to the world, even when this is interpreted as an affirmation of divine transcendence. Unrelated and unaffected by the world, such a theistic God limns the ultimate patriarchal ideal, the solitary, dominant male.[27]

She critiques classical theism for modeling divine being on the root metaphor of motion derived from the non-personal physical world. "A different interpretation becomes possible when the root metaphor is taken from personal reality that is constitutively relational. Then the essence of God can be seen to consist in the motion of personal relations and the act that is love." Suffering now becomes not a movement from potentiality to act but "an expression of divine being insofar as it is an *act* freely engaged in as a consequence of care for others." Divine suffering is now interpretable as "Sophia-God's act of love freely overflowing in compassion."[28]

Love is absolutely central. "She Who Is" is "the dark radiance of love in solidarity with the struggle of denigrated persons."[29] Furthermore, "The being of God that we are speaking of *is essentially love*. God's being is identical with an act of communion, not with monolithic substance, and so is inherently relational."[30] God manifests a "power of suffering love to resist and create anew."[31] God is perceived as a "suffering Sophia-God of powerful compassionate love."[32]

So also, the title is intended to signify "*the creative, relational power of being* who enlivens, suffers with, sustains, and enfolds the universe."[33] Johnson's proposal for a feminist reshaping of the notion of omnipotence occupies only a page and half. "We seek an understanding that does not divide power and compassionate love in a dualistic framework that identifies love with a resignation of power and the exercise of power with a denial of love. Rather, we seek to integrate these two, seeing love as the shape in which divine power appears."[34] What is absent, however, is any investigation into how this reformulation can be constitutively understood, beyond notions of "power-with" and such phrases as "a vitality, an empowering vigor that reaches out and awakens freedom and strength in oneself and others . . . an energy that brings forth, stirs up, and fosters life," a transforming of people.[35]

Johnson is cautious about overemphasizing the value of love because of "the attention traditionally devoted to agapaic or self-giving love," without sufficiently equal regard for self-affirmation. Even so, "set within an inclusive context and continuously regulated by the value of relational autonomy . . . love may yet serve as a crystallization of the relational essence of God's being."[36] She offers a formidable twist on Anselm in suggesting that God is no less than that one "than whose power of love nothing greater can be conceived."[37]

This moves decisively in the direction my exploration desires to take us, toward a new unification of love and power at the very center of God in which love is allowed to redefine power. Johnson is pursuing "a resymbolization of divine power not as dominative or controlling power, nor as dialectical power in weakness, nor simply as persuasive power, but as the liberating power of connectedness that is effective in compassionate love. We can say: Sophia-God is in solidarity with those who suffer as a *mystery of empowerment*."³⁸ This points excitingly toward an understanding of a wholly other way of being powerful, for God. It blazes new trails into a wilderness of the reflective imagination that we are are invited to explore further.

ENDNOTES

1. Is it a coincidence that what we have been observing, that love has taken a backseat to power in traditional interpretations of God, reflects the dismissing of a "soft," receptive side of God for the sake of a harder, all-sufficient, self-contained, overpowering side of God?

2. For a brief but excellent overview of relevant resources, see Elizabeth A. Johnson, *Quest for the Living God* (London: Bloomsbury Publishing, 2007), 110–12.

3. Mary Daly, *Beyond God the Father: Toward a Philosophy of Women's Liberation* (Boston: Beacon Press, 1973), 12, and all of ch. 1.

4. Ibid., 13.

5. Ibid., 18.

6. Ibid., 19.

7. Ibid., 33ff.

8. Ibid., 32.

9. Ibid., 36.

10. Carter Heyward, *The Redemption of God: A Theology of Mutual Relation* (Washington, DC: University Press of America, 1982), 2.

11. Ibid., 11, emphasis original.

12. Ibid., 31f. 41.

13. Ibid., 41–43.

14. Rita Nakashima Brock, *Journeys by Heart: A Christology of Erotic Power* (New York: The Crossroad Publishing Co., 1988). See the section on Brock, below.

15. Heyward, *Touching Our Strength: The Erotic as Power and the Love of God* (San Francisco: Harper & Row, 1989), 3, emphasis mine.

16. Ibid., 187.

17. Ibid., 21.

18. Ibid., 191. We will visit this theme more extensively in the chapter on "Overtures to a Relational God." The conjoining of these two foci, feminists' and "process" theologians' understandings of power as relational, arises in the work of such scholars as Anne Carr, who wrote: "Feminist understanding of power in relational terms, as empowerment of the other, corresponds to process theology's distinction between two kinds of power, coercive power and persuasive power . . . God's liberating action occurs through human power and action that imitates the persuasive, nonviolent power of God, a power that, as human experience teaches and the symbol of the cross reveals, all too often fails in sinful human history. While women's experience underscores the compassion and so the gentle power of God, a power in the world that is apparently helpless without human cooperation, it also heightens awareness of human freedom and responsibility." Anne Carr, *Transforming Grace: Christian Tradition and Women's Experience* (San Francisco: Harper & Row, 1988), 151f.

19. Heyward, *Touching Our Strength*, 192.

20. Ibid., 24, emphases mine. The last sentence here was expanded that same year in a collection of Heyward's essays and sermons: "God is revealed as Lover and Beloved and as the creative, liberating, and sanctifying Spirit that draws us together in right relation." Heyward, *Speaking of Christ: A Lesbian Feminist Voice*, ed. Ellen C. Davis (New York: The Pilgrim Press, 1989), 69.

21. Rita Nakashima Brock, *Journeys by Heart: A Christology of Erotic Power* (New York: The Crossroad Publishing Co., 1988), 40.

22. Ibid.

23. Ibid., 26, both quotes. Brock derived this notion from Haunani-Kay Trask, *Eros and Power: The Promise of Feminist Theory* (Philadelphia: University of Pennsylvania Press, 1986), 92-93: "In the feminist vision, Eros is both love *and* power." (Quoted by Brock, 25.)

24. Ibid., 41.

25. Ibid., 36.

26. Elizabeth A. Johnson, *She Who Is: The Mystery of God in Feminist Theological Discourse* (New York: Crossroad, 1992), 21. See also Johnson's later summary of this critique in her *Quest for the Living God*, 14–16,

and all of ch. 5 (90–112).

27. Johnson, *She Who Is*, 225.

28. Ibid., 265, all three quotes; emphasis original.

29. Ibid., 244.

30. Ibid., 238, emphasis mine.

31. Ibid., 271.

32. Ibid., 272.

33. Ibid., 13, emphasis mine.

34. Ibid., 269.

35. Ibid.

36. Ibid., 265, both quotes.

37. Ibid., 268.

38. Ibid., 270, emphasis mine.

13

Inklings of an Impotent God

We have entertained responses to traditional Christian theism that proclaim the liberating death of such a deity, or at least the death of the supreme masculinity of that God. These are one way to challenge the hammerlock hold that divine omnipotence has held over its adherents. Another path was also available, taken by some, that endeavored to strike down the very notion of God's unlimited power itself, opting instead for a perception of the divine that its critics would disparage as an apparently *impotent* God. That option is now to be examined here.

This chapter proceeds by reversing the usual order of progression. I begin not with the earlier manifestations of proposals that solve the love/power riddle by negating divine omnipotence, thence to move forward in time. Rather I start with the 1981 publication of a book by an American Jewish rabbi that rocked the sensibilities of Christian pastors across the U.S. and initiated an exciting new dialogue on the problem—in traditional Jewish *and* Christian thought—of *theodicy*, and then look back at other earlier contributions along a similar track, concerning a possibly *limited* God.

WHEN BAD THINGS HAPPEN: HAROLD KUSHNER

Adam Kushner was born with a rare genetic disorder called "progeria," which causes rapid aging. Adam died at the age of fourteen, looking like a wizened old man. His father, Rabbi Harold Kushner (b. 1935), agonized over his son's innocent suffering and fate, and wound up dealing with it by writing a bestseller that, at first, no publishing house wanted. He called it *When Bad Things Happen to Good People* (1981).

Kushner drew on the sufferings of Job and the Holocaust, as well as his own family's suffering, in trying to make sense out of the senseless. He recognized that the Genesis story of creation emphasizes the emergence of order out of chaos and saw that as a process that is still underway.[1] So where is God in the unresolved chaos still rearing its ugly head in creation?

He came to recognize that "Christianity introduced the world to the idea of a God who suffers," and went on to confess that "I can worship a God who hates suffering but cannot eliminate it, more easily that I can worship a God who chooses to make children suffer and die, for whatever exalted reason."[2]

So Kushner refused to accept the idea that God causes human misfortune: "tragedy is not God's will."[3] But "If God does not cause the bad things that happen to good people, and if He cannot prevent them, what good is He at all? . . . How does God make a difference in our lives if He neither kills nor cures?"[4] Kushner's answer: "God inspires people to help other people who have been hurt in life . . . God, who neither causes nor prevents tragedies, helps by inspiring people to help."[5] "God may not prevent the calamity, but He gives us the strength and the perseverance to overcome it."[6]

In short, Kushner found himself on the horns of a dilemma. Either God has power over our misfortunes and chooses not to prevent them, or God cares about us in our misfortunes but is powerless to prevent them. His stance affirms the view of Archibald MacLeish in *J.B.*, that there is no justice, only love.[7] In the end, out of love, we are called to forgive God for not being perfect![8]

This hearkens back to the late medieval discussion about the duality of God's absolute power and God's ordained power. The latter assures that the world flows forward according to God's immutable laws concerning the proper order of things. The former provides the option that God's "power in reserve" is perfectly capable of overturning one or another of those laws whenever and however God so chooses. This is the distinction that allows for so-called "miracles." It also stands behind the understanding of an "interventionist" God who may upset the normal order by contravening what would otherwise naturally happen. Prayer to God often takes the form of pleading with God to intervene in the natural course of events and alter the outcome. Rabbi Kushner's pleas went unanswered. Adam died. The Holocaust and many other horrendous calamities in history are the cosmic extension of that, writ large.

So we have a God who has neither died nor been killed, but a God whose power is perceived to be unavailable except as an "inspiration"—the hint of an impotent God, who would not really be God at all. This way of resolving the seeming absence of God's power in the world was hardly original with Kushner. Let us trace it back to its earlier manifestations.

EARLIER PREDECESSORS IN THE CHRISTIAN TRADITION

Deism arose on the continent and in England toward the beginning of the Enlightenment. It does not designate a school of thought, and perspectives of the deists varied widely. The most prominent representatives of English deism were John Toland, author of *Christianity not Mysterious* (1696), and Matthew Tindal, whose *Christianity as Old as Creation* (1730) is often called the Bible of deism. It was published three years before his death; the only copy of a subsequent manuscript was burned by a bishop of the Church of England as being too hot for the faithful to handle.

Deism, generally, promoted an all-wise, all-good God who once in the deeply distant past set matters in motion and provided the laws by which the universe operates, but does nothing at all by way of interference in the natural course of the created order. Thus every notion of a *providential* role on God's part is emphatically negated. Deists therefore considered God to be power-*less* to alter the course of natural and human events.[9]

In 1759, four years after the devastation of the Lisbon earthquake, the French philosopher Voltaire (1694–1778) wrote his *Candide*, a hilarious puncturing of Leibniz's claim that things are for the best in this best of all possible worlds. The adventures and misadventures and calamitous misfortunes of Candide and his friends convey bitingly the utter nonsense of that point of view. Even the philosopher Pangloss comes to the realization that he still maintains that view, "without believing it."[10]

Voltaire did not present his views on God in a straightforward manner but seems to have come to the conclusion, particularly regarding the effects of the Lisbon earthquake, that he would rather worship a *limited* God than an *evil* one. James Collins concluded that:

> Voltaire even speculates about whether the necessity of the divine action may not betoken some limitation upon God's power. The divine power may be relatively supreme, in that it is not subject to any foreign agency, and yet it may also be limited in an internal way to what can be done in accordance with Newtonian mechanical laws. Thus the benevolent God can be regarded as infinite in durational existence, yet finite in power, knowledge, and presence.[11]

Similarly, a century later, John Stuart Mill (1806–73), in the third essay of his *Three Essays on Religion* (1874, posthumously), insisted that "natural theology can point only to a Creator with limited, not unlimited power."[12] He wrote of "the impossible problem of reconciling infinite benevolence and justice with infinite power in the Creator of such a world as this,"[13] and concluded: "the notion of a providential government by an omnipotent Being for the good of his creatures must be entirely dismissed."[14] Only if the power of God is limited is there "nothing to disprove the supposition that his goodness is complete."[15]

We have previously met Dostoyevsky's Karamazov brothers.[16] Following Ivan's rejection of a God who is seen to be responsible for the suffering of the innocent, he goes on to narrate his tale of Jesus Christ coming again during the time of the Spanish Inquisition, and promptly being thrown in prison by the aged Grand Inquisitor. The Inquisitor eventually comes to visit him in his cell, mocks him, berates him, denounces him for his failure and the failure of the ideas of love and servanthood and the exaltation of human freedom that he brought. The Inquisitor understands that the church has adopted the ways of Rome and the sword of Caesar. The Prisoner remains silent throughout, answering him, at the end, only with a kiss.[17] It is no less than the supplanting of power with love, poetically rendered.

And finally, the American philosopher and psychologist William James wrote in his *A Pluralistic Universe* (1909) that "there is a God, but . . . he is finite, either in power or in knowledge, or in both at once."[18] His explorations in this direction influenced the man we are about to meet.

A GOD OF LIMITED POWER: EDGAR BRIGHTMAN

Edgar Brightman (1884–1953) was an American Methodist scholar who followed in the train of Borden Parker Bowne in the philosophical school known as "Boston personalism." His most important work relevant to this exploration was his 1930 publication entitled *The Problem of God*.

For Brightman, "the expansion of God into an omnipotent being" restricted God's benevolence, even though classical theism asserted both "with equal assurance."[19] He found the traditional combination of the two to be "superficial."[20] Omnipotence is "derived predominantly from abstract thought."[21] It is not based on experience alone, whereas benevolence is more plainly rooted there. Moreover, "it is religiously *much more essential that God should be good than that he should be absolutely all-powerful*."[22]

> A God whose purpose it is to develop a society of free persons must forego some knowledge [foreknowledge] and some power if he is to attain his purpose. Expansion in either direction necessitates contraction in the other.[23]

Brightman's solution was to propose a God who is *limited* both by Godself (that which is within God's nature, the "The Eternally Given"), and that in relation to which God is at work and toward which God is in some respects "passive" (in contrast to God's "active will"), i.e., the free choices of other persons.[24]

All of this finally leads Brightman to say that worshiping a limited God elicits "belief in a *finite* God."[25] Even so, he still wanted to maintain that the active element in God is still *in control*, though it maintains that with "struggle and pain."[26] Raising motifs we are encountering throughout this exploration into the challenges to the Augustinian synthesis, Brightman recognized the vital importance of the *love* of God and the presence of *suffering* in God. "God is not simply a happy, loving Father; he is the struggle and the mysterious pain at the heart of life. He is indeed love; but *a suffering love* that redeems through a Cross."[27]

> It is *far more reasonable to deny the absolute omnipotence of the power manifesting itself in the world than to deny its goodness.* On our view, God is perfect in will, but not in achievement; perfect to derive good from all situations, but not in power to determine in detail what those situations will be.[28]

The problem with Brightman's heroic effort to limit God's power for the sake of being able to worship a God of supreme goodness shows its face on the final page of the book. Even after all he willingly surrendered, he still maintained at the very end that God is "the *controlling power* of the universe, guiding it through all struggles and delays toward an ever-enlarging value."[29] What restrains God's omnipotence, it seems, is something given within God, something in God's nature which necessitates God's working out of God's plans in relationship to creation and within time, but it still remains God who is working it out.

Because there is no fresh rendering of the meaning of power, all the expressions of limits on that divine power come to be cancelled out in the end. Justifying God as a God of well-intentioned benevolence by placing boundaries around the triumphant omnipotence of God finally collapses under the weight of its own insufficiently conceived alternative. How is a God who manifests barely an inkling of impotence even a God at all?

ENDNOTES

1. Harold S. Kushner, *When Bad Things Happen to Good People* (New York: Schocken Books, 1981), 51f.
2. Ibid., 134.

3. Ibid.

4. Ibid., 138f.

5. Ibid., 139f.

6. Ibid., 141.

7. Ibid., 145, referencing MacLeish, J. B., 151.

8. Ibid., 148.

9. The deists were influential well beyond the theological arena by virtue of the fact that a large number of this country's Founding Fathers were Deists, whether closeted or openly. Jefferson's "self-evident" truths were deistic ones: The pursuit of happiness is understood to be what God intended for humans from the creation, in contrast to traditional Christianity's understanding of the pre-eminent importance of glorifying God.

10. Voltaire, *Candide*, tr. Lowell Bair (New York: Bantam Books, 1959), 117.

11. James Collins, *God in Modern Philosophy* (Chicago: Henry Regnery Co., 1959), 148.

12. John Stuart Mill, *Three Essays on Religion* (New York: Henry Holt and Co., 1874)

13. Ibid., 186f.

14. Ibid., 243.

15. Ibid., 252.

16. See above, ch. 11.

17. Dostoyevsky, *The Brothers Karamazov*, 292–314.

18. William James, *A Pluralistic Universe* (New York : Longmans, Green, and Co., 1909), 311.

19. Edgar Sheffield Brightman, *The Problem of God* (New York: The Abingdon Press, 1930), 96.

20. Ibid., 97.

21. Ibid., 98.

22. Ibid., emphasis mine.

23. Ibid., 102. This is the choice that must be made, I insist, when one does not reconceive the *nature* of power whenever that power is wielded

and defined by *love*.

24. Ibid., 113, 124, 127.

25. Ibid., 127, emphasis mine.

26. Ibid., 135.

27. Ibid., 137, emphasis mine.

28. Ibid., emphasis mine.

29. Ibid., 193, emphasis mine. In regard to God's eventual conquering of evil, Brightman wrote, God "may delay, but he cannot fail" (122).

14

Breakthroughs to a Loving God

Themes that have been surfacing in the myriad of challenges to the Augustinian synthesis known as Christian theism overlap and interlock. The mystics' deity was more fully identified by love than by power. A God not hemmed in by a doctrine of immutability becomes open to the adventure of divine love. A God who is not apathetic is a God who suffers in love. The God beyond patriarchy is a God for whom love is at the center of the divine identity.

Thus we come to a focus that has already occupied a major amount of attention throughout these previous chapters but now becomes the direct object of our present concern. We come to a century and a half and more of rekindled and illuminating contributions to a God whose love can no longer be sacrificed on the altar of God's overwhelming power.

Reaching back into the eighteenth century, we encounter John Wesley, the founder of Methodism, who wrote in his *Explanatory Notes upon the New Testament*, regarding 1 John 4:8: "God is often styled holy, righteous, wise, but not holiness, righteousness, or wisdom in the abstract as he is said to be love: intimating that this is . . . his reigning attribute."[1] So could his brother Charles sing of "love divine, all loves excelling," and of Jesus, "thou art all compassion; pure, unbounded love thou art."² And early in the nineteenth century, the Scottish American churchman Alexander Campbell wrote in his *The Christian System* (1839), "God and *Love* [are] two names for one idea."³

> The grand principle, or means which God has adopted for the accomplishment of this moral regeneration, is the full demonstration and proof of a single proposition addressed to the reason of man. This sublime proposition is THAT GOD IS LOVE.⁴

For Campbell, "it is in the person and mission of the INCARNATE WORD that we learn that God is love."⁵

In addition, Frederick W. Faber, an Anglican turned Roman Catholic, a theologian and hymn writer who composed "Faith of Our Fathers" and "There's a Wideness in God's Mercy," observed in 1857 in his *The Creator and the Creature*: "Love is tantamount to the whole of God, and is co-extensive with him . . . Love is the perfection of the Uncreated in Himself."⁶

These were the forerunners, along with other voices we have already been listening to. Let us now give more extended attention to their conceptual companions, the number of whose voices worthy of being heard is sizeable indeed. I have tried to bring order into this array of insightful scholarship by grouping them according to certain predominant themes, even though they merit attention each in their own right—and some prominently so.

RECLAIMING THE INSIGHT THAT GOD *IS* LOVE

D. Z. Phillips asked perceptively, "What if religion means what it says, that God *is* love, no more and no less? It would follow that God does not have two separate attributes, power and love, but that the only power God has or is, *is* the power of love."⁷ Richard Garnett "the Younger," "Keeper of Printed Books" in the library of the British Museum where he toiled for forty-five years, engagingly announced at the beginning of his *De Flagello Myrteo* (1905) that "Love is God's essence; Power but his attribute; therefore is his love greater than his power."⁸ And Elizabeth Johnson recently has observed that if it were possible to sum up the rediscoveries of recent theologizing, "it would be the classic Christian belief that '*God is Love*' (1 John 4:16)."[9]

The absence of this recognition in the classical expressions of Christian theism has been strikingly reversed in theological reflections reaching back a century and a half. The selections that follow here each makes its own helpful contribution to the recovery of this vital conviction.

SØREN KIERKEGAARD: GOD'S PASSION TO LOVE AND TO *BE* LOVE

Søren Kierkegaard (1813–55) wrote in Danish under a variety of pseudonymns and published his explicitly anti-Hegelian tracts at his own personal expense—dying, at it turned out, just as the money, and presumably everything important that he had to say, ran out. In the twentieth century he came to be hailed as the father of Christian Existentialism.

"This is all I have known for certain," he wrote in his journal in 1850, "that God is love. Even if I have been mistaken on this or that point, God is nevertheless love."[10] And in a much earlier entry from 1839, he observed—correctly, I think—that "it is really remarkable that whereas all the other qualifications pronounced about God are adjectives, 'love' is the only substantive, and one would scarcely think of saying 'God is lovely.' Thus language itself has expressed the substantive character of love implied by this qualification."[11]

The notion that God is love, is the One Who Loves, is "unchanged love," "infinite love," pervades Kierkegaard's writings. God is no less than "the love which sustains all existence."[12] There is no systematic rendering of this notion because he rebelled against the very idea of systems of thought that betray the incarnational scandal of particularity. Chapter Two of his aptly named *Philosophical Fragments* (1844) is entitled "The God as Teacher and Saviour: An Essay of the Imagination." It is the now-familiar narrative of God, moved by love for humanity, wishing to reveal Godself but not in an overwhelming, overpowering way. So Kierkegaard imagined a king loving a humble maiden who, out of love for her, takes the form of a servant to disclose his great love. "Love is exultant when it unites equals, but it is triumphant when it makes that which was unequal equal in love."[13] And thus it was that God disclosed Godself to humankind in Jesus of Nazareth.

God can therefore be understood to be "like a poet," not "consenting" to all that happens among the characters in a poem but allowing it:

> poetically he permits everything possible to come forth... God's wanting to work as a poet in this fashion [discloses] God's passion to love and to be loved, yes, almost as if he were himself found in this passion, O, infinite love, so that in the power of this passion he cannot stop loving, almost as if it were a weakness, although it is rather his strength, his omnipotent love. This is the measure of his unswerving love.[14]

Kierkegaard wrestled throughout his pseudonymous writings with how to reconcile this centrality of God as Love with the doctrine of divine omnipotence, and specifically with holding onto both omnipotence and human freedom. He expanded upon the motif of God's reaching out unintimidatingly by claiming:

> For this is the unfathomable nature of love, that it desires equality with the beloved, not in jest merely, but in earnest and truth. And it is the *omnipotence of the love* which is so resolved that it is able to accomplish its purpose... This is the God as he stands upon the earth, like unto the humblest by the *power of his omnipotent love*.[15]

So we encounter already here the theme of the next section, divine power as the "power of omnipotent love." In a journal entry in 1846, he wrote:

> Only omnipotence can withdraw itself at the same time it gives itself away, and this relationship is the very independence of the receiver. God's omnipotence is therefore his goodness. For goodness is to give oneself away completely, but in such a way that by omnipotently taking oneself back one makes the recipient independent... Only a wretched and mundane conception of the dialectic of power holds that it is greater in proportion to its ability to compel and to make dependent.[16]

But Kierkegaard could not finally answer the question of whether the omnipotence of love assures a blessed outcome at the end, overcoming all residual opposition.[17] There is an "immutability" to God's love that is a matter of assured constancy,[18] but no certain conclusion of what power God's love has in reserve to confront intransigence non-compellingly.

ALBRECHT RITSCHL: THE ULTIMATE REIGN OF GOD'S LOVE

Albrecht Ritschl (1822–89) is noted for his concentration on the divine intent to usher in, with human contributions, God's eventual Reign—understood as an ellipse with two foci, as both gift and task. At the center of this expectation is the assurance that love constitutes the very nature of God and of God's coming Reign. The goodness of God:

> is embraced in the specific attribute of the Divine Fatherhood; or, in other words, the truth that He has revealed Himself to the Christian community as love. There is no other conception of equal worth beside this which need be taken into account . . . the conception of love is the only adequate conception of God.[19]

He went on to insist that this "conception of love . . . is the key to the revelation of God in Christianity,"[20] and the "character" of the divine will is only to be understood under the rubric of love.[21]

> When God is conceived as love . . . He is not conceived as being anything apart from and prior to His self-determination as love. He is either conceived as love, or simply not at all.[22]

Such love, as any valid loving, "aims at the promotion of the other's personal end, whether known or conjectured."[23]

Ritschl combined "freedom of action" and "dependence upon God" by maintaining that freedom is present only when our actions are directed toward the Reign of God as final end of our aspirations. Freedom is defined as "permanent self-determination by the good end," or, in Christian terms, "by the Kingdom of God as final end."[24] But this whole notion works only if dependence on God is interpreted in a way other than on the *absolute power* of God. The power-freedom dichotomy is not yet resolved. The not-yet of God's impending Reign is no way guaranteed, so long as human resistance is not futile.

A. M. FAIRBAIRN: AN ETHICIZED DEITY

The Scotsman Andrew Martin Fairbairn (1838–1912) was Principal of Mansfield College, Oxford. Lectures that he delivered at the end of the nineteenth century in the United States at Yale and at Union Seminary became *The Place of Christ in Modern Theology* (1903) in print.

Over against deism and pantheism, Fairbairn promoted what he called an "ethicized Deity."[25] His work was marred by a distinction between God and "Godhead": "God is deity conceived in relation, over against the universe, its cause or ground, it law and end; but the Godhead is deity conceived according to His own nature, as He is from within and for Himself." This "Godhead" has "completely ethicized the conception of God."[26] It is not that the former is elusive while only the latter is accessible to us. Rather, the Christian revelation is of the Godhead itself, as distinctly trinitarian.[27]

Thus the very God who is in relation to God's creation *is love*,[28] "not the eternal possibility but the eternal actuality of love."[29] Creation itself has arisen by virtue of the eternal love:

> since God is according to His essence love, He could not but be determined to the creative act . . . creation is due to the moral perfection of the Creator, who is so essentially love that He could not but create a world that He might create beatitude.[30]

Fairbairn went on to observe that "God does not love because He created, but He created because He loved."[31]

Fairbairn's work is instructive to us only as an additional indicator of how widespread the centrality of love was becoming over a century ago for understanding the divine nature, even though he did not address in any helpful way how this challenges traditional understandings of divine power.

NELS F. S. FERRÉ: LOVE IS THE POWER OF BECOMING

Nels Ferré was born in Sweden in 1908 and emigrated to the United States by himself at the age of thirteen. His life of prolific scholarship was spent in this country. He was strongly influenced by Edgar Brightman, and at Harvard he served as a graduate assistant to the process philosopher Alfred North Whitehead, whose work we will encounter two chapters from now. Ferré died in 1971.

Ferré's *The Christian Understanding of God* (1951) is the primary source for our focus here. He came to the notion of Love as ultimate being/becoming not from a biblical perspective but from the starting point of philosophical theology.[32] Love, for him, is "the ultimate category."[33] Love is "the form of being which acts out of complete concern not only for all, in all dimensions of life, and the conditions which sustain, promote and enhance life, but also for ever new life and new conditions of life."[34] God as love is "self-existing and self-directing. God as love, moreover, is both actual and potential. God is subject; and a subject is capable of both loving and being loved."[35] And the very nature of the ultimate as love is, precisely, "to have relations."[36] Gary Dorrien concludes that, for Ferré, "theology is about the transformation of the world through the love-transforming power of God's Spirit."[37]

God can in no way be perceived as static, as perpetual being without change. Rather, "only by becoming can being become what it is. God as reality both is and becomes by nature, for He is love."[38]

> If love is the principle and power of becoming, the very nature of love is to share His being. To love is to give. To love is to create. To love is to keep fulfilling. To love is to be by becoming.[39]

Ferré recognized that the divine love/power conundrum cannot be resolved from the power side,[40] but all he was able to put forward is that "He who is love by nature expresses Himself by sharing His power with us . . . Power is the capacity of love to effect its end."[41] But there is no real resolution, and Ferré even continued to use such terms as "sovereignty" and divine "control" positively.[42] Not only is the ultimate future of God's creation assured, because of the *sovereign* nature of God's love, but the ultimate victory of that love is "total."[43] If God "is sovereign love, the question as to the outcome [of history] is completely closed. Love will win unconditional surrender from all that is not love."[44]

Essentially, Ferré represents no real advance over the internal conflicts in Ritschl's thought, in that love is understood to be a power other than controlling and yet love's ultimate victory is somehow assured at the end. It is similar to the unresolved tension we have seen also in Moltmann.

What we have encountered among the pioneers in this section is a clarion call to reclaim the New Testament's bold assertion, in 1 John, that love itself is no mere divine attribute but characterizes the very being of God. That is indeed a giant leap forward from theism's attempts to "shoehorn" love into the essential being of a God who is omnipotent Lord of all. Where efforts were seen here to reconstitute the Love/Power relationship, very little significant progress is visible. But that work was going on as well. To a selection of those breakthrough efforts I now turn.

THE POWER OF OMNIPOTENT LOVE

CLARENCE EDWIN ROLT: LOVE *IS* GOD'S POWER

Born in 1880, the British theologian C. E. Rolt studied at Oxford and went on to a life of promising scholarship cut short by death from a lingering illness, only months before his translation into English of the major works of pseudo-Dionysius appeared in print, in 1917. He was 37 years old. His own masterpiece, *The World's Redemption*,[45] came out in 1913, shortly before war broke out all over Europe. It fell pretty much into obscurity until the German theologian of hope, Jürgen Moltmann, gave it serious attention in his *The Trinity and the Kingdom*[46] in 1980. Much of Rolt's most important insight into the power and love of God might well have been developed more probingly, had he lived long enough to accomplish it.

Rolt began his study with a rejection of the traditional understanding of power as compulsion or "brute force," which leads to the realization that "the mind is brought at last to One Who is yet stronger than the universe itself, and Who . . . by the act of an almighty will, which nothing can resist, bends all things to His purposes and compels the whole material system to obey His irresistible commands."[47] In such a perspective, God's power "consists of infinite force."[48] Rolt went on to spell this out in richly metaphoric detail.

> This conception of the nature of omnipotence is accepted by most Christians as a part of the Divine revelation. It is firmly

embedded in all popular theology, and unhappily finds a place in most theology that claims to be philosophic. True, the philosophic theologian does his best as a rule to explain it away so far as he can with much talk about God's "self-limitation" or the necessity of His obeying the laws He has Himself made for His universe. Nevertheless the fact remains that this conception of despotic force is for him, as for the generality of mankind, the only conception of Divine Power. He may, in practice, treat it as a piece of lumber, but he regards it in theory as a piece of necessary lumber, however useless and inconvenient. And therefore he allows it to remain blocking out the light and air in his theological edifice, instead of boldly throwing it out of the window. And hence when he becomes vaguely conscious that it does not harmonise with the main lines of the building it occupies or with the rest of the furniture around it, instead of turning the useless thing out and casting it on to the rubbish-heap, he contents himself with raising a dust of words which serve, for the moment, to disguise its hideous outlines and hide them from his sight.[49]

By way of contrast, Rolt insisted that this way of conceiving of divine power is "immoral, irrational and anti-Christian," from which have sprung some of the most egregious travesties in the Christian faith.[50]

Rolt's initial answer is very pessimistic: since God's power cannot be expected to "crush opposing forces," it can only be "bent and broken and yet remain unconquered . . . it can only hope and wait."[51] But the breakthrough is coming: it is "love, at its truest"[52] that suffers patiently:

> Hence it would seem that the omnipotence of God . . . is therefore nothing else than *love itself*. It consists in love, and has no other quality whatsoever. *Love is, in fact, the only real power*, and force is not power at all . . . To say that God has infinite love, and that to this love is added infinite power, is totally and utterly false. He has nothing besides that perfect Love which is Himself. *God is Love, and this Love is itself His power*, nor can we truly conceive of Him as possessing any other power besides.[53]

So, Jesus' depiction in the Gospel story is that of "a God Whose omnipotence consisted not in coercive force but in enduring love."[54] The secret of the "essential power of Christ" was simply "love made perfect through suffering."[55] Ergo, "God is love, and love alone; and this is the sum total of His power."[56]

Rolt correctly recognized that creation, both initially and ongoingly, is a process of order being wrestled out of chaos. Evil, the resistance to love's power, is not so much an aspect of divine action but a manifestion of the chaos still being overcome.[57]

The tragedy is that Rolt did not live long enough to investigate more deeply the dynamics of love as powerful. What he did produce is a tantalizing fillip crying out to be expanded upon. Precisely *how* love wields the only power at God's disposal is the issue demanding elaboration. That task is still underway.

GORDON KAUFMAN: A HISTORICIST COUPLING OF DIVINE POWER AND LOVE

Gordon Kaufman (1925–2011) grew up in a Mennonite household and served as a conscientious objector in World War II. His pacifist morality was of one piece with what emerged in his initial reflections about the nature of God's power. The "early" Kaufman is the part of his work that interests us here, even though he was already moving away from his conclusions in *Systematic Theology: A Historicist Perspective* (1968) before it was published. Although much of what he wrote about God's power and love is continuous with what we have just seen in C. E. Rolt, Kaufman did not indicate any awareness of Rolt's work.

In his early—and subsequently rejected—phase, Kaufman focused on what can be known about divine matters by reflection on matters historical. And God's acting in history "has a very specific character: it is *an act of love* . . . This God, then, is one whose purposes are characterized by lovingkindness."[58] God, in accordance with God's love, is willing to sacrifice God's "absolute power."[59] When we speak of the power of God, "our ordinary conceptions may be very misleading."[60] But even so, he believed that God "modulates" his power when dealing with free beings as opposed to his *coercing* others to conform to the divine will. Consequently, we are to understand that God's power is:

the power to give, *the power to love,* the paradoxical power of "weakness" . . . God's power is thus much greater than the compelling force of a tyrant who makes others submit against their will . . . his power is sufficient to transform a willful person from self-centeredness to love, without destroying or even violating the tender plant of freedom.[61]

When we talk about omnipotence, etc., "we must always make certain that it is to this reality, and not some other, that we are referring . . . Too often in Christian history this simple but all-important rule has been forgotten." So any notion of God's omnipotence "must be seen as *the omnipotence of God's love.*"[62] Kaufman's ringing conclusion is that the "first cause" of the universe itself "is no abstract, empty concept of God but *God's all-powerful love.*"[63]

Not literally, of course, but analogically, and symbolically, the *power of God* is treated as the "second" of the perfections of God's freedom.[64] It is rather apparent that Kaufman attempted, unsuccessfully, to have it both ways. On the one hand, he contended, correctly, that it is *as* love that God is powerful.[65] But on the other hand, God's power remains *undeconstructed.* It is "power over," "all-powerful in the world."[66] He rightly observed that God "is *omnicompetent,* that he can appropriately deal with any circumstance that arises; nothing can ultimately defeat or destroy him,"[67] but he believed this is only a working out of the inherent meaning of omnipotence while, elsewhere, he gave that word its far more classical tonalities.

There are many reasons why Kaufman went on to "de-reify" God and surrender his conviction that God is any reality other than a dimension of "our *interpersonal* relationships with our fellow humans."[68] But clearly his inability or refusal to decouple divine power from all vestiges of its inherited meaning as power-over crippled the long-term benefit of his early insights.

Geddes MacGregor: The Powerful Love of a Kenotic God

The work of Geddes MacGregor (1909–98) is strikingly prescient, though insufficient attention was paid to his 1975 work, *He Who Lets Us Be.*[69] Originally from Scotland, he spent most of his long academic career in the United States.

MacGregor pursued a theology of kenosis, God's sacrificial self-emptying. He boldly endorsed Patripassianism and regarded the doctrine of God's impassibility as one of the crucial errors of orthodoxy: "the One whom we call God must be *par excellence* dynamic, not impassible."[70] He observed that Christian theologians from the beginning "seem to have been reluctant to take 'God is love' seriously as a theological proposition."[71] He wrote that "a profound misunderstanding of the nature of both the power and the love of God has radically distorted the traditional view of the situation." The power of God is not "the ability to do everything (*omnipotere*) or to control everything (*pantokratein*)" but rather "the infinite power that springs from creative love," and "sacrificial love . . . The divine almightiness consists…of unlimited capacity for creative love."[72] Further along, he explicitly affirmed that "the omnipotence of God is the power of love . . . To say that God is omnipotent can only mean that nothing diminishes his love."[73]

In moving beyond kenotic christology to kenotic theology, MacGregor called God "kenotic Being" and considered kenosis to be "the root principle of Being."[74] In this regard, his position was limited to identifying *how God exercises power differently*, rather than seeing how the very *nature* of God's power is to be reinterpreted (reconstructed) through the lens of God as love. Kenosis becomes a matter of God's self-abnegation of a mode of power that God wills not to utilize. In that respect, MacGregor could still hold on to an assurance of God's "providential intervention."[75]

EBERHARD JÜNGEL: THE POWER OF LOVE IN WEAKNESS

Eberhard Jüngel was born in Germany, in 1934, on what eventually became the "wrong" side of the Iron Curtain, but managed to study under Karl Barth and the New Testament scholar Ernst Fuchs before the Wall went up. His facility in matters both theological and biblical contributes significantly to his subsequent work. In the Foreword to the First and Second Editions of his *God as the Mystery of the World* (originally, 1976), he wrote: "Basically the intent of all the studies in this book is nothing else than to exposit consequently this one statement from First John: God is love (1 John 4:8)."[76] Indeed, "To think God as love" is no less than "the task of theology."[77]

Drawing out insights from the last writings of Dietrich Bonhoeffer, Jüngel rejected the notion of a "worldly necessity of God" on the grounds that:

> The God who is necessary in the world is always conceived of as *God the Lord*. And it appeared that there was general agreement as to what a lord is. God's lordship was discussed in the sense of his exercise of omnipotence. The God who is necessary in the world was understood as the almighty Lord whose love and mercy appear to be fundamentally secondary and subsidiary to his claim to lordship. This is the earthly way of thinking of a lord: first he has all power and then perhaps he can be merciful—but then again, perhaps not. God's lordliness and lordship are thought of in the same general way. He is mighty, able, and free to love or not to love . . . one must not conclude that freedom or power is superior to love, while the love of God becomes a secondary attribute. The thesis of the worldly nonnecessity of God is directed precisely against this view of God according to which God, as the almighty Lord who can be differentiated from his love, is necessary to the world.[78]

So Jüngel was driven to reverse this way of thinking that "lordship" can be said to define adequately the essence of God. Starting with the understanding that God is love, he concluded: "Thus, godly power and godly love are related to one another neither through subordination nor dialectically. Rather, God's mightiness is understood as the power of his love. *Only love is almighty*."[79]

The self-determination of God to *be* love is particularly discerned by us in the cross, but it does not first *become* the truth about God in that event. That conclusion would represent a "self-distortion" of God. "What happened on the cross of Jesus is an event which in its uniqueness discloses the depths of deity. The special eschatological event of the identification of God with the man Jesus is at the same time the innermost mystery of divine being."[80]

Jüngel found in Paul's words on power in weakness, reflected in the cross (1 Cor. 1:18ff.), a "stringent rejection of all deification of self-willing power"[81] and an affirmation of its obverse:

love does not even fear its own weakness. The one who does not *want* to share in the weakness of love is basically incapable of love. For the strength of love consists of the certainty that love can be helped to victory only by love. To be sure, when opposed by everything which is not love, it is totally unprotected and vulnerable . . . But it is the very *power* of love which implies its weakness against everything which is not love. For love does not assert itself in any other way than through love. And that is both its strength and its weakness. Since love asserts itself only lovingly, it is highly vulnerable from outside, but inwardly it is profoundly indestructible. It remains within its element, and it radiates in order to draw into itself. It cannot destroy what opposes it, but can only *transform* it.[82]

There may well be earlier theological reflections on Paul's assertion that God's weakness is more powerful than what we typically understand as power, but I have not surfaced them. I think Jüngel's dual role as theologian and biblical scholar stood him very well in calling attention to the importance of this insight in the biblical narrative.

THE TRANSFORMING POWER OF LOVE: TEILHARD DE CHARDIN

Pierre Teilhard de Chardin (1881–1955) was a Jesuit paleontologist who developed an evolutionary vision of God and God's universe that was so far removed from conventional Roman Catholic thinking that he was prohibited from publishing this aspect of his work during his lifetime. That meant, of course, that he could not benefit from peer review. He wrote without the rigor of academic theology and never attempted to organize his work into systematic shape. Nevertheless, the originality and depth of his imaginative proposals warrant careful attention.

For Teilhard, the whole of reality is continuously evolving toward its final destiny, a cosmic "Omega point" that includes the dynamic participation of a God who is anything but static or fully complete already in Godself.[83] God *is* Omega, the eschatological end of history and of all of creation.[84]

The theme of love is completely at the heart of Teilhard's cosmic reconceptualizing. Love "is undoubtedly the single higher form towards which, as they are transformed, all the other sorts of spiritual energy converge."[85] Therefore Teilhard uses his term "amorization" to identify the evolutionary direction in which all reality is moving.[86]

As early as 1920, in an essay entitled "The Modes of Divine Action in the Universe," Teilhard guardedly called into question traditional notions of divine omnipotence. The decision to create a *soul* surely places constraints on divine power no more and no less restrictive than the physical impossibility of creating a square circle,[87] wherefore "the supreme miracle of the divine power . . . consists in being able, through a deep-reaching and all-embracing influence, incessantly to *integrate*, on a higher plane, all good and all evil in the reality which that power builds up by means of secondary causes."[88]

He went on to conclude in 1931 that "Love is the most universal, the most tremendous and the most mysterious of the cosmic forces."[89] Love, like thought, "is still in full growth in the noosphere . . . (It demands to be released, so that it may flow irresistibly towards the true and the beautiful. Its awakening is certain."[90] And another six years later he pondered upon "not force but love above us; and therefore, *at the beginning*, the recognized existence of an Omega that makes possible a universal love."[91]

As his ideas continued to develop, he wrote in an essay on "The Rise of the Other" in 1942:

> In its most general form and from the point of view of physics, love is the internal, affectively apprehended, aspect of the affinity which links and draws together the elements of the world, *centre to centre* . . . Love is power of producing inter-centric relationship. It is present, therefore (at least in a rudimentary state), in all the natural centres, living and pre-living, which make up the world; and it represents, too, the most profound, most direct, and most creative form of inter-action that it is possible to conceive between those centres. Love, in fact, is the expression and the agent of universal synthesis. Love, again, is centric power.[92]

And in 1951, four years before his death, he identified God specifically as "love-energy."[93]

The year before, Teilhard wrote an autobiographical essay in which he depicted the process of how he arrived at his overall vision. It became the title essay in the collection entitled *The Heart of the Matter:*

> it is only in the Christo-centric area of a noogenetic Universe that it [love] is released in the pure state and so displays its astonishing power to *transform* everything and *replace* everything . . . A current of love is all at once released, to spread over the whole breadth and depth of the World; and this it does not as though it were some super-added warmth or fragrance, but as a fundamental essence that will metamorphose all things, assimilate and take the place of all.[94]

And here is precisely the crux of the problem that characterizes Teilhard's unfulfilled promise. In the end, Love *has to* prevail, otherwise the culmination of all in Omega does not transpire. And if Love *must* prove successful in the end in overcoming all lingering resistance, then does it not cease to maintain its own essential qualities? There remains, in other words, a vestige of compulsion in Love's deployment of power that renders the whole picture suspect. As radical as Teilhard's thought was, it was not truly radical enough to break through all the way to an all-encompassing vision of Love being the *only* mode of divine power.[95]

LETTING LOVE FULLY REDEFINE POWER

WILLIAM H. VANSTONE: LOVE PRECARIOUS AND VULNERABLE

A chapter in William Vanstone's *The Risk of Love*,[96] originally published in Great Britain in 1977 under the title *Love's Endeavour, Love's Expense: The Response of Being to the Love of God*, led to the Templeton Foundation's sponsoring of a conference of theologians and scientists at Queens' College, Cambridge, in October 1998, with a follow-up in New York City the following year, the results of which are in *The Work of Love: Creation as Kenosis*.[97] Born in 1923, Vanstone died between these two meetings, in March of 1999.

Turning down numerous offers of teaching posts, Vanstone was a canon in the Church of England and not a formal academician. Even so, his reflections on the nature of love and what that implies for the nature of God are truly trailblazing. What he embarked upon was a thoughtful inquiry into what a "phenomenology of love" would reveal. What he found were what he determined to be three marks of authentic love: without limit, without control of the one loved, without detachment.[98] Therefore authentic love is to be understood "as limitless, as precarious, and as vulnerable."[99]

With regard to the second "mark," love is "distorted by the assurance of possession or control." There is "no assurance or certainty of completion . . . each step that is taken, whether it 'succeeds' or 'fails', becomes the basis for the next, and equally precarious, step which must follow,."[100]

> Love aspires to reach that which, being truly an '"other," cannot be controlled. The aspiration of love is that the other, which cannot be controlled, may receive; and the greatness of love lies in its endless and unfailing improvisation in hope that the other may receive. As aspiration, love never fails; for there is no internal limit to its will to endeavour, to venture and to expend. But as specific achievement, love must often fail; and each step it takes is poignant of the possibility of failure.[101]

Regarding the third mark, love gives to its object power over itself. "To that which is loved power is given which it would not otherwise possess and which otherwise would be unaccountable."[102] This creates a new vulnerability in the one who loves—not in the sense that it can be diminished or destroyed.

> But love is vulnerable in and through the beloved in the sense that in him its issue is at stake—its completion or frustration, its triumph or tragedy. He who loves surrenders into other hands the issue and outcome of his own aspiration . . . Where there is no such surrender or gift of power the falsity of love is exposed.[103]

Vanstone then extended these reflections, into what seemed to him the unequivocal nature of love phenomenologically, into the very being of God. If God is indeed, as we consider God to be, essentially love, then what has just been identified also characterizes love in God. The "activity of God in creation must be limitless creativity." There is no superabundance of divine power held in reserve. "From His self-giving nothing is held back; nothing remains in God unexpended."[104] The activity of God in creation must also be *precarious*:

> Its progress, like every progress of love, must be an angular progress—in which each step is a precarious step into the unknown; in which each triumph contains a new potential of tragedy, and each tragedy may be redeemed into a wider triumph; in which, for the making of that which is truly an "other," control is jeopardised, lost, and, through activity yet more intense and vision yet more sublime, regained; in which the divine creativity ever extends and enlarges itself, and in which its endeavour is ever poised upon the brink of failure. If creation is the work of love, then its shape cannot be predetermined by the Creator, nor its triumph foreknown.[105]

The presence of evil in creation must be understood as a consequence of the precariousness of God's creative activity.[106]

> If the creation is the work of love, its "security'" lies not in its conformity to some predetermined plan but in the unsparing love which will not abandon a single fragment of it, and man's assurance must be the assurance not that all that happens is determined by God's plan but that all that happens is encompassed by His love.[107]

And finally, and perhaps most critically, the activity of God in creation must be *vulnerable*.

> We know only that God is love. We know only the *activity* of God. We know that God is vulnerable only in the sense in which the activity of love may be said to be vulnerable . . . The power which love gives to the other is power to determine the issue of love—its completion or frustration, its triumph or tragedy. This is the vulnerability of authentic love—that it surrenders to the other power over its own issue, power to determine the triumph or the tragedy of love. The vulnerability of God

means that the issue of His love as triumph or tragedy depends upon His creation. There is given to the creation the power to determine the love of God as either triumphant or tragic love. This power may be called "power of response": upon the response of the creation the love of God depends for its triumph or its tragedy.[108]

I have quoted extensively from Vanstone's work because I think it is not widely known and is worthy of considerable attention. The two key marks of love as precarious and vulnerable set the discussion of God's powerful love moving in an entirely new direction. There is no holding back, no antiquarian retaining of a residue of non-precarious, non-vulnerable power on God's part. I remain deeply indebted to his insights.

He closed his book with a reprinting of his "A Hymn to the Creator." Here are the final three stanzas:

Drained is love in making full;
Bound in setting others free;
Poor in making many rich;
Weak in giving power to be.

Therefore He Who Thee reveals
Hangs, O Father, on that Tree
Helpless; and the nails and thorns
Tell of what Thy love must be.

Thou art God; no monarch Thou
Thron'd in easy state to reign;
Thou art God, Whose arms of love
Aching, spent, the world sustain.[109]

WENDY FARLEY: LOVE'S POWER AS *EMPOWERMENT*

The work of Wendy Farley (b. 1958) is so inclusive that it could well be presented in at least three different places in this treatise, embracing a post-patriarchal God, a God who suffers, as well as the God of essential love. I have chosen to give attention to her writings here, because they particularly reinforce the directions we have just been exploring.

Similarly to Vanstone, in her *Tragic Vision and Divine Compassion* (1990), Farley explores a "phenomenology of compassion."[110] She sees the key issue in Tolkien's *The Lord of the Rings* to be a matter of how the power of domination corrupts even the most benevolent attempt to use it.[111] Compassion is "a power [that] cannot coerce."[112] Compassion represents "a fundamentally different *kind* of power than the power of coercion."[113] Compassion, as redemptive power, "gives power to someone else: it is *empowering* rather than controlling,."[114]

Her recognition of the positive virtue of the role of *empowering* is an extremely vital step, in my estimation. When I first surfaced this notion in an essay in 1973,[115] it was typically dismissed by confusing it with *enabling*, a negative action relating to the inappropriate support of persons suffering from various addictions. That the idea has since received significant traction is a very positive development.

In her chapter on "A Phenomenology of Divine Love," Farley insists, rightly, that love and power cannot be juxtaposed as "two alien entities." Recognizing the reluctance of theologians to ascribe love to God,[116] she goes on to observe: "As a noncoercive form of power, love creates the possibility of evil by leaving freedom and the future undetermined."[117]

Farley distinguishes "the power of love expressed in creation (eros)" and the power present "in providence (tragic love)," which are complimented by "the power of redemption. Compassion is divine power in a new guise the guise of redemption."[118] She goes on to explain:

> Eros is the power of God to bring being from nothingness; tragic love is providential care for a cosmos immersed in inevitable suffering and conflict. Compassion immerses itself in evil in order to struggle against it . . . Tragic love cares for the world, but it is compassion that mediates redemptive power. Redemptive love presupposes sympathetic knowledge of suffering. But in compassion this sympathetic participation in suffering is accompanied by *power* that struggles to transform evil into a locus of healing . . . According to Christian theology, God's knowledge of suffering is radicalized in the incarnation. The immediacy of knowledge of suffering and evil is here again, accompanied by transforming power . . . Compassion is the intensity of divine being as it enters into suffering, guilt, and

evil to mediate the power to overcome them. As human beings and communities apprehend the presence of divine compassion for them and with them, they experience power to resist the degrading effects of suffering, to defy structures and policies that institutionalize injustice, and to confront their own guilt . . . the compassion of God *empowers*. Divine compassion is not a form of paternalistic charity but a more radical love that offers liberating power.[119]

Divine compassion, then, is understood as God's "empowering presence."[120] "It is the risk and folly of the power of love to create that over which it has only relative control," thus disclosing "the nonabsolute power of God."[121]

No guarantee can be provided for a final victory by God over the forces that oppose God. "The problem of theodicy is history's power to reject God."[122] Any meaningful theodicy "can only hope to illuminate the radical love of God that is not overcome by evil, that is poured out inexhaustibly over all creation."[123]

I merely ask, *how* does God as love, as compassion, empower? How does love as empowerment actually make a difference in how the ongoing creation continues to unfold, filled as it is with unspeakable acts of depravity? How is God actually acting in an empowering way? "Through interhuman compassion and justice, the reality and power of God are present to resist evil in history."[124] I still wish to probe deeper for an explanation of how this happens in a way that is more than human resilience.

THOMAS JAY OORD: LOVE THAT EMPOWERS WELL-BEING

Having studied process theology under David Griffin at Claremont, and working extensively with the Templeton Foundation on the "science" of love, Thomas Oord (b. 1965) brings an investigative mind to his stance with the "open theology" group of Evangelical theologians.[125] Almost all of his scholarly output focuses in one way or another on the topic of love divine and human.

An encompassing definition of love underlies all of Oord's treatments of the subject: "To love is to act intentionally, in sympathetic/empathetic response to God and others, to promote overall well-being."[126] The key components of this definition are the centrality of *action* as opposed to mere passion or emotion, the responsive interrelationship between the lover and the beloved, and the goal of promoting well-being—the biblical notion of "shalom."

Oord is in company with those, over against Anders Nygren,[127] who recognize the key role of *eros* for God, not just *agape*, championing the importance, contrary to Augustine, of *desire* as a valid component of divine love.

> To the tradition speaking of God as perfect and thus without need, adherents of divine *eros* argue that maximal perfection involves perfect desiring and receiving. Our conception of a maximal human lover is not of someone detached and without desire; a great lover is someone who desires appropriately and who is appropriately influenced by others. The maximally perfect lover must be a maximally perfect giver *and* maximally perfect receiver, say advocates of divine *eros* theology.[128]

Oord also carries through consistently on the critical necessity of absolving God of any and all residual power that is not the power present in divine love. He challenges the kenotic approach we have already surfaced, denying that to be love God emptied himself of all non-loving power. Rather, love characterizes the nature of all the power God ever has, without some presumed act of divine self-limitation: "noncoercion is an *essential* feature of how God lovingly relates to creation . . . Self-giving love is part of God's very nature, not an arbitrary divine choice."[129] This, of course, legitimates the genuine reality of human freedom to accept or refuse God's offer of a love that empowers: "God's essential love relations with the cosmos entails that God cannot fail to offer, withdraw, or override the power for freedom that creatures require in their moment-by-moment life decisions."[130]

It is *The Nature of Love* (2010) where Oord shines most brightly in aiming a laser beam at the power of divine love. "The gift of Godself to creation is essential to what it means to be God. God necessarily relates with and gives to creatures, because God necessarily loves us."[131] God "empowers" rather than "overpowers."[132]

God always exerts almighty power in love. A steadfastly loving God exerts maximal power and yet never entirely controls others. *We best understand God's power through the lens of God's love, not vice versa.*[133]

The consequence of these reflections is the full recognition that to have been created in God's image means, for human beings, that we are created in the image of God as Love.[134] That has all-encompassing implications for the way in which we are invited to exercise power in our relationships with one another and with all of creation on our home planet. The highest form of power is found in so relating as not to diminish in any way the power of the recipient of our actions.

I am greatly indebted to Tom Oord for the penetrating work he has accomplished. Proposals for explicating the empowering love of God that appear in the final chapter of this book are continuous with the orientation he has brought forward.[135]

ENDNOTES

1. As quoted in Mildred Bangs Wynkoop, *A Theology of Love: The Dynamic of Wesleyanism* (Kansas City, Mo.: Beacon Hill Press of Kansas City, 1972), 93f.

2. First published in a collection of Charles Wesley's hymns in 1747.

3. Alexander Campbell, *The Christian System*, 2nd ed. (Pittsburg: Forrester & Campbell, 1839), 92. Online: www.mun.ca/rels/restmov/texts/acampbell/cs/

4. Ibid., 220, emphasis original.

5. Ibid., 222, emphasis original.

6. Frederick W. Faber, *The Creator and the Creature* (1857), 176, as cited in Nels F. S. Ferré, *The Christian Understanding of God* (New York: Harper & Brothers, 1951), 253, note 7.

7. D. Z. Phillips, *The Problem of Evil and the Problem of God* (Minneapolis: Fortress Press, 2004), 199, emphases original.

8. Richard Garnett, *De Flagello Myrteo: 360 Thoughts and Fancies on Love*, 3rd ed. (London: Elkin Mathews, 1906), 10.

9. Elizabeth A. Johnson, *Quest for the Living God: Mapping Frontiers in the Theology of God* (New York: Bloomsbury Publishing, 2007), 17, emphasis original.

10. Søren Kierkegaard, *The Journals of Kierkegaard, 1834–1854*, ed. and tr. Alexander Dru (London: Fontana Books, 1958), 194.

11. *Søren Kierkegaard's Journals and Papers*, 7 vol., ed. and tr. Howard V. Hong and Edna H. Hong (Bloomington: Indiana University Press, 1967–1978), vol. II, 90f.

12. Kierkegaard, *Works of Love*, tr. Howard and Edna Hong (New York: Harper & Row, 1962), 280.

13. Kierkegaard, *Philosophical Fragments*, 2nd ed., tr. David Swenson (Princeton: Princeton University Press, 1962), 33.

14. Kierkegaard, *Journals and Papers*, vol. II, 147 (from 1854).

15. Kierkegaard, *Philosophical Fragments*, 39f., emphases mine.

16. Kierkegaard, *Journals and Papers*, vol. II, 62f.

17. See, e.g., Arnold B. Come, "Kierkegaard's Ontology of Love," in Robert L. Perkins, ed., *Works of Love: International Kierkegaard Commentary*, vol. 16 (Macon, Ga.: Mercer University Press, 1999), 118.

18. See Kierkegaard's sermon on "The Unchangeableness of God," tr. David F. Swenson, in Robert Bretall, ed., *A Kierkegaard Anthology* (New York: The Modern Library, 1946), particularly 470–78.

19. Albrecht Ritschl, *The Christian Doctrine of Justification and Reconciliation: The Positive Development of the Doctrine*, tr. H.R. Mackintosh and A.B. Macauly (Edinburgh: T. and T. Clark, 1900; republished in 1966 by Reference Book Publishers, Inc., Clifton, NJ), 273f.

20. Ibid., 276.

21. Ibid., 279.

22. Ibid., 282.

23. Ibid., 277.

24. Ibid., 293.

25. Andrew Martin Fairbairn, *The Place of Christ in Modern Theology* (New York: Charles Scribner's Sons, 1903), 403–06, 415, 417 *et al.*

26. Ibid., 439.

27. Ibid., 385.

28. Ibid., 394.

29. Ibid., 410.

30. Ibid., 413.

31. Ibid., 417.

32. Nels F. S. Ferré, *The Christian Understanding of God* (New York: Harper & Brothers, 1951), 6–10, 15–29.

33. Ibid., 45.

34. Ibid., 15f. This focus on novelty is no doubt an influence from Whitehead.

35. Ibid., 17f.

36 Ibid., 19.

37. Gary Dorrien, *The Making of American Liberal Theology: Crisis, Irony and Postmodernity, 1950-2005* (Louisville: Westminster John Knox Press, 2006), 42. See Dorrien's excellent summary of Ferré's life and thought, op. cit., 39–57.

38. Ferré, op cit., 23.

39. Ibid., 26.

40. Ibid., 98–101.

41. Ibid., 101.

42. Ibid., chapter 5.

43. Ibid., 219.

44. Ibid.

45. Clarence Edwin Rolt, *The World's Redemption* (New York: Longman's, Green, 1913).

46. Moltmann, *The Trinity and the Kingdom*, 31–34.

47. Rolt, op. cit., 12.

48. Ibid., 13.

49. Ibid.

50. Ibid.

51. Ibid., 14.

52. Ibid., 15.

53. Ibid., 16, all emphases my own.

54. Ibid., 27.

55. Ibid., 35.

56. Ibid., 37.

57. See ibid., 124–26, and Moltmann's comment on Rolt in *The Trinity and the Kingdom*, 34.

58. Gordon D. Kaufman, *Systematic Theology: A Historicist Perspective* (New York: Charles Scribner's Sons, 1968), 88, emphasis mine.

59. Ibid., 89.

60. Ibid., 91.

61. Ibid., 92.

62. Ibid., 92f., both quotes; emphasis mine.

63. Ibid., 113, emphasis mine.

64. Ibid., 151–54.

65. Ibid., 152.

66. Ibid., 152, 154.

67. Ibid., 153, emphasis mine.

68. Kaufman, *In Face of Mystery: A Constructive Theology* (Cambridge: Harvard University Press, 1993), 333, emphasis original.

69. Geddes MacGregor, *He Who Lets Us Be: A Theology of Love* (New York: The Seabury Press, 1975). The unreconstructed identifying of a God of masculinity surely did not help MacGregor's cause.

70. Ibid., 5.

71. Ibid., 11.

72. Ibid., 15, all quotes after preceding footnote.

73. Ibid., 128.

74. Ibid., 107.

75. Ibid., 161; see also 127, and all of chapter 9 on "Providence and Prayer." MacGregor's focus on kenosis can also be seen in the work of many of the current theologians who are interacting productively with

scientists in pursing a shared vision. See, in particular, the essays in the volume edited by John Polkinghorne, *The Work of Love: Creation as Kenosis* (Grand Rapids: Wm. B. Eerdmans, 2001). The problem is the same in both places: Kenosis appears to speak of a willful act on God's part to "give up" power-over for the sake of power-with, but that still entails that God's (unexercised) power includes that possibility. My investigation pursues an alternative understanding, that this in no way characterizes the power of God in the first place.

76. Eberhard Jüngel, *God as the Mystery of the World*, tr. Darrell L. Guder (Grand Rapids: Eerdmans, 1983), x.

77. Ibid., 315.

78. Ibid., 21.

79. Ibid., 22, emphasis mine.

80. Ibid., 220.

81. Ibid., 206.

82. Ibid., 325, emphases original.

83. This summary sentence is based on numerous passages in Teilhard's writings. See, in particular, Pierre Teilhard de Chardin, *Human Energy*, tr. J. M. Cohen (New York: Harcourt Brace Jovanovich, 1971), 145; and *The Heart of Matter*, tr. René Hague (New York: Harcourt Brace Jovanovich, 1979), 53: God "in some way 'transforms himself' as he incorporates us . . . All around us, and within our own selves, God is in process of 'changing', as a result of the coincidence of his magnetic power and our own Thought."

84. Emile Rideau, *The Thought of Teilhard de Chardin*, tr. René Hague (New York: Harper & Row, 1967), 147–50.

85. Teilhard de Chardin, *Christianity and Evolution*, tr. René Hague (New York: Harcourt Brace Jovanovich, 1971), 186.

86. Teilhard de Chardin, *Science and Christ*, tr. René Hague (New York: Harper & Row, 1968), 171.

87. Teilhard de Chardin, *Christianity and Evolution*, 32f.

88. *Ibid.*, 34.

89. Teilhard de Chardin, *Human Energy*, 32.

90. Ibid., 129.

91. Ibid., 152.

92. Teilhard de Chardin, *Activation of Energy*, tr. René Hague (New York: Harcourt Brace Jovanovich, 1970), 70f.

93. Ibid., 280.

94. Teilhard de Chardin, *The Heart of the Matter*, 51.

95. Teilhard's vision is being powerfully presented in the early 21st century by the Franciscan scholar Ilia Delio, whose most recent work champions and elaborates on his relevance for today. See her *The Unbearable Wholeness of Being: God, Evolution, and the Power of Love* (Maryknoll, NY: Orbis Books, 2013), especially chapter three.

96. William H. Vanstone, *The Risk of Love* (New York: Oxford Univ., Press, 1978).

97. John Polkinghorne, ed. *The Work of Love*, x. The book was dedicated to Canon Vanstone's memory and each chapter begins with a quote from *The Risk of Love*.

98. Vanstone, *The Risk of Love*, 42–54.

99. Ibid., 53.

100. Ibid., 46.

101. Ibid., 49.

102. Ibid., 51.

103 Ibid., 52.

104. Ibid., 59f.

105. Ibid., 62f.

106. Ibid., 63.

107. Ibid., 66.

108. Ibid., 67.

109. Ibid., 119f.

110. Wendy Farley, *Tragic Vision and Divine Compassion: A Contemporary Theodicy* (Louisville: Westminster/John Knox Press, 1990). See chapter three, especially pp. 75–81.

111. Ibid., 89–92.

112. Ibid., 93.

113. Ibid., 97.

114. Ibid., 94, emphasis mine.

115. David P. Polk, "Empowering Love," *Lexington Theological Quarterly*, April, 1973 (vol. VIII, No. 2), 60–67. The biblical witness to Jesus proclaims "not simply that God is love, but that God's love is powerful—and that God's power is characterized by love! . . . The majesty of Jesus' vision of God's truth is that God's love is not something extraneous to [God's] power but the very nature of it" (63).

116. Farley, op. cit., 96.

117. Ibid., 98.

118. Ibid., 111.

119. Ibid., 111f.

120. Ibid., 114.

121. Ibid., 124.

122. Ibid., 125.

123. Ibid., 133.

124. Ibid., 114.

125. See Thomas Jay Oord, ed., *Creation Made Free: Open Theology Engaging Science* (Eugene, OR: Pickwick Publications, 2008), for a helpful overview of this orientation.

126. Oord, *The Nature of Love: a Theology* (St. Louis: Chalice Press, 2010), 17. A slightly different, earlier variant appeared in his *Science of Love* (Philadelphia: Templeton Foundation Press, 2004), 9: "To love is to act intentionally, in sympathetic response to others (including God), to promote overall well-being."

127. The massive undertaking of Anders Nygren in his *Agape and Eros* has not received individual attention in this overview for two primary reasons: He did not actually address in any cogent way the relationship between love and power in God—"power" is not even an entry in the extensive subject index—and his assessment of the unreality of *eros* in God has been subsequently determined to be unacceptably one-sided. See the whole of chapter two in Oord's *The Nature of Love* for a helpful summary of Nygren's position and the problems it contains.

128. Oord, "Divine Love," in Thomas Jay Oord, ed., *Philosophy of*

Religion: Introductory Essays (Kansas City, Mo.: Beacon Hill Press of Kansas City, 2003), 103.

129. Oord, *Science of Love*, 17f.

130. Ibid., 18. Oord also maintains that this aspect of God did not begin with the Big Bang but was eternally true of God all along (18f.). "The creation of this universe did not entail divine coercion. The Big Bang suggests that God's creative energy would have been extremely influential at the origin of our universe. But divine influence, even in the Big Bang, would not have been strictly coercive" (20).

131. Oord, *The Nature of Love*, 125. Although this appeared in print only in 2010, it is a revision of Oord's doctoral dissertation at Claremont.

132. Ibid., 126.

133. Ibid., 128, emphasis mine.

134. Oord, *Defining Love: A Philosophical, Scientific, and Theological Engagement* (Grand Rapids, MI: Brazos Press, 2010), 179.

135. Many other contributions on the subject of this chapter that were made toward the end of the twentieth century have not been included here not because they are not relevant but because of space limitations and a sense that they present ideas already dealt with here. They nevertheless merit mention: Daniel Migliori, *The Power of God* (Philadelphia: Westminster Press, 1983), and its later revision, *The Power of God and the gods of Power* (Louisville: WJK Press, 2008). Paul S. Fiddes, *The Creative Suffering of God* (Oxford: Clarendon Press, 1988). Vincent Brümmer, *The Model of Love: A Study in Philosophical Theology* (New York: Cambridge Univ. Press, 1993). George M. Newlands, *God in Christian Perspective* (Edinburgh: T&T Clark, 1994), and his earlier but less helpful *Theology of the Love of God* (Atlanta: John Knox Press, 1980). Edward Collins Vacek, S.J., *Love, Human and Divine: The Heart of Christian Ethics* (Washington, D.C.: Georgetown University Press, 1994). Kevin J. Vanhoozer, ed., *Nothing Greater, Nothing Better: Theological Essays on the Love of God* (Grand Rapids: Wm. B. Eerdmans, 2001).

15

Hunger for a Liberating God

Impulses for developing a theological understanding that is liberating for victims of a variety of types of oppression burst on the scene almost simultaneously. Three that came to prominence in the 1970s were the struggles against patriarchal oppression of women, racial oppression of Blacks in the United States, and economic and political oppression of the underclass, especially in Latin American countries. The first of these has already been covered in the chapter on a post-patriarchal theology. It is time now to focus on the remaining two.

Mary Daly published *Beyond God the Father* in 1973. The English translation of Gustavo Gutiérrez's *A Theology of Liberation* was published by Orbis in the same year. James Cone had brought out *A Black Theology of Liberation* a year before the original Spanish edition of Gutiérrez's work. The Medellín Conference of Latin American Catholic bishops, oficially known as the Latin American Episcopal Council (CELAM II) took place in 1968 in Medellín, Columbia. Puebla (CELAM III) did not follow until 1979. The official statement from Puebla included the famous reference to God's "preferential option for the poor." Impetus can be clearly traced to the liberating atmosphere of the Second Vatican Council in 1962. Gutiérrez was already at work in 1964 in starting to develop the notion of theology as "critical reflection on praxis."[1]

I begin here with an examination of James Cone's work as highly influential and indicative of the direction Black liberation theology took, then turn to key representatives of Latin American theology of liberation. At the end of this exploration, I ask the paired questions: How fruitful has this effort turned out to be, and what limits its potential impact?

A BLACK THEOLOGY OF LIBERATION: JAMES CONE

When James H. Cone (b. 1938) shocked readers by announcing that God, and Christ, are "black," he was only doing what women theologians were also examining at the time: that the way to get beyond a narrow understanding of God as male, or white, is to conceive God as the opposite of that, as black, or female ("She Who Is"). We can move beyond a God of specific "color" only after inherited and implied notions of a White God have been punctured by concentration on a Black God, which Cone provided.

White theological critics initially overreacted to Cone out of fear, I think. Cone did not invent Black Power. He was merely interpreting to whites an already-existing and rather threatening movement by identifying that struggle with the Gospel. Except for his unquestioning dependence on the very white theologians who needed deconstructing, I think he hit the nail squarely on the head.

In 1969, Cone fired his opening salvo with *Black Theology and Black Power*. Jesus, he announced, "is God himself coming into the very depths of human existence for the sole purpose of striking off the chains of slavery, thereby freeing man from ungodly principalities and powers that hinder his relationship with God . . . Jesus' work is essentially one of liberation."[2]

Cone then went on to ask how it is possible to reconcile this focus on Black Power, and on emancipation at any cost, with Christ's message of love.

> For God to love the black man means that God has made him somebody. The black man does not need to hate himself because he is not white . . . hrough God's love, the black man is given the power to *become*, the power to make others recognize him.[3]

In other words, blacks cannot even begin to consider loving their white oppressors until they can experience a love of self and other blacks that flows from God's freely given *agape*.

> Therefore the new black man refuses to speak of love without justice and power. Love without the power to guarantee justice in human relations is meaningless. Indeed, there is no place in Christian theology for sentimental love, love without risk or cost. Love demands all, the whole of one's being. Thus, for the black man to believe the Word of God about his love revealed in Christ, he must be prepared to meet head-on the sentimental "Christian" love of whites, which would make him a nonperson.[4]

Repudiating utterly the notion that God directs the flow of history whatever twists and turns it may take, Cone asserted emphatically that Black theology "refuses to embrace any concept of God which makes black suffering the will of God."[5]

In his subsequent publication of *A Black Theology of Liberation* (1970), Cone traced his position back to the liberating activity of Yahweh in the Old Testament and expanded his understanding of blackness to an ontoloigical symbol of all who are oppressed: Blackness "stands for all victims of oppression who realize that their humanity is inseparable from man's liberation from whiteness."[6] Furthermore:

> The blackness of God means that God has made the oppressed condition his own condition . . . the liberation of the oppressed is part of the innermost nature of God himself. This means that liberation is not an afterthought, but the essence of divine activity. The blackness of God then means that the essence of the nature of God is to be found in the concept of liberation.[7]

In regard to this liberating activity in God, *love* is essential to God's nature. But because of violations of God's intentions among the oppressor, love must include the dimension of divine wrath.[8] At this point, Cone really began to push the limits of understanding:

> Black theology cannot accept a view of God which does not represent him as being for blacks and thus against whites . . . black

> people have no time for a neutral God . . . There is no use for a God who loves whites the *same* as blacks . . . What we need is the divine love as expressed in Black Power which is the power of black people to destroy their oppressors, here and now, by any means at their disposal. Unless God is participating in this holy activity, we must reject his love.[9]

Clearly this represents an awkward interpretation of the all-embracing quality of divine love, though it is not entirely beyond the pale of the scathing indictments by the Old Testament prophets concerning those who violate the covenant with God.

Cone affirmed the doctrine of divine omnipotence, but with a twist. "Omnipotence does not refer to God's absolute power to accomplish what he wants . . . God's omnipotence is the power to let black people stand out from whiteness and to be."[10]

In *God of the Oppressed* (1975), Cone finally got around to addressing directly the issue of theodicy, expanding on the problem of a presumably all-powerful God. "The persistence of suffering seems to require us to deny either God's perfect goodness or his unlimited power." He began by observing that taking an either/or stand regarding God's power and God's "goodness" is unacceptable: "It is a violation of black faith to weaken either divine love or divine power."[11] Cone acknowledged that, in fact, his position is "in company with all the classic theologies of the Christian tradition," though, of course, with a different point of departure: the plight of the oppressed.[12] Biblically, he focused on the redemptive suffering of Jesus (coupled with his resurrection as a defeat of suffering) and expressed the eschatological point that God has in fact defeated the powers of evil even though we still encounter them and are called to fight against them, "becoming God's suffering servants in the world."[13]

"God's power and judgment," Cone insisted, "*will* create justice and order out of chaos."[14] The question, of course, is: How? What is the actual nature of God's liberating power? The problem for Cone was that he was too dependent upon the traditions of the very White theology he was seeking to repudiate, finding no way to reconceive the *nature* of divine power that matched the vigor with which he challenged conventional notions of the *purposes* to which God directs that power. Discussions in the chapter previous to this have shown how that impasse has already begun to be surmounted.

GOD'S PREFERENTIAL OPTION FOR THE POOR: LATIN AMERICAN VOICES

It is almost treasonous to deal with Latin American theologies of liberation by lifting up individual thinkers who successfully wrote for publication. At its heart, the movement that undergirds these written reflections arose out of the gatherings and shared reflections of the oppressed poor themselves, in groups called *comunidades eclesiales de base*—communities of the Christian wretched who met together to study scripture in light of their own impoverished situations and reflect on how each one informs the other (*praxis*).[15] But our access to their groundbreaking work is through the printed page, and so I proceed with a full awareness that the persons under consideration here are as much reporters as originators.

GOD'S LOVE FOR THE OPPRESSED

Our Idea of God was originally published in 1968, shortly after CELEM II in Medellín. It is a transitional work, recognizing the growing importance of the issues liberation theology would deal with but still developed as a theology from the groves of academe, not from the barrio. Its author, the Uruguayan Jesuit Juan Luis Segundo (1925–96), was particularly concerned with rejecting North American death-of-God theology, but already present were the beginnings of an awareness that the church needs to lend its resources not to the reinforcement of society and its present (repressive) values but to its liberation.[16]

Segundo focused his attentions sharply on God as trinitarian, but he recognized that the Christian conviction that God is love *starts* in the interrelationships of the Trinity but hardly ends there.[17] God's love toward us is, indeed, liberating: "The poor, the sick, the marginal people do construct the future earth, if they expend their forces to the limit in the work of liberating love . . . in the history we share with God no love is lost."[18] Segundo emphasized that any "conception of God, which views him solely as some immutable, self-sufficient nature without any real interest in what he himself brought about, is nothing but the rationalization of our own alienated societal relationships."[19]

On the relationship between love and violence, Segundo was insightful:

> Love and violence are the two opposite poles of any interpersonal relationship. To love is to give something to a person. To do violence is to obtain something from a person. To love is to make that person the center of our action. To do violence is to make that person an instrument for obtaining something.[20]

Gustavo Gutiérrez (b. 1928) is a Dominican from Peru who is widely regarded as the initiator of Latin American liberation theology. Although his premiere work, *A Theology of Liberation*,[21] appeared originally in 1971, it is to two later works that I turn for a clearer picture of his key contributions: *The Power of the Poor in History* (in Spanish: 1979) and *The God of Life* (in Spanish: 1989).

Jesus Christ "is the full manifestation of the God who is love: the Father."[22] In fact, Jesus "is precisely *God become poor*."[23] This points Gutiérrez in the direction of where God as love is to be recognized in our presence: "To believe in the God who reveals himself in history, and pitches his tent in its midst, means to live in this tent—in Christ Jesus—and to proclaim from there the liberating love of the Father."[24]

A decade later, Gutiérrez offered up a series of riffs on key biblical passages that extensively spell out the background perspective on God that informs his earlier explorations into liberation theology. Part One is entitled "God Is Love" and begins with the 1 John 4:8 quote, specifically tying this understanding of God as love to Jesus' proclamation of God as *Abba*, Father—actually, "papa" or "daddy."[25] Quoting Jeremiah, Isaiah, and Hosea, he lifted up the God of tender love, womb love.[26] On the basis of these reflections, Gutiérrez sharply criticized his church's Thomistic predominance, based on the philosophy of Aristotle, that finds it "difficult to say that God is love."[27]

His overview of God's fundamental concern for the poor and the suffering is summarized powerfully in this later book:

God's preferential option for the poor, the weak, the least members of society, runs throughout the Bible and cannot be understood apart from the absolute freedom and gratuitousness of God's love . . . Universality and preference mark the proclamation of the kingdom. God addresses a message of life to every human being without exception, while at the same time God shows preference for the poor and the oppressed . . . It is not easy to preserve both universality and preference, but that is the challenge we must meet if we would be faithful to the God of the kingdom that Jesus proclaims—namely, to be able to love every human being while retaining a preferential option for the poor and the oppressed.[28]

GOD'S EMPOWERING OF THE OPPRESSED

In words that will find strong support further along in this study, Juan Luis Segundo offered a very provocative notion at the very end of his book.

> God is a continuing summons in our lives to a never-ending search for authentic solutions, for sincere solutions that are not a mixture of good and bad but a discovery of the good in all its purity . . . God is *the unrest in us* that does not allow us to be tranquil and content, that *keeps prodding us* toward the better course that remains ahead of us. It is in this unrest, in this anxious desire to arrive a authentic solutions, pure values, and uncompromised agreements, that we gradually come to know and recognize the God in whom we believe.[29]

This proposal that God "prods" us forward, generates "unrest" in us, seems to me to offer up a key element in the manner in which divine love works on us and in us to generate effective consequences, without overwhelming or overpowering us at the same time. I intend to "unpack" this more thoroughly to examine just how that process can be explained as an empowering one.[30]

One year after Segundo's work appeared, the young Brazilian Protestant Rubem A. Alves (1933–2014) appropriated Jürgen Moltmann's theology of hope for his constituents. Writing in Portugese but also fluent in English, with a Ph.D. from Princeton, he and his work were perhaps less well known in Spanish-speaking Latin America than they should have been.

The central issue for Alves is the "freedom to create history."[31] And "the creation of history is possible only through power." Therefore, language about God becomes "a language about events, their power and their promise."[32] In regard to the Israelites of the Old Testament, "where the events were expressions of liberating efficacy 'in spite of', there was their God."[33] The Gospel is understood as "the annunciation of the historical reality of the ongoing politics of God, which expressed itself . . . as a power that invades history."[34]

> As the messianic events of liberation in the Old Testament were not a result of human efficacy but rather a gift, an act of power that transcended the given possibilities of history, the Christian communities saw in Jesus an act of God's freedom . . . the power that creates a new future is something new, it is freedom from beyond history that is freedom for history. Only thus do the messianic power and hope for history remain as such.[35]

Moving marginally beyond Moltmann, Alves represented God as a presence of the ultimate Future putting *pressure* on the present to move toward the "new tomorrow" that is, in fact, "the sole determination of the present."[36]

Alves seems conflicted on just what sense it makes to speak of God's love as a powerful force moving the present toward its intended future. On the one hand, love cannot serve as a principle for liberating transformation. But, on the other, "Love is what *God* does in order to make man free."[37] Regarding, then, the interplay between power divine and human:

> If action is the midwife of the future, then human activity can add the new to the world. It can indeed be an act of creation. God's grace, instead of making human creativity superfluous or impossible, is therefore the politics that makes it possible and necessary. That is so because in the context of the politics of human liberation man encounters a God who remains open, who has not yet arrived, who is *determined and helped by human activity. God needs man for the creation of his future.*[38]

Thus the future "is not simply a future created by God for man, but by God and man, in historical dialogical cooperation."[39]

Three years later, in *Tomorrow's Child*, Alves contrasted "the love of power" that characterizes the predominant theme of our times with "the power of love," and went on to state:

> Love looks for effectiveness. Love demands power. The gifts of the future enjoyed in community must function like the preliminaries of love: they must create the excitement that prepares one for the great experience still to come. They are its *sacrament*, the *aperitif* of the absent, of the possible, of that which does not yet exist. And therefore they contain *the ethical and political imperative of creative love*.[40]

Gutiérrez picked up on this theme in an unresolved manner, stating that "God is a love that ever transcends us," manifesting Godself as a "God of might" but most especially as "a God who dwells in the heart that can love."[41] Reaching into the Old Testament, he accepted equally that "God manifests himself in awe as a God of power (Exod. 19:18) or makes himself heard gently and discreetly in a breath of the wind (1 Kings 19:12)."[42]

In the final analysis, Gutiérrez could only acknowledge "the transcendence of God and the utter freedom with which God loves," whereby "God will act, utterly freely, if it pleases God to do so."[43] There is no external conditioning of the activity of God in creation and history: "God's reign is universal, over the cosmos . . . and over history."[44] But he did not stop there. The lack of a consistent resolution of the problem of how God acts is seen explicitly in an extended analysis of the dilemma of Job. Even though Job himself recognizes God as "all-powerful" (42:2), God's "power is limited by human freedom . . . God's love, like all true love, operates in a world not of cause and effect but of freedom and gratuitousness."[45]

Unfortunately, it is clear that Gutiérrez was unable to move consistently away from traditional notions of the *nature* of God's power. His alteration of focus was essentially in regard to those *on whose behalf* that power is wielded in history, namely, the poor and the oppressed. The dynamic of love/life/liberation and *power* remained insufficiently explored.

José Míguez Bonino (1924–2012) was an Argentinian Methodist who wrote *Doing Theology in a Revolutionary Setting* in 1975 and *Toward a Christian Political Ethics* eight years later. His key contribution to this inquiry is his understanding that the Reign of God in and over history is "a *pressure that impels*."[46] We speak of "'love', 'liberation', 'the new man' as the signs which allow us to identify the active sovereignty of God in history."[47]

The Christian faith has always claimed that power belongs to God. But Míguez Bonino insists that omnipotence, as that has typically been understood, is not specifically present in the Bible and is never affirmed in the abstract. God is conveyed as an active presence who acts, in history and in creation, in faithfulness to humankind. God's power "is the power that prevails over the chaos, that sets limits to the onslaught of the forces of destruction and ensures the conditions needed for human life and prosperity . . . God's power is his 'justice' in action," as exemplified particularly in the Magnificat.[48]

But two other features emerge in this biblical portrait:

> God's righteous power is affirmed in the midst of conflict. God is engaged in a struggle—his power is manifest in this struggle and is the guarantee of the final triumph of that righteousness of God which is disclosed and presently active in 'the mighty acts'. Second, such acts are related to human agents . . . human mediation is the way in which God's power operates in history.[49]

However, this mediation always eventually oversteps itself, absolutizing itself and negating justice. "Jesus understood his mission . . . as one of incarnating in a paradigmatic way God's just and liberating rule."[50]

The audacity of Leonardo Boff (b. 1938), a Brazilian Franciscan, in writing *Church: Charism and Power* (1981), got him in trouble with ecclesiastical authorities. It was so critical of the Roman Catholic Church's use of ecclesial power that he was summoned to Rome and, for a time, silenced. Eventually he left the Franciscans and resigned his priesthood. He has worked since as a Catholic lay theologian.

Boff provides us with a perceptive historical overview of the church's misuse of power. The early established church, after Constantine, did not abolish the existing order and the modes of power that sustained it;

instead the church itself adapted itself to that order. The key category is *potestas*, power. The church simply appropriated secular expressions of power from the Roman world and gave them a stamp of divine approval, a sacralization.[51] This culminated in the eleventh century with Pope Gregory VII (*Dictatus Papae*, 1075), who instituted the ideology of the absolute power of the papacy.

> Support for this was not the figure of the poor, humble, and weak jesus but rather God himself, omnipotent Lord of the universe and sole source of power. The Pope was to be understood as the unique reflection of divine power in creation, God's vicar and representative . . . the Church's exercise of power followed the patterns of pagan power in terms of domination, centralization, marginalization, triumphalism, human *hybris* beneath a sacred mantle.[52]

Boff's contribution on this topic penetrates beyond what we have witnessed up to now in regard to the abandonment of all traces of sovereign divinity as classic omnipotence:

> Jesus did not preach the Church but rather the Kingdom of God that included liberation for the poor, comfort for those who cry, justice, peace, forgiveness, and love . . . he did not call others to be rulers but to be submissive, humble, and loyal. He liberates for freedom and love that allow one to be submissive yet free, critical, and loyal without being servile, that call those in power to be servants and brothers free from the appetites for greater power. Fraternity, open communication with everyone, solidarity with all people, with the little ones, the least of the earth, sinners and even enemies, goodness, undiscriminating love, unlimited forgiveness are the great ideals put forth by Jesus. . . . The *exousia*, that is, the sovereignty, that appears in his attitudes and words in not power in terms of human power. It is *the power of love* . . . It is *the power of God*. . . . What is the power of God? . . . Power is the power to love. The power of love is different in nature from the power of *domination*; it is *fragile, vulnerable*, conquering through its weakness and its capacity for giving and forgiveness.[53]

In refusing to use divine power to alter his own impending death, Jesus "de-divinized power . . . It is in weakness that the love of God and the God of love are revealed (1 Cor 1:25; 2 Cor 13:4; Phil 2:7),"[54]

I find that Boff has gone the furthest in repudiating all vestiges of conventional power in lifting up the liberating work of God. He does not delve into the nagging question of *how* fragile and vulnerable love is powerful over against the forces of domination, but he sets us firmly on the right track. In that respect, he moves beyond the conceptual limitations that burdened his colleagues.

Elizabeth Johnson has observed perceptively that, with the work of the theologians of human liberation, "Naming God the liberator does not just craft one more symbol to add to the treasury of divine images. It puts a question mark next to every other idea of God that ignores the very concrete suffering of peoples due to economic, social, and politically structured deprivation."[55]

By and large, however, it seems to me that the weakness in these proposals is that they do not challenge the conventional theistic notion of God's power as that which ultimately will prevail. They merely—and this is a big "merely"—shift the focus of that power to divine activity on behalf of the black, the poor, the oppressed in history and in concrete historical settings. As we saw, Alves wrote of "the *pressure* of the spirit, of freedom, as it seeks its goal, [which] can never be stopped,"[56] and Míguez Bonino wrote of a "pressure that impels."[57] The question remains whether, in their vision, this pressure ever slides over into the notion of irresistibility.

Except for Boff, I find the work of these dedicated individuals unsatisfying on this key point. There is certainly comfort to be found in the expectation that the work carried on in the midst of crushing oppression contributes to the intentionality of God to fulfill for *all* the promises to God's chosen ones in the Exodus. But any assurance of a final outcome overtrumps the perception of the vulnerability of God's empowering love.

ENDNOTES

1. Leonardo Boff and Clodovis Boff, *Introducing Liberation Theology*, tr. Paul Burns (Maryknoll, New York: Orbis Books, 1987), 66ff.

2. James H. Cone, *Black Theology and Black Power* (New York: The Seabury Press, 1969), 35.

3. Ibid., 52.

4. Ibid., 53f.

5. Ibid., 124.

6. Cone, *A Black Theology of Liberation* (Philadelphia: J. B. Lippencott Co., 1970), 28.

7. Ibid., 121.

8. Ibid., 130.

9. Ibid., 131f.

10. Ibid., 150.

11. Cone, *God of the Oppressed* (New York: The Seabury Press, 1975), 163, both quotations.

12. Ibid.

13. Ibid., 177.

14. Ibid., 9.

15. See Elizabeth Johnson, *Quest for the Living God*, 73, and all of chapter four.

16. Juan Luis Segundo, *Our Idea of God*, vol. 3 of *A Theology for a New Humanity*, tr. John Drury Barr (Maryknoll, New York: Orbis Books, 1973), 131–33.

17. Ibid., 66.

18. Ibid., 46.

19. Ibid., 133.

20. Ibid., 164. A few years later, Paulo Freire would observe: "Every relationship of domination, of exploitation, of oppression, is by definition violent, whether or not the violence is expressed by drastic means. In such a relationship, dominator and dominated alike are reduced to things—the former dehumanized by an excess of power, the latter by a lack of it. And things cannot love." Freire, *Education for Critical Consciousness*, tr. Myra Bergman Ramos (New York: The Continuum Publishing Co., 1973), 10–11, footnote.

21. Gustavo Gutiérrez, *A Theology of Liberation: History, Politics, and*

Salvation, tr. Sr. Caridad Inda and John Eagleson (Maryknoll, New York: Orbis Books, 1973).

22. Gutiérrez, *The Power of the Poor in History*, tr. Robert R. Barr (Maryknoll, New York: Orbis Books, 1983), 12f.

23. Ibid., 13, emphasis original.

24. Ibid., 16.

25. Gutiérrez, *The God of Life*, tr. Matthew J. O'Connell (Maryknoll, New York: Orbis Books, 1990), 1f.

26. Ibid., 42–45.

27. Ibid., xiii.

28. Ibid., 116f.

29. Segundo, op. cit., 181, emphases mine.

30. I recast this perspective in my final chapter, 18, page 242, utilizing categories drawn from the philosophy of A. N. Whitehead.

31. Rubem A. Alves, *A Theology of Human Hope* (Washington: Corpus Books, 1969), 12.

32. Ibid., 90.

33. Ibid., 91.

34. Ibid., 92.

35. Ibid.

36. Ibid., 94.

37. Ibid., 126, emphasis mine.

38. Ibid., 144, emphasis mine.

39. Ibid.

40. Alves, *Tomorrow's Child: Imagination, Creativity, and the Rebirth of Culture* (New York: Harper & Row, 1972), 203, emphases original.

41. Gutiérrez, *The Power of the Poor in History*, 209.

42. Ibid., 19,

43. Gutiérrez, *The God of Life*, 80.

44. Ibid., 108.

45. Ibid., 161f.

46. José Míguez Bonino, *Doing Theology in a Revolutionary Situation* (Philadelphia: Fortress Press, 1975), 143, emphasis mine.

47. Ibid., 138.

48. Míguez Bonino, *Toward a Christian Political Ethics* (Philadelphia: Fortress Press, 1983), 96.

49. Ibid., 97.

50. Ibid., 98.

51. Leonardo Boff, *Church: Charism and Power: Liberation Theology and the Institutional Church*, tr. John W. Diercksmeier (New York: The Crossroad Publishing Co., 1986), 50f.

52. Ibid., 56.

53. Ibid., 59, emphases mine.

54. Ibid., 60.

55. Elizabeth Johnson, *Quest for the Living God*, 86.

56. Alves, *A Theology of Human Hope*, 94.

57. Míguez Bonino, *Doing Theology in a Revolutionary Situation*, 143.

16

Overtures to a Relational God

We have examined how, one by one, elements of the Augustinian superstructure have crumbled away under the assault of competing ideas. God's immutability has been disputed by the preferability of a divine nature that is open to, and responsive to, new developments, in continuity with the biblical witness. God's stoic apathy under the doctrine of divine impassibility has been supplanted by a strong endorsement of a God who suffers, championing the very heresy of patripassianism. God's overwhelmingly masculine qualities have been brought to heel by the additional understanding of a post-patriarchal affirmation of a fuller and more complete divinity. The diminishment of the vital importance of love as an essential aspect of the being of God has been widely repudiated by a return to the New Testament conviction that God is none other than Love itself, with resulting challenges to the established doctrine of divine omnipotence.

There remains but one further component to be brought to light before the edifice collapses of its own unsupportable weight. And that is the critical importance of *relationality* for God, not just in an eternal innertrinitarian relationship between Father, Son, and Spirit but also, and essentially, in God's constitutive relationships with God's creation.

To that I now turn, by introducing the contributions of scholars who have seen the possibility of a fresh way of understanding reality under the influence of the visionary philosophy of Alfred North Whitehead.

Whitehead entitled his explosively original "essay in cosmology," *Process and Reality*.[1] The title led to a subsequent emphasis on a way of thinking called "process thought," or "process theology," among those who came under his towering influence. That accurately reflects his seminal shift of attention from the ancient and enduring focus on "being" and substance and permanence to the more helpful category of "becoming," particularly in light of scientific advances in the twentieth century that recognized the essentially fluid character of what we call reality.

But a second mode of revolutionary thinking also found a foundational presence in Whitehead's "exercise" in "imaginative thought,"[2] namely, the emphasis on *relations* as internal to and constitutive of all that becomes and is, including the very reality of God. Therefore, more recently, his followers in the theological arena typically name this orientation "process-relational" thought. Both of these aspects of his work are important here, but especially the latter.

I begin with attention to the philosophical underpinnings, not only in Whitehead but also in Charles Hartshorne, and then move to those who have built on this work to bring forth their own vital theological appropriations that inform the focus of this book.

PHILOSOPHICAL UNDERPINNINGS: WHITEHEAD AND HARTSHORNE

ALFRED NORTH WHITEHEAD: THE GOD OF CAESAR AND THE GOD OF THE GALILEAN

A. N. Whitehead (1861–1947) retired in 1924 from an academic career in England in the fields of mathematics and education and promptly accepted an invitation to join the faculty in philosophy at Harvard University, where his work took off in a totally unexpected direction. His objective was to accomplish a philosophical foundation for the various sciences to be able to talk with one another. He gave the Lowell Lectures in 1925, which were published that same year under the title *Science and the Modern World*. Strikingly, he added two chapters before publication, and these are the only places in the book where the subject of God is addressed. It became clear that, for Whitehead to bring his cosmological vision to completion, he needed to posit a source for the becoming of novelty,[3] and he found no better name for that reality than "God."[4]

My very brief overview of Whitehead's interpretation of the cosmic process is drawn from throughout the pages of his *Process and Reality*. Every single moment of becoming is impacted by its inheritance of all that has gone before, some influences highly significant, the vast majority of them quite negligible. It is in this way that the world of the past weighs heavily on the becoming of the new, typically bringing about a resistance to the actualizing of genuine novelty. Similarly, every occasion of experience, once it has completed itself, becomes in turn an influence on that which follows after it.

In Whitehead's vision, God is by no means inactive in this becoming. God provides for each new occasion its "initial aim," the maximal good that this occasion can accomplish as it actualizes itself. But God does not determine what this actual occasion will *do* with that aim. In its fundamental freedom—true not just for the becoming of each moment of the human consciousness but for *all* of creation—everything that emerges into a new present is not bound either by its past (fatalism) or by God (determinism). It modifies what is given to it in the combination of past pressure and divine *lure*. And, in Whitehead's fully encompassing cosmology, God *also* receives and is influenced by that occasion's act of becoming.

Therefore two complimentary "natures" are posited for God: the "Primordial Nature," that aspect of God which is, indeed, totally beyond change, and the "Consequent Nature," that aspect of God which is perfectly receptive of change because of its openness to whatever the moments of creation have done with God's maximal proposals. The Primordial Nature is God's eternal envisagement of pure possibility, not unlike Plato's "forms." The Consequent Nature is that aspect of God's supreme relatedness in which nothing that transpires in all of creation is lost to God's indefatigable receptivity. So Whitehead could write in the next-to-the-last paragraph of his *magnum opus*:

> What is done in the world is transformed into a reality in heaven, and the reality in heaven passes back into the world.

> By reason of this *reciprocal relation*, the love in the world passes into the love in heaven, and floods back again into the world. In this sense, God is *the great companion—the fellow-sufferer who understands.*[5]

Finally, one additional dimension of this philosophical vision must be clarified. Relations are not *incidental* to that which becomes, nor are they external aspects. Rather, relations *constitute* becoming. To become is to relate to all, including God, in just *this* particular way and not in any other. A freely constituted decision to respond to the past's weight and the divine lure is no other than the particular emergence of a complex bundle of relatedness.

Whitehead insisted that God cannot be an exception to the ontological categories but must be their supreme exemplification. Therefore he was able to conclude that what is true for all that becomes throughout creation is absolutely true for God as well. Not only is God not secure in God's own being apart from all that transpires. God *is* who God is precisely in the manner of God's relations with what God has set into motion but not circumvented with impositional restrictions. God proposes. The becoming occasion disposes. God receives the result, and is forever after affected by that.

With this as structural background, what did the mature Whitehead have to say specifically about divine power?

> When the Western world accepted Christianity, Caesar conquered; and the received text of Western theology was edited by his lawyers . . . The brief Galilean vision of humility flickered throughout the ages, uncertainly . . . The Church gave unto God the attributes which belonged exclusively to Caesar.[6]

Whitehead saw in traditional theology three dominant ways of thinking about God: as imperial ruler, as moral energy, and as ultimate philosophical principle, but he did not favor any of them.

> There is, however, in the Galilean origin of Christianity, yet another suggestion which does not fit very well with any of the three main strands of thought. It does not emphasize the ruling Caesar, or the ruthless moralist, or the unmoved mover.

It dwells upon the tender elements in the world, which slowly and in quietness operate by love.[7]

Clearly Whitehead's understanding of the passion of God to offer ever new possibilities of becoming locates love at the center of God's eternal becoming. Love "involves deep feeling of an aim in the Universe, winning such triumph as is possible to it."[8] So could he say, God "is the poet of the world, with tender patience leading it by his vision of truth, beauty, and goodness."[9]

CHARLES HARTSHORNE: THE MAXIMAL POWER OF DIVINE RELATEDNESS

The American philosopher of religion Charles Hartshorne (1897–2000) was already pursuing patterns of thought along lines similar to Whitehead when he arrived at Harvard for post-doctoral work in 1925 and became Whitehead's teaching assistant. Hartshorne went on to become the center of a cluster of scholars in Chicago—including Bernard Loomer and Daniel Day Williams—that introduced process thought to a new generation of theologians.

Hartshorne had grown up in a family milieu that led him early to the perception that God is love.[10] As he wrote in his Preface to *Man's Vision of God* (1941), "a magnificent intellectual content—far surpassing that of such systems as Thomism, Spinozism, German idealism, positivism (old or new)—is implicit in the religious faith most briefly expressed in the three words, God is love."[11] He pointed out what has subsequently begun to become obvious but which was still a fresh insight back then:

> We say, God is holy, not that he is holiness. Only "love" is an abstraction which implies the final concrete truth. God '"is" love, he is not merely loving, as he is merely righteous or wise . . . It is not an accident that love was the abstraction least often appealed to in technical theology, though frequently suggested in the high points of Scripture and other genuinely religious writing.[12]

Reinforcing in advance the claim I have put forth at the end of Part Two, Hartshorne went on to point out: "Just as the Stoics said the ideal was to have good will toward all but not in such fashion as to depend in any degree for happiness upon their fortunes or misfortunes, so Christian theologians, who scarcely accepted this idea in their ethics, nevertheless adhered to it in characterizing God."[13]

Regarding the relationship between love and power, Hartshorne began by stating that "the real trouble is not in attributing too much power to God, but in an oversimple or too mechanical conception of the nature of power in general."[14]

> The dilemma appears final: *either value is social* [relational], and then its perfection cannot be wholly within the power of any one being, even God; *or it is not social at all,* and then the saying "God is love," is in error.[15]

God's power can be understood as "perfect" in that it is "unsurpassable": "No conceivable being could do more with us than God can."[16] But it remains a power unique in its capacity to absorb all creaturely responses to that gift of power. He expressed this throughout his book on *The Divine Relativity* (1948). One passage sums up that understanding:

> The notion of a cosmic power that determines all decisions fails to make sense . . . Instead of saying that God's power is limited, suggesting that it is less than some conceivable power, we should rather say: his power is absolutely maximal, the greatest possible, but even the greatest possible power is still one power among others, is not the only power.[17]

Nearly half a century on, in his wittily entitled *Omnipotence and Other Theological Mistakes* (1984), Hartshorne reviewed two meanings of "all-powerful": the traditional, of course—the (benevolent) tyrant ideal of absolute, all determining, irresistible power[18]—and what he previously had identified as the greatest possible power in a universe of multiple centers of power: "The only livable doctrine of divine power is that it *influences* all that happens but *determines nothing* in its concrete particularity."[19] And this he characterized crisply: "God's power simply is the appeal of unsurpassable love."[20]

Hartshorne's primary concern was to explode the classic notion of divine perfection as something self-contained within an unchanging, unaffected deity, and to posit instead a much larger God who is perfect precisely in including the encompassing scope of God's relatedness to all that becomes. In that regard, he developed a position he called "dipolar" theism, parallel to Whitehead's distinguishing of the Primordial and Consequent Natures in God. For Hartshorne, to conceive of God only as perfectly self-contained would be to conceive of half a God—the half championed by traditional theism. A truly unsurpassable deity is one who is simultaneously transcendent to all else that is—the "absolute" pole—but also maximally responsive to all that is not-God—the "relative" pole. This dipolarity in God is what enabled Hartshorne to see love at the heart of the divine being *and* becoming—an unchanging love that reliably underlies the very essence of God, an ever-interacting love that is capable of receiving into God that which creation does in response to it.[21] So he named one of the chapters in *The Divine Relativity*, "God as Absolute, Yet Related to All."[22]

A PROCESS THEOLOGY OF LOVE: DANIEL DAY WILLIAMS

Daniel Day Williams (1910–73) joined Hartshorne on the faculty at Chicago Theological Seminary in 1939 but he was no stranger to that milieu, having done pre-doctoral work there in the early thirties. He became, for a time, part of a notable group of scholars who advanced the perspectives of process philosophy into the theological arena. Distracted by other projects, and always gracious to the demands of others on his time, he did not complete what came to be recognized as the first systematic theology shaped by process thought until 1967. He named it *The Spirit and the Forms of Love*.

Accepting the biblical understanding of love as central to any human concept of the divine is at the heart of Williams' enterprise, directly challenging the Augustinian formulation as a corruption of this.[23] Love is "spirit taking form in history."[24] Since God's being "is love itself," God is always "the Holy Spirit, the spirit of unqualified love."[25] Love is "the very being of God in an eternally outgoing, creative life."[26]

Furthermore, to love is to facilitate the freedom of the one loved "with all its consequences, even for God."[27] Love necessarily involves suffering, which may well occur when one allows the consequence of being acted upon by the other, wherefore Williams wrote of the "suffering love of God":

> The disclosure of who God is has come through…his self-identification with the suffering of the world for the sake of love: God does not surrender his deity, his everlastingness, the perfection of his power and love. God remains God . . . God is revealed in Jesus' suffering because in him suffering is the authentic expression and communication of love.[28]

Freedom to love in response to God's loving of us calls for "a revision of the traditional view of the exercise of the divine sovereignty."[29] God risks the refusal of love.

> What the analogy of causality excludes from the doctrine of God is his exercise of sheer power to create without becoming involved with the creature, and without being subject to the suffering which follows upon the creature's freedom. Causality without involvement is incompatible with love . . . a will which allows no effective power to any other cannot be a loving will.[30]

Williams conjoined divine power and love in a way that does not violate the notion of what love is while assuring that power truly is an aspect of God's being as love. The power of God:

> is not that of absolute omnipotence to do anything. It is the power to do everything that the loving ground of all being can do to express and to communicate and fulfill the society of loving beings. God's power expresses his love, it does not violate it. Therefore it is the kind of power which holds the world together in one society, setting limits to the freedom of the creatures without destroying that freedom.[31]

He then utilized terminology that for decades informed the basic stance of process theology on the nature of true power, though, as we shall see, that is open to challenge: God "*persuades* the world by an act of suffering with the kind of power which leaves its object free to respond in humility and love."[32] Persuasion is affirmed as a positive alternative to coercion or compulsion, surrendering the illusion of control and intending not to violate the freedom of the one being persuaded.

In a posthumously published volume, *The Demonic and the Divine*, written in 1973 but only made available in 1990, Williams contrasted the notion of divine power with "the demonic":

> The demonic feeds on the divine power of being and distorts it . . . [It] always moves toward final self-destruction. It cannot destroy the creative good, though it can destroy particular structures of good . . . The divine power outlasts every power that in any way blocks it.[33]

The notion of "outlasting" echoes the modest reassurance in John 1:5, that "the light shines in the darkness, but the darkness has not overcome it." It is not a claim that darkness was conquered by the light of the Word become flesh. It is that this light of God is indefatigable; it cannot be extinguished. It "outlasts" all assaults on its illuminating power.

Therefore Williams explicitly repudiated the validity of the inherited tradition of classic Christian theism.

> If genuine freedom involves risk and loss, then traditional theology leaves us unfree. If genuine creativity involves the uncertainty of not knowing the outcome beforehand, not having it guaranteed, then traditional theology takes away from God the creator's greatest dignity and glory, which is not absolute power to make everything come out right, but absolute love that involves God in the risks of an unfinished and suffering world.[34]

Love entails risk. God embraces the vulnerability of risk, in being true to the divine nature as Love. The only assurance is that God's love, ultimately, cannot be cancelled out by forces that oppose it. History is the arena of the conflict between love and not-love, with all the pain that this has entailed.

UNILATERAL AND RELATIONAL POWER: BERNARD LOOMER

Bernard Loomer (1912–85) became dean of the University of Chicago Divinity School in 1945, only three years after finishing his doctoral dissertation. He did not publish extensively, but his essay on "Two

Conceptions of Power" in the journal *Process Studies* (1976) became a pivot around which considerable reflection turned.

Loomer distinguished between "unilateral" (or "linear") power, which is understood to move only in one direction, with a capacity to influence another without in turn being influenced, and "relational" power, about which much more will be said shortly. Neither "type" actually exists in its purity,[35] but power when it is conceived as unilateral is a "truncated" view, "demonic in its destructiveness."[36] And in a "competition of power, our relative strength or size can be ascertained by the degree to which the freedom of the other is curtailed. The reduction of freedom is an attenuation of power."[37]

When love is contrasted with power, we need to be aware that "it is the linear [unilateral] conception of power that is regarded as the antithesis of love."[38] In fact, "the god of unilateral power . . . is a demonic god."[39]

Loomer is mistakenly credited with having surfaced a distinction between "persuasive" and "coercive" power, but this does not represent the thrust of his argument.

> The issue between love and linear power is not finally the issue between persuasion and coercion . . . In some interpretations of love, especially Christian love, it would appear that love is as unilateral and nonrelational in its way as linear power is in its way. The interpretation of divine love, as being a concern for the other with no concern for itself, may be the ultimate instance . . . this kind of love, like this kind of power, needs an alternative conception.[40]

In pursuit of this, Loomer moved on to his analysis of relational power, "the ability both to produce and to undergo an effect. It is the capacity both to influence others and to be influenced by others. Relational power involves both a giving and a receiving."[41] To explain what he has in mind, Loomer introduced the category of "size," which involves "the enlargement of the freedom of all the members to both give and receive." In other words, the greater the extent of freedom is experienced in the recipient of relational power, the larger the size. The more the freedom of the other is curtailed, size shrinks.

> [In a] competition of power, our relative strength or size can be ascertained by the degree to which the freedom of the other is curtailed. The reduction of freedom is an attenuation of power,[42]

> Under the relational conception of power what is truly for the good of any one or all of the relational partners is not a preconceived good. The true good is not a function of controlling or dominating influence. The true good is an emergent from deeply mutual relationships.[43]

This analysis provides a significant foundation for comprehending the superiority of an understanding of power that is other than controlling, dominating, "almighty." In Loomer's view, pure "unilateral" power does not even exist. There is always some counter-influence, however miniscule. But to be able to see that maximal power is the power to offer greater, not less, freedom to the other—in short, to *empower*—is the hallmark of power that involves a mutuality of relatedness.

Loomer's explorations challenge the widespread conviction that power is a "zero-sum" game, characterized by the coupling, "the more, the less": The more power I have, the less you have. The pie is of finite size and must be divided up. This was, indeed, the very issue that led Nietzsche to proclaim the death of a God who limits God's creatures in precisely this way. Loomer's reflections on "size" clearly point in the opposite direction. Relational power—power that, in my preferred term, is *empowering*—results in a coupling of "the more, the more." The more my actions empower you, the greater the amount of power now present in the room. The *more* God acts effectively upon me, the freer I become. This will be unpacked more thoroughly in the final chapter.

GOD AS CREATIVE-RESPONSIVE LOVE: JOHN B. COBB, JR.

John Cobb (b. 1925) grew up in pre-war Japan as the son of Methodist missionaries. He did his doctorate at the University of Chicago where he discovered the philosophy of Whitehead through his own teachers, Charles Hartshorne and Daniel Day Williams. Thus has the tradition been transmitted, now spilling out globally from Claremont where Cobb primarily taught before retirement.

Cobb published *God and the World* in 1969, pointing out to his students what readers and critics alike tended to miss: that the word "and" in the title was specifically italicized. It is the interrelationship between the two that he finds crucial.

Quoting Nikos Kazantzakis' imaginative rendering of the "Cry" in *Report to Greco*, Cobb identifies God centrally as the One Who Calls us forward,[44] "the One Who Calls us beyond ourselves to the more that is possible,"[45] allowing for a "sense of movement into the open future" whereby "God as understood in this way is not a repressive force but a liberating one."[46] The problem of evil, therefore, loses much of its force.

> The world is not seen any longer as embodying an omnipotent sovereign's will but rather as responding ever anew to a possibility offered. That the response is imperfect does not imply the imperfection of what is offered. There is no world that does not reflect the influence of God's past agency, but there is also no world that is the product of that agency alone.[47]

Cobb's conviction is "that the proper conception of divine power holds the key to the Christian solution of the problem of evil."[48] As long as power is conceived in the conventional sense of "the ability to determine what is to be and how it is to be . . . there can be no satisfactory explanation of the evil in the world that does not reject the power of God,"[49] not simply the omni-power of God but any power of God at all. So, "we need a basic reconception of what is meant by power." Cobb finds this to be present in the work of Hartshorne. If God is "omnipotent in the sense of being the only power there is . . . where there is not competing power, omnipotence means little . . . *The power that counts is the power to influence the exercise of power by others.*"[50]

Cobb calls this "persuasion"; God "exercises the optimum persuasive power in relation to whatever is."[51] In his discussion of how both God *and* world operate upon a becoming occasion, God always is working with the "given," that is, the actuality of past decisions for good or for ill and all qualities inbetween. So what God *can* offer is always conditioned by past actual decisions made in response to God's past offers of an optimal becoming.

Cobb and his colleague (and former student) David Griffin co-wrote *Process Theology: An Introductory Exposition* in 1976, where the identification of God as "creative-responsive love" appears.[52] To say with the New Testament that God is love requires, in their estimation, the further clarification that God is love both creatively, in the way in which God offers an opening to new emergence in the unfolding moment, and responsively: "God enjoys our enjoyments, and suffers with our sufferings. This is the kind of responsiveness which is truly divine and belongs to the very nature of perfection."[53] A dynamic and interrelational God receives into Godself whatever response we have made to the divine lure (Whitehead's initial aim), thus being enlarged by it.

Cobb later summed up his assessment of the attributing of love to the being and becoming of God in an unpublished essay in 2006, on "The Contribution of Process Thought to Reflection on Love."

> I believe that in its broadest and most general meaning love is central to all reality and order, and that it is grounded in the very nature of reality. I also believe that God is the supreme instance of the love that is to be found everywhere. Of course, just as human love is far transcendent of the attraction of quanta to one another; so God's love is far transcendent of anything we can actually experience as love. But that does not entail that the word "love" is not literally applied to God. As Charles Hartshorne used to say, it is only to God that it can be applied literally. That is, all our emotions and motives are so mixed that to call any of them "love" is not truly accurate. Yet we are not lacking in an idea of what love in its purity would be. It is that ideal love that we Christians attribute to God. It is to that purer and all inclusive love that we aspire.[54]

In the same paper, commenting on the final pages of *Process and Reality*, Cobb wrote "some of us think, following Whitehead here, that John's assertion that 'God is love' is a profound metaphysical truth."[55] As do I.

A GOD WHO IS OMNI-AMOROUS: CATHERINE KELLER

Catherine Keller (b. 1953) represents here the current generation's leadership among process-relational theologians. She studied with Cobb at Claremont and now teaches at Drew University. A wide range of publications in feminist thought preceded her *God and Power* in 2005 and *On the Mystery* in 2008. Of these two works I wish to concentrate attention on the first of these, *God and Power*.

Keller scathingly rejects Calvin's defense of an omnipotent God who controls all, untouched by all that we experience on Earth as injustice: "the logic-defying logic of omnipotence twinned with good/ness ultimately sanctions *every* injustice as the will of God."[55]

> A theology of omnipotence electrifies the halo of American domination. Where then does the idolatry lie—in the fact that the United States plays God or, as I would put it, in the fact that it imitates a *false* God? Does the idolatry lie in our emulation of a divine superpower or in our confusion of God with omnipotence in the first place?[56]

Over against an impotent God, "another alternative discerns at the heart of the universe a wisdom of open ends, a strange attractor amid indeterminacy and its complex determinations."[57] Calvin got it half right. God is there in every event—but *participating* rather than controlling.

> Why reduce the mystery to an all-too-human, all-too-masculine, and all-too-imperial idol of *power*? Why turn a humbling mystery into a mystification of injustice? . . . [We can see] on the one *hand a manic will to power called omnipotence* and on the other a *depressive sentimentality called lov*e. For the classical fusion of goodness with omnipotence creates in fact not unity but a profoundly conflicted entity . . . To heal the internally contradictory religious combination of love and power, *power itself first needs recoding*.[58]

This is the project underway here. The "recoding" of power so that an understanding of it becomes consistent with, not opposed to, essential love is precisely the unfinished but well pursued task at hand. Reaching back to the original biblical understanding of creation involving the increasing emergence of order out of chaos, Keller writes:

> Let the hierarchical universe of unilateral and omnipotent sovereignty fade into a more wildly democratic cosmos of

unpredictable and uncontrollable—but never unordered—interrelations. God is called upon not as a unilateral superpower but as a relational force, not an omnipotent creator from nothing, imposing order upon chaos, but the lure to a self-organizing complexity, creating out of the chaos.[59]

Three years later, Keller defined power as "the energy of influence."[60] It is reciprocal and interactive, as we have been encountering. It is a "power made perfect in weakness" (2 Cor. 12:9), a power that "does not overpower but *empowers*."[61] Keller invites the displacing of our love of power with what she has represented as the power of love, combining *eros* and *agape*: the divine *Eros* attracts, calls, invites; the divine *Agape* responds, receives, feels our feelings compassionately.[62]

It is in light of the foregoing that Keller dares finally to state what should have been obvious for two millennia but was never explicitly articulated: that the "omni" that most fully identifies what is "all" in God is none other than *omnilove*, or what she calls a God who is omni-amorous.[63]

TRANSITION: FROM CHALLENGE TO RECONSTRUCTION

The thesis directing the content of these pages can be stated succinctly. The biblical witness brought forth a way of thinking about the nature of God as a living and interacting God who is predominantly and even essentially love. The prevailing structure of theological interpretation in the West lost that vision, replacing it with static categories of divine completedness necessitating a view of absolute omnipotence. The edifice thus erected and defended for twenty centuries gradually has been seen to crumble to ruins under the multi-directional assault against a theism unable to sustain its own dead weight. Therefore the question arises: How are we to move forward to a fresh synthesis of God as Powerful Love that builds on the criticisms of Augustinian theism that we have observed? In a phrase, it is by identifying what is meant when one proclaims God as *Empowering Love*. The task of explicating what that can mean is now what lies ahead.

ENDNOTES

1. Originally published in 1929; Corrected Edition edited by David Ray Griffin and Donald W. Sherburne (New York: The Free Press, 1978).

2. Alfred North Whitehead, *Process and Reality*, 5.

3. Whitehead challenged the conventional ontological question, "Why is there anything rather than nothing at all?" with what he considered much more penetrating: "Why is there ever anything *new*?"

4. Whitehead, *Science and the Modern World*, 2nd ed. (New York: Macmillan, 1926), viii. Lewis Ford writes that Whitehead "studied theology exhaustively for eight years in the 1890s, then sold off his entire theology library out of dismay over the failure of theologians to resolve the problem of God's omnipotence and the presence of evil in the world." Ford, *The Lure of God: A Biblical Background for Process Theism* (Philadelphia: Fortress Press, 1978), 2.

5. Whitehead, *Process and Reality*, 351, emphases mine.

6. Ibid., 342.

7. Ibid., 343.

8. Whitehead, *Adventures of Ideas* (New York: Macmillan, 1933); 288 (page reference from the Mentor edition of 1955).

9. Whitehead, *Process and Reality*, 346.

10. See David Griffin's summary regarding the influence of Hartshorne's parents on his worldview, in "Charles Hartshorne," *A New Handbook of Christian Theologians*, ed. Donald W. Musser and Joseph L. Price (Nashville: Abingdon Press, 1996), 200.

11. Charles Hartshorne, *Man's Vision of God* (New York: Harper & Brothers, 1941), ix.

12. Ibid., 111f. Late in his very long life, Hartshorne came to an awakening of his inappropriate use of gender-specific terminology and expressed the wish that he could rewrite everything he had put into print in order to eliminate that unintended bias.

13. Ibid., 116.

14. Ibid., xv.

15. Ibid., 14.

16. Ibid., 294.

17. Hartshorne, *The Divine Relativity: A Social Conception of God* (New Haven: Yale University Press, 1948), 138.

18. Hartshorne, *Omnipotence and Other Theological Mistakes* (Albany: State University of New York Press, 1984), 11.

19. Ibid., 25, emphases mine.

20. Ibid., 14.

21. See David Griffin's summary of this aspect of Hartshorne's position in *A New Handbook*, 209–12.

22. Hartshorne, *The Divine Relativity*, chapter two.

23. Daniel Day Williams, *The Spirit and the Forms of Love* (New York: Harper & Row, 1968), chapters III and V.

24. Ibid., 3.

25. Ibid., 4.

26. Ibid., 36.

27. Ibid., 162.

28. Ibid., 167.

29. Ibid., 127.

30. Ibid., 128.

31. Ibid., 137.

32. Ibid., 138, emphasis mine.

33. Williams, *The Demonic and the Divine* (Minneapolis: Fortress Press, 1990), 36.

34. Ibid., 34.

35. Bernard Loomer, "Two Conceptions of Power," *Process Studies* 6:1 (1976), 8.

36. Ibid., 6. David Griffin has incisively investigated the genuine reality of "demonic power" in chapter eight of his *Christian Faith and the Truth Behind 9/11: A Call to Reflection and Action* (Louisville: WJK Press, 2006).

37. Loomer, op. cit., 11.

38. Ibid., 15.

39. Ibid., 32.

40. Ibid., 15f.

41. Ibid., 17.

42. Ibid., 11.

43. Ibid., 19.

44. John B. Cobb, Jr., *God and the World* (Philadelphia: The Westminster Press, 1969), 61, 45.

45. Ibid., 64.

46. Ibid., 63f.

47. Ibid., 64.

48. Ibid., 87.

49. Ibid., 88.

50. Ibid., 89, emphasis mine.

51. Ibid., 91f.

52. John B. Cobb, Jr., and David Ray Griffin, *Process Theology: An Introductory Exposition* (Philadelphia: The Westminster Press, 1976), the title of chapter three. The initial draft of this chapter was written by Griffin, according to the Preface, but both signed off on all the chapters.

53. Ibid., 48.

54. Cobb, "The Contribution of Process Thought to Reflection on Love," unpublished essay, 2006, 10. Available at the Center for Process Studies.

55. Ibid., 1.

56. Catherine Keller, *God and Power: Counter-Apocalyptic Journeys* (Minneapolis: Fortress Press, 2005), 17.

57. Ibid., 29.

58. Ibid.

59. Ibid., 30, first two emphases original, final emphasis mine.

60. Ibid., 31.

61. Ibid., 81.

62. Ibid., 85, emphasis mine.

63. Ibid., 99.

64. Ibid.

Part IV

The Reunification of Love with Power

17

Glimpses of a Revealed God

To begin the task of reconceiving not a God whose power is loving but a God whose love is powerful requires a return to where we began, with another look back at the biblical witness that surely must underlie all theological formulation to some degree or other. If the concern in Part One was to listen to Scripture's multifaceted testimony on this topic, the focus shifts here to a theological appropriation of what has been heard. That the primary attention here is to the New Testament witness does not for one second deny that what has surfaced in the Old Testament narratives remains of paramount importance for comprehending what emerged in the New.

Christian theologians are often fond of saying that to know who God is, look at Jesus. Do not look *only* at Jesus. That would be too limiting and parochial. But look *particularly* at the God Jesus disclosed in order to discern the full reality of God more accurately. Wolfhart Pannenberg made this claim very explicitly: "As Christians we know God only as he has been revealed in and through Jesus. All other talk about God can have, at most, provisional significance."[1] And further, "If God is revealed through Jesus Christ, then who or what God is becomes defined only through the Christ event."[2] Even the philosopher of religion Charles

Hartshorne could maintain that we should not simply "add" Jesus to an unreconstructed idea of a non-loving God; rather, we should take Jesus as "proof that God really *is love*."[3]

So I find it fair that the portrayal of the divine that is reflected through the lens of Jesus' life, teachings, and eventual demise should be accepted as a key element in any inquiry into the nature of God. The tragedy, of course, is that it becomes very easy to give lip service to this notion without a genuine openness to where the testimony might lead us. That seems particularly true in the case of Pannenberg, as we have seen.[4]

I am persuaded that the God disclosed by Jesus in the Gospel record and the church's canonical witness to him can be identified as a *God who is Empowering Love*. My position is that genuine openness to this perception enables us to peel back the layers of misinterpretation that resulted from the church's turning away from this central thesis and to recapture the vital message of a living, interactive, supremely relational deity to whom Jesus consistently pointed, a God who wills to be intimately interconnected with God's people and God's world, i.e., the entire cosmos. To that end, I wish to examine anew the New Testament's championing of a God who is love, with an eye to discerning the theological implications of the themes we have previously encountered in Part One.

GOD IS LOVE: REAFFIRMING I JOHN

God is love. I join the ranks of those who perceive this to be not merely one assessment among others concerning the very being of God but regard it as central and all encompassing. Love, here, is not an adjective, characterizing a particular quality of the divine. It is a far more embracing assertion that its corollaries, "God is loving," or "God loves," although these are also true. Mary Daly proposed that we consider God a "verb."[5] Partly I agree. God *acts*, lovingly. But that does not tell the whole story by itself. God as love is more than just a divine action. God is *more than* just a verb. If we start with the realization that love defines the very essence of deity, consequences fall into place like a row of tumbling dominoes.

Clearly we "know" love only from our human perspective. We know love as *agape*, self-sacrificing, utterly unselfish. We also know love as *eros*, desiring, self-oriented. On a somewhat lesser level of importance, we know love as *philia*, friendship, camaraderie.[6] It is not wrong to attribute all these aspects of love to God. Indeed, it often seems our ability to comprehend the meaning of love depends on the language we use, since a single word in English embraces all three. 1 John proposes that we only know or experience love derivatively. We are not its originators but its *recipients*, realizing what love means only because of God's reaching out to us: "We love because [God] first loved us" (4:19). This is a bold assertion but one I think we need to take as seriously as his proclamation that the very reality of God is love. We discern something happening to us and in us from beyond us, and name that something "love."

When we reach across the abyss from finite to infinite reality, all our concepts, of course, finally fall short. They *point* more successfully than they define. Even so, some ways of pointing are more helpful than others. The imaging of a God who is "love" only in God's own internal (trinitarian) relations and has no need of us and is not affected in any way by us—as we have seen in Augustine's synthesis—does not do justice to the richness of the concept as we typically experience it and reflect upon it. So I find Tom Oord's previously presented definition as helpful a "pointer" as any: "To love is to act intentionally, in sympathetic/empathetic response to God and others, to promote overall well-being."[7] To apply this definition to God's initiative and extend it, I think it would read like this: For *God* to love is for God to act intentionally toward each becoming occasion of experience to promote its maximal well-being, including a sympathetic/empathetic response to its self-actualization.

The strength of this way of thinking is that it describes more than a mere *disposition*; it expresses an *action*. For God to love us is more than taking kindly to us in spite of, or even because of, our infirmities. For God to love us is to act toward us in a manner that promotes maximal shalom. For God to *be* love is to acknowledge that *all* of God's actions are marked by this constitutive character.

GOD'S EMPOWERING REIGN OF LOVE: REACCESSING JESUS

In the Synoptic Gospels, the primary focus of Jesus' message is on the impending arrival of the eschatological Reign of God—*basileia tou theou*, as we saw in Chapter Two. In light of what we have just considered, it is now possible to express this more pointedly: Jesus proclaims no less than *the elusive presence of the empowering love of God* in the midst of his hearers.[8] Jesus conveys by word and deed the conviction that the sovereignty of love is making itself felt there and then, as the foretaste of a fullness of love's sovereignty still to come.[9]

> When John heard in prison what the Messiah was doing, he sent word by his disciples and said to him, "Are you the one who is to come, or are we to wait for another?" Jesus answered them, "Go and tell John what you hear and see: the blind receive their sight, the lame walk, the lepers are cleansed, the deaf hear, the dead are raised, and the poor have good news brought to them. (Mt 11:2–5)

The witness of the Gospels consistently portrays Jesus as one who embodies, here and now, the power of a compassionate God who provides a foretaste of the coming fullness of the inbreaking reign of God. The apocalyptic expectation of all-powerful deity establishing emphatically God's rule on Earth is transformed by Jesus' appropriation of it into something entirely other: God is active already in furthering God's intentions for a creation in travail, but not in the ultimate, decisive way envisioned by champions of divine triumphalism. Rather, this God works mysteriously, in and with the conditions of the times. Where there are positive responses to what Jesus, on God's behalf, lifts up as desirable, surprising results happen. I need not take the healings literally. That is not the point. The church's kerygma is witnessing to its conviction that for those who accept Jesus' promise of the inbreaking reign of empowering love, the impact of that promise can be experienced already, proleptically.

The witness wavers between this sense of a partial realization of God's reign of love and the expectation that it will yet arrive "with power" at some time in the not very distant future (Mk 9:1). This tension reflects the unreconstructed hope in the apocalyptic tradition that all adversity now being experienced will eventually be overcome by the restoration of God's overwhelming might. It is hardly coincidental that this passage was not accepted into the other two Synoptic Gospels dependent on Mark.

Elusively, love's power is already having an impact. Where there is response to Jesus' invitation and challenge, lives are fundamentally changed. Peter and John leave their fishing nets to accept his call to be disciples. The despised tax-collector Zacchaeus is so awestruck at being affirmed by this strange Galilean that he throws open his doors, puts on a feast, and becomes a philanthropist. The "woman taken in adultery" finds herself befriended and defended, to the shame of her male accusers. In every instance and so many more, an invitation is made, an offer is extended. The response is not pre-ordained. It is made out of a degree of freedom—not total freedom, for we are always burdened and limited by the impact of our past decisions—and responding to the empowering offer becomes itself a moment in a sequence of ever more empowering offers. They constitute offers to live here and now *as if* the reign of God's love were really present—which, mysteriously, it is, in the occasions of positive response to it.

The supplanting of traditional power by empowerment has already been announced by Mary in her Magnificat: "He has brought down the powerful from their thrones, and lifted up the lowly" (Lk 1:52). Her son directs his followers' attention to the mystery that is divine intimacy with the hurting and the oppressed, assuring a constant presence that is insurmountable. Reversal of fortune does not come by magic. Where the empowering offer to experience a life lived harmoniously with others is rejected, God does not unilaterally intervene.

Let us not misinterpret what is being claimed here. It is not as though the mysterious availability of God's empowering love *began* with Jesus. That would represent a dangerously false reading. The power of love taught by Jesus is totally continuous with what we have previously examined in the Old Testament's witness to God's unquenchable *hesed*. As we saw, the conjoining of God's power and God's love is fully recognizable in the Old Testament. So what is new?

One answer to this is that Jesus does not limit the beneficiaries of this gift of empowering love to the people of the covenant. Jesus' proclamation reaches beyond the descendents of Abraham and Sarah to anyone who would pay attention. The other answer is that Jesus boldly declares an intimate and unmediated access to the gift of divinely derived empowerment, in the very midst of suffering and oppression. It represents an invitation to live fully *out of* the assurance of the promise, with a concomitant sense that so to do results in an effective anticipation of love's triumph: Outcasts are received back into the community *now*, the feast of inclusivity is shared *now*, wholeness that includes bodily healing occurs *now*, as a "living into" the eschatological banquet of God's reign. Contrary to the apocalyptic tradition Jesus inherited, waiting for God's return is a chimera. Live *now* the eschatological hope, because living *as if* God were powerfully present precisely enhances the effective power of a very present God. "The more, the more": Responding to God's love expands the capacity of that love to empower others—the domino theory in reverse.

POWER IN WEAKNESS: RE-VIEWING THE FIRST EASTER

Friday came, and then Sunday.

Friday and Sunday must be treated in tandem. Sunday without Friday would hardly have been necessary, but Friday without Sunday is catastrophic.

Clearly there came a time in the church's wrestling with the ignominy of its leader having died the death of a common criminal, a rebel against the rule of Rome, that transformed its negativity into something so positive it could be named "Good Friday." But the church did not begin there. Indeed, a very early remnant of the witnessing tradition posited a striking contrast, as we have had occasion to notice before in Chapter Two: "The God of our ancestors raised up Jesus, whom *you* had killed by hanging him on a tree" (Acts 5:30, emphasis mine). The thrust of this piece of a sermon, ostensibly by Simon Peter, is unmistakable: Sunday cancelled out Friday. Sunday overtrumped Friday. What happened on Sunday was God's way of dealing with what had occurred on Friday.

Pursuing this distinction brings us face to face with the non-interventional character of empowering love: It is the way of such love not to cancel out the bad, but to absorb it within God's very own being, and never be prevented from bringing forth the possibility of new creation over and over again.

Why is that still so fundamentally important, in spite of our uncertainty about what to do with the singular claims about something called a "resurrection"? It is because, for Friday to have the last word, the claim in Jesus' teaching that God's power is love and God's love is powerful *is totally denied*. Pannenberg is one who perceived this very clearly: "After the crucifixion of Jesus the question of the legitimacy of his mission was no longer open; on the contrary, until something else happened, it was negatively decided."[10]

The message pervading the New Testament is that God acted not to *prevent* Jesus' crucifixion, but to prevent Jesus' crucifixion from having the last word. Revisiting the claim at the beginning of John's Gospel that "the light shines in the darkness, and *the darkness did not overcome it*" (1:5, emphasis mine) leads me to assert that the event of Easter Sunday was God's response to the intent of the world to extinguish the light that was Jesus. Easter is the promise that the light of life-giving love still shines.

I do not pretend to comprehend the complexity of what transpired between the individual that was Jesus and the love that is God on that first Easter. But it is not an easy problem to wish away. Much about the church's initial claims about the event cannot easily be explained away, particularly the insistence that it was none other than a *woman*, or women, who were the initial witnesses to this singular happening when, in the judicial principles of that day, women could not under any circumstances be called as witnesses to anything. Certainly the growing reception of the reality underlying the first Easter empowered defeated followers to become stalwart devotees, often to the point of martyrdom.

I am avoiding naming that event "resurrection" because this was simply the only category at hand among Jesus' followers for dealing with the radically new character of this singular overcoming of death's finality. "Resurrection" is a term taken from the apocalyptic tradition, a tradition that Jesus had more than passing familiarity with but which he persistently transformed, as we have observed—emphasizing God's present immediacy and intimacy. Whatever it is that transpired between the burial of Jesus' body in the tomb and the growing conviction among his followers that somehow the power of his presence still permeated their very lives, it can only be comprehended as something utterly novel. The empowering love that is God found a way to offer yet new opportunities for becoming that was not restricted to the electromagnetic continuum. That, indeed, is the meaning of the "Easter event."

It is in regard to this set of considerations that I make sense of Paul's disorienting reversal of power and weakness in 1 Corinthians 1:17–25.[11] There, the cross is neither God's counterintuitive triumph nor God's ignominious defeat. Viewed in light of its aftermath, the Easter event, the cross stands as a signpost on the path to understanding God's true power not in crushing evil but in surmounting its finality in what appears to human wisdom as foolishness and weakness. Power in weakness is not overpowering the strong but empowering all, the weak and the strong, to fulfill their best possible destinies.[2] For love, as Paul maintains later, "never ends" (1 Cor 13:8). Nor does its power.

ENDNOTES

1. Wolfhart Pannenberg, *Jesus—God and Man*, tr. Lewis L. Wilkens and Duane Priebe (Philadelphia: The Westminster Press, 1968), 19.

2. Ibid., 140.

3. Hartshorne, *Man's Vision of God*, 165.

4. See Chapter Six, above.

5. Daly, *Beyond God the Father*, 33ff.

6. See, e.g., Oord, *The Nature of Love*, chapter two, especially 49–51.

7. Ibid., 9.

8. I do not presume here to establish this focus of Jesus' proclamation as the teaching of the "historical Jesus" behind the post-Easter Gospels, although I have, in fact, previously argued this to be the case. See David P. Polk, *On the Way to God: An Exploration into the Theology of Wolfhart Pannenberg* (Lanham, Maryland: University Press of America, 1989), 183–96.

9. This paragraph and much of what follows in this section is a rephrasing of the position presented in my essay on "Empowering Love," *Lexington Theological Quarterly*, 1973. My original title of the essay was "The Gospel of Empowering Love," the beginning of my long journey to this present text.

10. Quoted from personal communication with Pannenberg by Frank Tupper in his *The Theology of Wolfhart Pannenberg* (Philadelphia: The Westminster Press, 1973), 146. See also Pannenberg, *Jesus—God and Man,* tr. Lewis L. Wilkens and Duane Priebe (Philadelphia: The Westminster Press, 1968), 112.

11. Ron Farmer even finds support for this reversal in the counter-testimony of Revelation 5:6–14, at odds with conventional apocalyptic notions of divine power. See his insightful commentary on this passage in his *Revelation* (Chalice Commentaries for Today; St. Louis: Chalice Press, 2005), 63–69.

12. I have previously identified Eberhard Jüngel's important recognition of this dynamic in his *God as the Mystery of the World*. See the quote in Chapter 14 above, n. 82.

18

The Love of an Empowering God

ENVISIONING A FRESH ALTERNATIVE: KEY COMPONENTS

We are coming to an end of a long and fruitful journey, which is in turn a new beginning. The task that remains is to flesh out an understanding of *how* the love that is God empowers every becoming occasion to maximize its own exercise of power. I begin with reminders of what is being rejected, before moving forward to what is being affirmed.

I began at Dachau. Overwhelming suffering and the callous destruction of human life bring to the fore Leibniz's problem of theodicy: How can one believe in a God of love if the seeming exercise of God's power results in such repeated calamity? Power seems to cancel out love. How does one surmount that?

I have insisted that beginning with a preformed notion of divine power that includes omnipotent control of all that becomes simply does not allow any notion of divine love to be shoehorned in. Starting with conventional understandings of the exercise of power leads to a dead end. The dilemma of affirming a powerful God who is also a God of love cannot be resolved by starting on the power side of the issue.

It can only be resolved by starting instead with the affirmation that God is fully and unconditionally love and then asking the question in reverse: If God *is* love, what does power *mean* when applied to a loving God?

The first element that is surrendered is the matter of *control*. A loving God does not presume to determine all by God's self the *outcome* of the movement to momentary novelty that arises within the temporal flow. God *influences* every moment of becoming but finally *decides* the precise nature of no moment of becoming. In Whitehead's terms, the "initial" aim that God offers each new becoming, or "concrescence," does not simply become automatically the "actualized" aim. God *proposes* without *imposing*. Or, to put it in the apostle Paul's ringing terms, love "does not insist on its own way" (1 Cor 13:4).

As an issue, theodicy dissolves into thin air when God is not weighed down by the responsibility of determining every outcome and controlling every decision. But I aver that this does not render God impotent. Power as *empowerment* alters the landscape of the discussion radically.

I affirm Genesis' proposal that creation is a matter of generating order out of chaos, rather than the church's post-biblical proclamation of *creatio ex nihilo*. This appears to me to be a dimension of all of God's ongoing creative activity. God never works with a "clean slate" in offering new possibilities of becoming. Just as I have a world of the past behind me pressing forward upon me, limiting my options, providing a concrete context for the shape of a new possible "me" that God is proposing, so does God have degrees of chaotic disorder to take account of in every specific lure God initiates. Even the physicists' Big Bang theory of the origination of the universe does not negate the understanding that there was that out of which the primal explosion arose, even if only a "singularity." Therefore, every instance of God's empowering offer for a new becoming is conditioned by the raw materials of the past of which God necessarily takes account. Evil as embodying the forces of chaos is that which God is ever endeavoring to overcome but in responsive freedom we are significant participants in that ongoing process.

One additional element of the Augustinian synthesis that I am rejecting remains to be surfaced. *Time* is experienced from "within" time as a moment-by-moment migration from what has gone before to what is occurring now to what is not yet. To rephrase this in Whiteheadian terms, what has gone before is what is able to have an *influence* on what is occurring now. What is not yet is that which is able to *be influenced* by what is occurring now. And every simultaneous occurrence in the present moment is regarded as "contemporaneous," neither influential upon nor influenced by this momentary actualization.

The question then becomes: Is time real for God? The classic response has been that God is "outside of" time, that temporal progression is a process that God in God's eternity embraces as a whole, with no distinctions of already and not yet. It is for this reason that God is said to be "omniscient" regarding even matters that, from our time-bound perspective, have not "happened" yet. But if God is acting out of love to empower my new becoming with no control over my free response, then the new of my becoming is *new also for God*. God's omniscience is not "inaccurate": that is, God is not confused about matters already settled, possibilities unresolved, and the current moment of self-actualization. In other words, God is precisely omniscient in knowing the past as past, the present as present, and the future as future. God works *within* time to affect the way in which time is filled out. As the interactions between the God of love and the beneficiaries of that empowering love occur successively in temporal sequence, with movement taking place in both directions—from God to us, from us to God, as I explain later in this chapter—so is God a part of the temporal continuum. Time is very real for the God who is love. Tom Oord, in criticizing Augustine, puts it quite nicely: "Love takes time."[1]

I wish to introduce at this point a shift of metaphor. The primary metaphor I have been using is one of architectural construction, writing of crumbling foundations weakened by the varying confrontations with the theistic synthesis originating with Augustine. That is not a purely masculine activity, but it does have a primarily masculine tone about it. I think a preferable and gender-shifting metaphor to utilize as we move forward is the action of weaving a tapestry. I am indebted to O. I. Cricket Harrison for an insightful hymn text that sings of the "Restless Weaver, ever spinning threads of justice and shalom, dreaming patterns of creation . . . gathering up life's varied fibers—every texture, every hue."[2] That seems a more suitable image for expressing the new unifying task for "weaving" a post-theistic alternative to the inherited but discredited tradition concerning God's power and God's love. And so I ask next: What fabrics and textures and threads can be appropriated from the challenges explored above in Part Three that contribute to a vision of a God of empowering love?

WEAVING A NEW TAPESTRY: CONTRIBUTIONS FROM THE COUNTERTESTIMONY

My work of constructing an alternative answer to the divine power/love conundrum draws on a vast array of predecessors whose breakthroughs into fresh modes of understanding underlie what I now present. Eight basic threads are identified here, with acknowledgment to those who originally recognized and began to interweave them.

LOVE CHARACTERIZES THE ESSENTIAL REALITY OF GOD.

This insight can be traced all the way back to the Medieval mystics, starting with Dionysius and Bonaventure but also especially prevalent among the women mystics. Significant contributions to this pivotal understanding were provided, at least *in nuce,* by such varied individuals as the Wesley brothers, the American reformer Alexander Campbell, and Søren Kierkegaard, as well as Albrecht Ritschl and Pierre Teilhard de Chardin among others. William Vanstone's probing analyses of the subject are noted below.

GOD'S POWER IS AN OMNIPOTENCE OF LOVE.

We are primarily indebted to Clarence Rolt for initially championing this insistence that the *only* power God *has* is a power of love, though he did not live long enough to pursue this idea in richer detail. Others who picked up on his challenge include Jürgen Moltmann, Nels F. S. Ferré, Eberhard Jüngel, and a rich company of Whiteheadian process/relational thinkers who benefited from the teaching of John B. Cobb, Jr.

THE POWERFUL LOVE OF GOD IS AN EMPOWERING LOVE.

I quietly initiated a discussion of this theme four decades ago. Those who have pursued it in their own way particularly include Wendy Farley (the first, I think, in 1990), Elizabeth Johnson, Thomas Oord, and especially Catherine Keller. The contribution I am making here, in the remaining sections of this book, is to attempt to spell out more explicitly just what it means to speak of God in this way.

PATHOS IS AT THE HEART OF A GOD WHO IS LOVE.

The breakthrough to the recovery of a biblical God who shares in creation's suffering came particularly in the World War I reflections of the Irish-Anglican Geoffrey Studdert-Kennedy, later championed by Jürgen Moltmann. Dorothee Sölle and Wendy Farley have been among the leading voices within a widespread community of scholarship who have elevated this vital insight into contemporary prominence.

A GOD WHO IS LOVE IS A LIVING GOD IN DYNAMIC INTERRELATION

John Cobb and those of us he mentored, as well as Daniel Day Williams, have appropriated the philosophical vision of Whitehead and Hartshorne in putting theology back into contact with the biblical understanding of a God in dynamic interrelation with all of creation. Trinitarians recognized this essential quality in God's own internal relations but did not always extend it outward to that which is other than God. That God *is* love includes the realization that God is in intimate relation with all that is, not incidentally but constitutively.

GOD TRANSCENDS BUT ALSO EMBRACES GENDER IDENTITY.

The overturning of the classic patriarchal model for conceiving of God provided space for generating fresh ways of understanding the mode of divine activity in the human and cosmic sphere. Feminine characteristics of God were greatly in need to counterbalance and constrain the overwhelmingly masculine values attributed to divinity. As we have seen, trailblazing work from such women scholars as Mary Daly, Carter Heyward, Rita Nakashima Brock, Elizabeth Johnson, Wendy Farley, and Catherine Keller, among so many others, paved the way for a more embracing view of God's indefatigable love.

GOD'S EMPOWERING LOVE CHAMPIONS THE MARGINALIZED AND THE DISPOSSESSED.

For God as love to desire and act positively toward the well-being of all includes an understanding with liberation theologians that God wills the well-being particularly of those who are most lacking in that quality of being. This conviction can be traced all the way back to Micah and Hannah in the witness of the Old Testament as well as in the pronouncements attributed to Jesus. My departure from the positions generally taken within liberation theology is the recognition that conventional notions of divine power are no solution for the plight of the disenfranchised. God by Godself does not reverse those conditions of oppression. That remains an open-ended process in which all of us, in our response to God's lure, make our contributions for good or for ill.

GOD'S EMPOWERING LOVE ACTS PERSUASIVELY WITHOUT CANCELING OUT THE SELF-DETERMINATION OF THE BELOVED.

The insufficiently-known and underrated work of the Anglican canon William Vanstone remains of vital importance in recognizing a continuity between a phenomenology of love as we experience it and a phenomenology of love at work in God. In particular, the realization that, truly to *be* love, God's power is one that surrenders the illusion of invulnerability and control remains a key component in any theology of a God of empowering love. But, of course, it is already there in Paul: "Love . . . does not insist on its own way" (1 Cor 13:5).

In what now follows, I put into play Catherine Keller's use of the Greek words *eros* and *agape* in distinguishing the two movements of God's empowering love, as initiating and receiving. The divine *eros* attracts, calls, invites.[3] The divine *agape* responds, receives, feels our feelings compassionately.[4] How do these two movements helpfully redefine divine power?

THE MOVEMENT OF EROS: THE GIFT OF NEW POSSIBILITY

I am new every day, every moment. Of course, I am not brand new. I am the result of decisions made by me, and by decisions made by others that affect me, from the time I was born and even before. In this new moment of my "deciding" myself, I am deeply influenced by that staggering array of past becomings. I may well be "addicted" to repeating those past decisions, even apart from the technical definition of addiction.

But I am not condemned to repeat my previous decisions on and on into every new moment of my life. In the peculiarity of the human consciousness, I have something called "imagination." That is the capacity, for good or for ill, to entertain possibilities beyond my present self-actualization. I may "imagine" a healthful life of veganism in contrast to my current dependency on nutrition that increases my weight and my susceptibility to diabetes. I may even imagine something so new that it sets in motion a whole new complex of emergent realities, in the vein of a Steve Jobs or a Bill Gates—or a Martin Luther King, Jr., or a Mahatma Gandhi. Or, perversely, an Adolf Hitler. The imagination runs both to progress and to regress, to the diminishing of chaos or its servitude.

Belief in the reality of One who interrelates empoweringly with every miniscule component of the cosmos is the conviction that I am not totally on my own in those acts of imagining. I am being "pointed" in a certain consistent direction, moment by moment. The shape that "pointing" takes is what might be called "case specific." That is to say, the direction in which my imagination is being encouraged to flow is one that is both personally enriching and potentially enriching as well for everything "not me" that I influence. It is what Whitehead regarded as the aim toward an increasing presence of Peace, Beauty, and Harmony in the universe.[5]

This pointing is not the same as asserting that God "has a plan for me." That is far too limiting of God. A deeper truth is that God has a plan for me *in this particular moment*, and it is shaped both by God's desires for the best way in which I can become but also by my individual bundle of past decisions and decisions by others that also "in-form" me. God may well, and does, have an overall proposal in mind for the person I can become, but the specifics of how I may move in the direction of embodying that proposal are determined by how far I have come and where I am and what is happening to me in this present moment.

The gift God's love bestows on my present becoming is precisely that God opens up before me a future possibility I had not previously entertained.

John Cobb expressed it this way. Imagine a room full of people wrestling together to reach a consensus on a way out of a paralyzing conflict of wills. Who, Cobb asks, is the most powerful person in the room? Is it the one who has brought the most chits to call in? Is it the one with the most persuasive vocabulary, the loudest voice, the most powerful bearing? Not at all. It may well prove to be that the most powerful person in that room is the one who is able to entertain an alternative way to overcome the conflict, a possibility not hitherto perceived by any of the other participants. Cobb called this "leadership by proposal," but more fully, "leadership by proposal and the Holy Spirit."[6] His understanding is that the way God who is love empowers us is by opening us up to future possibilities beyond our current comprehending. The proposal may be rejected, or ignored, or derided. But once it is "in the air," it is now a factor in the "new past" of every participant in the room. It may well be that some months later someone else makes that same proposal and this time it gains traction, with perhaps no awareness that it had surfaced before. "Love takes time."

In love, God does not leave me floundering about on my own. In love, God gathers up all the influences on my present reality and offers to me a maximal proposal for how I might so organize them as to constitute my new self in the most gratifying way possible. That is what I call "empowerment." I am empowered by God *not* to repeat past mistakes; *not* to lash out at those who are persecuting me; *not* to seek vengeance in a perpetuation of the cycle of death and destruction; *not* to sink into despair over my own seeming powerlessness against whatever forces are defeating me. But the degree to which I do so is not predetermined by God. This is where empowerment triumphs over coercion. My own freedom is enhanced, not diminished, by God's offer to embark upon a new and more fulfilling movement into my future.

I am not satisfied with calling this the power of "persuasion," which tended to become paramount in much of process-relational theology. I think we all have had experiences in which persuasion transformed, perhaps very subtly, into *manipulation*. Manipulation is my attempt to get you to do what I want, without regard to what you might want. Manipulation treats the other not as an equally free subject but as an object precisely to be manipulated, like moving toy soldiers around on a table. Persuasion is presumably my attempt to influence your free choice without violating it. I am simply not comfortable with attributing that activity to God.[7] Empowerment, in my estimation, *offers*. The degree to which I respond positively to the offer *enhances* the power of the offer to influence me in the next moment and the moment after that.

By virtue of the potential of the sum total of the past that impinges upon my present becoming, it is accurate to speak of a "power struggle." Power as empowerment is in conflict with power as "power over," power to dominate, power that threatens to "force" itself upon me. Once again, God's power does not negate or nullify that very real power opposing it. In love, God's resources for my new beginning are an offer to checkmate the hold that conventional ways of being powerful have over me, but they are not an over-powering of them. That history is strewn with the corpses of power gone awry is very real testimony to the fact that God only and ever acts in an empowering way, never in a controlling, all-determining way. Resistance to God's offer happens. Suffering and loss bedevil God's creation. Love's assurance, once again, is that these are not ever allowed to have the final say. God's capacity to lure the world (cosmos) to its own continuing transformation is inexhaustible.

It is self-evident that this perspective allows no misunderstanding that God wills the bad in order to promote a greater good. That is vastly different from recognizing that, from God's loving empowerment, good can emerge from what seems irredeemable evil. A vivid case in point is the impact that Bull Conner's attacks on the civil rights marchers, and the Ku Klux Klan's murder of four African-American girls in the bombing of a church—among many other such atrocities—had on the unfolding of events, including the 1963 March on Washington for Jobs and Freedom. Americans awoke from their uncaring slumbers to rally behind changes in the law that brought new opportunities in the promotion of racial equality. Nothing more decisively embodies the position being outlined here than Martin Luther King Jr.'s ringing affirmation, "I have a dream."[8]

Regarding human and divine love, I must make a careful distinction here. I may well think I know what is best for my beloved so that I act in such a way as to bring about what I regard as the most appropriate self-actualization. But that is presumptuous on my part. I am human, not God. No individual's understanding can be that absolute. What I offer to my beloved must remain open to be modified or even enhanced by my beloved's response. What is explicitly true of *God*, however, is that God's discernment of the maximal possibility of actualization for God's beloved is *indeed* understandable as absolute, unsurpassable. The problem of our putting ourselves in God's place litters history with misdirected acts of "love": "I'm doing this for your benefit, not mine." "I'm destroying your mortal flesh for the sake of your immortal soul." Or even, "You'll thank me in the morning." Examples pile up higher than Everest.

Here, once again, is the power of the expression, "the more, the more." The more effective God is in luring us with an initial aim for actualizing ourselves—that is to say, the greater the extent of our enacting with minimal modification what God points us toward—then the greater the possibilities of God empowering us even more effectively in the next moment and beyond. The more our exercise of freedom corresponds with God's desires for us, the more God is able to offer us in future aims. The "adoptionist" heresy in Christology actually embodies precisely this understanding in the life of Jesus. One could readily maintain that Jesus so opened himself up to the leading of his "Father" that he began to see his world more and more from God's perspective, rather than seeing God from the world's perspective as the rest of us do.[9] This is one more instance, like patripassianism, where heresy may one day be received as orthodoxy.

To sum up: God *loves* me into moment-by-moment existence, never giving up on me, never being defeated by what I do with God's gifts or what the world does to me in opposition to those gifts. This is indeed *creatio ex amore*, and it is not a one-time matter in the beginning of history. It occurs over and over in God's offer for me to share in the bringing of order out of the chaos of my life. God *empowers* me in how I definitely shape my moment-by-moment existence, offering me (preconsciously) the maximal possibility of how I incarnate value and harmony and love in my own becoming. But what is true of the human individual is also true of all of creation. Evolution, even of the galaxies and the stars and the planets, is nothing other than God's patient luring of all that is into newly emerging fulfillments of possibility.

THE MOVEMENT OF AGAPE: THE GIFT OF DIVINE EMBRACE

God, in love, gives. Does God, in love, receive? Is there anything about the way we implement God's empowering gift of possibility that somehow contributes to the very being of God? The traditional declaration, that God is perfectly self-contained and aloof from every response of God's creatures to what God makes possible for us, collapses under the realization of the necessarily *interrelated* and *interactive* character of love. It moves in both directions, from God to us, from us to God. Love that is not also open receptively is half-love, uncompleted love.

What I am here calling God's receptive love is what Whitehead termed the "consequent" nature of God. It is that aspect of God that is totally inclusive of change, denying God's immutability. It is that aspect of God that takes account of what happened as a result of God's initiating move toward us and receives it fully, lovingly, into God's own being.

God's loving receptivity does not occur without *valuation*. This is what Christians have traditionally called *judgment*. God, indeed, judges moment by moment the adequacy of each actualized response, assessing the degree of fidelity to God's initial aim. But an equally vital theme in the Christian tradition is that God *forgives* the wrong we do. That is a key component of the receptive love of God that empowers. We are continually being judged *and* forgiven, freeing us from carrying around the heavy burden of our past misdeeds that, unchecked, would weigh us down unendurably. The new gift of empowering possibility already includes within itself the lovingly bestowed gift of empowering forgiveness.

The receptive love of God is what requires us to endorse the counter-affirmation of God as a God who *suffers*. That God "feels" our becoming in the depths of intensity denotes a God who is the very opposite of apathetic. God not only suffered with Jesus on the cross. God suffers with *every* element of creation that experiences its own suffering of one kind or another. Whitehead could write glowingly of God as "the great companion—the fellow-sufferer who understands."[10] The healing that God offers to those who suffer emerges out of God's own shared pain over creation's chaotic brokenness and the individual manifestations of that brokenness.

And so Jesus follows Moses in encouraging his hearers to "love the Lord your God with all your heart, and with all your soul, and with all your mind" (Mt 22:37). Is that only for our own sakes? I do not believe so. I believe it is also for the sake of God. Loving God contributes to God, as not loving God diminishes God. The greater the love that flows back to God, the greater are the possibilities for fresh embodiments of love with which God can grace us.

The mystery of prayer completes this dual movement. Genuine prayer is not an attempt to "change God's mind" or persuade God to act in a way God would not otherwise have done. Nor is prayer utterly inconsequential to anyone but the one who is praying.[11] Joseph Bracken writes that prayer "somehow releases positive energy, the power of love, into the world which God . . . can tailor to fit the needs of specific people in specific situations."[12] Prayer, in short, *empowers God*. Praying sends into God a reinforcement of the best that God is continually offering, contributing to the fullness of God's receptivity in a positive way.

I now bring these extended reflections to a close with the observation that, for anyone who receives these proposals for rethinking the power and love of God in a positive way, the next essential work to be done involves the development of a Christian ethic of responsive and responsible love that incarnates fully the understanding that *we are created in the image of God who is Empowering Love.*

ENDNOTES

1. Thomas Oord, *The Nature of Love*, 79. He also calls God's love "time-full love" (79f).

2. O. I. Cricket Harrison, "Restless Weaver," in *Chalice Hymnal*, #658 (St. Louis: Chalice Press, 1995).

3. Wendy Farley describes this movement of divine eros incisively in

her *The Wounding and Healing of Desire: Weaving Heaven and Earth* (Louisville: Westminster John Knox Press, 2005), chapter 6 on "The Divine Eros."

4. Catherine Keller, *On the Mystery*, 99.

5. Whitehead, *Adventures of Ideas*, 294f.

6. John Cobb, "The Holy Spirit and Leadership by Proposal," in his *Can Christ Become Good News Again?* (St. Louis: Chalice Press, 1991), 131–33.

7. Critics of process theology have carped that God, by history's standards, is not a very effective persuader.

8. Coincidentally, this paragraph is being written on the fiftieth anniversary of that speech.

9. See John B. Cobb, Jr., *The Process Perspective II* (St. Louis: Chalice Press, 2011), 111–15.

10. Whitehead, *Process and Reality*, 351.

11. See Marjorie Suchocki's marvelous survey of this topic in her *In God's Presence: Theological Reflections on Prayer* (St. Louis, Chalice Press, 1996).

12. Joseph A. Bracken, S.J., *Christianity and Process Thought: Spirituality for a Changing World* (Philadelphia: Templeton Foundation Press, 2006), 95.

For Further Reading

Rather than duplicate information already available in the footnote references by providing an extended bibliography, I have opted to offer suggestions for further reading in key areas of this enterprise.

For a crisp and very accessible introduction to the philosophy of A. N. Whitehead, I recommend C. Robert Mesle's *Process-Relational Philosophy: An Introduction to Alfred North Whitehead* (Templeton Foundation Press, 2008). Mesle's earlier volume on *Process Theology: A Basic Introduction* (Chalice Press, 1993) is the easiest to read among multiple options in this area, but I also find *The Process Perspective: Frequently Asked Questions about Process Theology* by John B. Cobb, Jr., edited by Jeanyne B. Slettom (Chalice, 2003), to be a gem of an introduction. A follow-up volume, *The Process Perspective II*, came out in 2011 with new questions and responses.

A list of vitally important resources that embody a vision parallel to this book has to begin with W. H. Vanstone's *The Risk of Love* (Oxford University Press, 1978). Regarding fresh alternatives to conventional approaches to the story of God in the Old Testament, see Terence Fretheim's groundbreaking *The Suffering of God: An Old Testament Perspective* (Fortress, 1984). And on the topic of suffering, consider

The Transforming God: An Interpretation of Suffering and Evil by Tyrone Inbody (Westminster John Knox Press, 1997).

Excellent inquiries into the history of how love has been treated in the traditions of Christian theology are to be found in Thomas Oord's *The Nature of Love: A Theology* (Chalice, 2010), along with his own insightful formulations. His other works on the subject of love also merit investigation.

Expanding and deepening her earlier work on *Tragic Vision and Divine Compassion: A Contemporary Theodicy* (Westminster John Knox, 1990), Wendy Farley has created a masterpiece of depth and beauty with her more recent *The Wounding and Healing of Desire: Weaving Heaven and Earth* (Westminster John Knox, 2005). Both are greatly recommended.

Tracing many of the same developments treated here in Part Three but going well beyond them into other important areas as well, Elizabeth A. Johnson's *Quest for the Living God: Mapping Frontiers in the Theology of God* (Bloomsbury Press, 2007) is worthy of serious attention.

Finally, I lift up the incisively imaginative work of Catherine Keller, from her *God and Power: Counter-Apocalyptic Journeys* (Fortress Press, 2005)—particularly Part Three on constructing a political theology of love—to most especially her brilliant *On the Mystery: Discerning God in Process* (Fortress, 2008), so revelatory that it almost rendered this book unnecessary.

SCRIPTURE INDEX

OLD TESTAMENT

Genesis
1:1–2	7f., 18
1:2	44
1:6	8
1:26–2	9
1:27	9, 153
1:28	9
3:1	8
3:8	8
6–8	8
19:24–25	13
45:4–9	13

Exodus
3:14	11
6:7	6
7:14–12:32	14
15:1–18	10
15:11	20
15:11–13	20
15:15	18
19:18	209
20:3	7
32:1–10	11
32:11–12	11f.
32:12	12
32:14	2

Deuteronomy
5:7	7
7:8	18
7:9	7
10:15	18
26:6–8	10
28	7

Numbers
11:13	4

Judges
7:22	4
8:23	5

1 Samuel
2:4,8	10
2:7	28

1 Kings
8:23	20
18:20–40	1
18:29	1
18:36–39	2
19:11–12	2, 209

2 Kings
19:15	7

1 Chronicles
29:11–12   5

2 Chronicles
25:8   4

Nehemiah
9:17   18

Job
6–7   12
7:11   12
16–17   12
40:4   12
42:2   209

Psalms
7:9–11   8
11:7   8
29:4   5
33:5   18
35:10   20
42:2   15
47:7–9   5
62:11–12   19
63:2–3   19
68:35   21
74:9–11   15
84:2   15
86:8   20f.
86:10,13   21
93–100   5
93:1–2   5
95:3   5
96:10   5
97:1   5
98   19
99:4   5
100   19
104   8
106:45   18
110:5–6   4
111:3   8
113:5–8   20
116:5   8
119:137   8
130:7   19
136   18
147:8–9   4

Isaiah
1:2   19
1:24   14
6:1,5   5
10:33f.   3
24–27   14
40:26   21
40:28–31   21
41:17–20   8
41:29   7
43:19   7
45:1,13   3
45:5,6   7
45:7   3
45:12   3
45:18   3
46:9   7
51:22   14
65:17   8
66:22   8

Jeremiah
2:11   7

9:24	8
10:1–16	20
10:10	15
10:16	20
18:8,10	13
20:7	12
26:3,13,19	13
31:20	135
32:17	3

Lamentations
3:32	18

Ezekiel
30:3	15

Hosea
1:2	16
1:6–9	16
1:9–10	16
2:19	17
6:4	17
9:1	16
11:1–2,4	16
11:5–7	16f.
11:8–9	17
13:14	17
14:4–9	17

Joel
1:15	15
2:11,31	15

Jonah
3:9–10	12f.

Micah
3:8	21

7:18–20	20
7:19	20

Zephaniah
1:7	15

Zechariah
8:8	8

NEW TESTAMENT

Matthew
1:23	27
5:43–44	30
11:2–5	240
19:24	28
22:29	27
22:37	257
26:64	27

Mark
9:1	29, 240
13:15	27

Luke
1:35	27
1:52–53	28, 241
4:16–21	29
23:35	31
24:49	27

John
1:5	224, 243
1:12	27
1:14	113
3:16	31
10:30	137
13:34	30

14:9	27	6:7	27
14:28	58	12:9	31, 230
14:30	29	13:3	27
15:9	31	13:4	212
16:27	31		
17:23–25	31	*Philippians*	
17:26	31	2:7	212

Acts
5:30 30, 242
10:39–40 30

Colossians
1:15 27

Hebrews
1:3 27

Romans
5:8 31

1 Corinthians
1:17-25 183f., 244
1:18 31, 91
1:24 31, 91
1:25 30f., 212
13:4–8 32, 45, 244, 247, 251

1 John
4:8 32, 45f., 65, 83, 89, 27, 143, 171, 178, 182, 206, 228
4:16 32, 45, 52, 77, 83, 89, 127, 143
4:19 32, 239

2 Corinthians
5:14 31

Author Index

Altizer, Thomas J. J., 145, 148–51
Alves, Rubem A. , 207–09, 212
Anderson, Bernhard, 5, 8
Anselm of Canterbury, 72f., 159
Aquinas, Thomas, i, 72, 74–79, 88, 94, 101, 115, 134
Aristides of Athens, 39, 45
Aristotle, 72, 74, 76, 94
Athenagoras, 39, 46
Augustine of Hippo, i–ii, 53, 56-71, 74, 78f., 96, 101, 114f., 124, 127, 171, 192, 239, 248

Barth, Karl, 89–92
Basil of Caesarea, 56
Berdyaev, Nicolas, 133f.
Blake, William, 144f., 149, 151
Boff, Leonardo, 210–12
Bonaventure, 112f., 249
Bonhoeffer, Dietrich, i, 183
Bowne, Borden Parker, 167
Bracken, Joseph, 257
Brady, Bernard, 26, 33, 115
Brightman, Edgar, 167f., 176
Brock, Rita Nakashima, 155–57, 250
Brueggemann, Walter, 7f., 13, 20f.
Burnaby, John, 65f.

Bushnell, Horace, 124, 126

Calvin, John, 72, 80–83, 136, 229
Campbell, Alexander, 172, 249
Carr, Anne, 161
Case-Winters, Anna, 83, 90f.
Catherine of Siena, 117f.
Clement of Alexandria, 41f., 47
Clement of Rome, 38f., 145
Cobb, John B., Jr., 226–28, 249f., 253, 259
Collins, James, 166
Cone, James H., 201–05
Copernicus, Nicolaus, 87f.
Cottret, Bernard, 81

Daly, Mary, 154f., 201, 238, 250
Davaney, Shiela Greene, 91
Delio, Ilia, 112f.
Dinsmore, Charles Allen, 126
Dionysius, 110–13, 178, 249
Dodd, C. H., 32
Dorrien, Gary, 177
Dostoyevsky, Fyodor, i, 144, 166f.
Doyle, Arthur Conan, 57

Edwards, Denis, 73
Eichrodt, Walther, 6, 19, 23

Epictetus, 101

Faber, Frederick W., 172
Fairbairn, A. M., 125f., 176
Farley, Wendy, 189-91, 250, 260
Farmer, Ron, 245
Ferré, Nels F. S., 94, 176, 249
Feuerbach, Ludwig, 141–43, 147
Frank, Anne, i
Fretheim, Terence, 3, 7, 9, 11f., 27, 259
Friere, Paulo, 213
Fuchs, Ernst, 182
Furnish, Victor, 31, 34

Garnett, Richard, 172
Gertrude of Helfta, 116f.
Good, Edwin, 19
Grant, Robert, 38
Gregory VII, 211
Gregory of Nazianzus, 56
Gregory of Nyssa, 53–56, 63
Griffin, David Ray, 191, 228, 232
Gunton, Colin, 48f.
Gutiérrez, Gustavo, 201, 206f., 209

Hadewijch of Antwerp, 115f.
Harnack, Adolf von, 460
Harrison, O. I. Cricket, 249
Hartshorne, Charles, 103, 217, 220–22, 226–28, 237f., 250
Hegel, G. W. F., 141, 173
Heschel, Abraham, 10f., 23, 102, 126
Heyward, Carter, 155f., 250
Hick, John, 79

Hildegard of Bingen, 114f.
Hippolytus of Rome, 45f.

Inbody, Tyrone, 260
Irenaeus of Lyons. 40f., 44, 46f.

James, William, 167
Johnson, Elizabeth, 157–60, 172f., 212, 250, 260
Johnston, George, 34
Julian of Norwich, 118f.
Jüngel, Eberhard, 143, 182–84, 249
Justin Martyr, 39, 46

Kant, Immanuel, 88
Kaufman, Gordon, 104, 180f.
Kazantzakis, Nikos, 227
Keller, Catherine, 228–30, 250f., 260
Kierkegaard, Søren, 173–75, 249
King, Martin Luther, Jr., 252, 254
Kitamori, Kazoh, 134f.
Kushner, Harold, I, 163-65

Lee, Jung Young, 134–36
Leff, Gordon, 79f.
Leibnitz, Gottfried, 64, 109, 166
Letter to Diognetus (anon.), 45
Loomer, Bernard, 220, 224–26
Luther, Martin, 80

MacGregor, Geddes, 181f.
MacLeish, Archibald, 109, 164
Marcion, 38, 46
Marcus Aurelius, 101f.
Martensen, Hans, 125

McDermott, Timothy, 76
Mesle, C. Robert, 259
Migliori, Daniel, 30f.
Míguez Bonino, José, 210, 212
Mill, John Stuart, 166
Miller, Patrick, 14
Moltmann, Jürgen, 18, 95, 103f., 126–28, 178, 207, 249f.
Mozley, John Kenneth, 124, 132

Newman, Barbara, 114
Nietzsche, Friedrich, i, 145–48, 226
Nygren, Anders, 157, 192, 199

Oord, Thomas Jay, 64-66, 191–93, 239, 248, 250, 260
Origen, 42–44, 48
Outler, Albert, 63

Pannenberg, Wolfhart, 2, 33, 49f., 95–97, 127f., 237f., 243
Pelikan, Jaroslav, 38, 46, 66
Phillips, D. Z., 172
Philo, 41
Plato, 44f., 47, 74, 218
Plotinus, 57
Polk, David P., 199, 244f.

Rad, Gerhard von, 13
Richard of St. Victor, 72f., 112
Ritschl, Albrecht, 175, 177, 249
Rolt, Clarence Edwin, 178–80, 249
Rubenstein, Richard L., 148
Schleiermacher, Friedrich, 87–89
Segundo, Juan Luis, 205–07
Sheel, Otto, 64

Simonov, Konstantin, 138
Sölle, Dorothee, 136–38, 250
Studdert-Kennedy, G. A., 126, 130–32, 250

Tacitus, 10
Tatian, 39
Teilhard de Chardin, Pierre, 184–86, 249
Teresa of Avila, 117, 119f.
Tertullian, 37, 46, 52
Theophilus of Antioch, 40, 44, 50f.
Tillich, Paul, 89, 92–94, 97f., 154
Tindal, Matthew, 165
Toland, John, 165

Upjohn, Shiela, 119

Valentinus, 40, 46
Vanstone, William H., 186–90, 249, 251, 259
Voltaire, 166

Wesley, Charles, 171f., 249
Wesley, John, 171, 249
Whitehead, Alfred North, 177, 217–20, 222, 228, 247–50, 252, 256f.
Wiesel, Elie, i, 137
William of Ockham, 79f.
Williams, Daniel Day, 220, 222–24, 226, 250
Wink, Walter, 134
Wolterstorff, Nicholas, 103

Zeno, 101f.

Subject Index

actual occasions of experience, 218f., 239, 246–48
adoptionism, 255
amorization, 185
apatheia, apathy, iii, 48, 101–04, 126, 130, 132, 136, 171, 216, 256f.
apocalyptic, apocalypse, 14f., 28f., 149f., 240–44
Aristotelianism, 74, 101, 206
atheism, 104f., 127, 132
Augustinianism, Augustinian synthesis, 73, 87, 103, 105, 124, 168, 171, 216, 222, 224, 230, 239, 248

basileia tou theou, reign of God: see God
being and becoming, 217–19, 222, 247f., 251f.
Big Bang, 247
Black Power, 202–05

chaos (primordial and ongoing), 8, 15, 44, 164, 180, 210, 229f., 247, 252, 255
Copernican Revolution, 87f.
cosmology, 217f.

Council of Nicaea, 54
counter-testimony, 105, 110
covenant, 4, 6–8, 18f., 26, 45, 47
creatio ex amore, creation out of love, 18, 32, 66, 176, 255
creatio ex nihilo, creation out of nothing, 18, 44, 61, 247

deconstruction, iii, 110
Deism, 165f., 176
determinism, 90, 96, 218, 221, 227, 247, 253f.
dipolar theism, 222
dunamis, 27, 29, 155

evil, 63f., 82, 111, 119, 133, 145, 180, 185, 188, 190f., 204, 224, 227, 247, 254
Existentialism, 173
exousia, 27, 155

fatalism, 218
forgiveness, 256
free will, human freedom, 61–64, 81, 83, 96, 133f., 175, 190, 192, 218, 222–26, 241, 247f., 253, 255

Gnosticism, 40

God, a living God, ii, 13, 15, 37, 45, 47f., 56, 66, 77, 91, 92, 97, 110, 141, 230, 250;
  anthropomorphized, 5f.;
  as *actus purus*, pure act, 74f., 77, 88;
  as being-itself, ground of being, 92–94;
  as Creator, 3, 7–10, 18, 38f., 40f., 44, 54, 61, 164, 176, 228–30, 247;
  as divine monarch, 4f., 7, 9, 19, 81, 83, 131f., 183, 219;
  as enemy, 144f., 147;
  as human projection, 142f.;
  as the power of the future, 95-97, 127, 208;
  basileia tou theou, reign of God, 27–30, 95, 134, 175, 210f., 240–42;
  controlling, 247f., 254;
  crucified, 124–28, 132f., 137, 148f., 183;
  death of God, 141–50, 163, 205, 226;
  divine abuse of power, 11f.;
  divine judgment, 256;
  divine love in Aquinas' writings, 77–79;
  divine love in Augustine's writings, 64–66;
  divine love in process-relational thought, 191–93, 219f.,

God, cont.
  222–24, 228;
  divine love in the NT, 26f., 31f., 216, 238f., 244;
  divine love in the OT, 15–21, 26f., 204, 241, 251;
  divine lure (the call forward), invitation, 207f., 218f., 227f., 241f., 247, 251–56;
  divine power in the NT, 27, 30f., 210, 241;
  divine power in the OT, 2–15, 19–21, 27, 47, 82f., 209, 241;
  divine receptivity, 218f., 221–23, 225, 228, 230, 248, 251, 256f.;
  divine repentance, 12f., 47, 82f.;
  divine simplicity, 42, 60f., 77f.;
  divine suffering, 48, 119, 130–38, 158, 164, 168, 171, 189, 216, 219, 222f., 228, 250, 256f.;
  empowering love, ii–iv, 21, 29, 32, 110, 156, 189–93, 212, 226, 230, 238, 240–44, 246–57;
  empowering the powerless, 10, 21, 28, 207–12, 241, 244, 251;
  "God is love," iii, 27, 31f., 38, 45f., 65, 77, 83, 89, 93, 116, 118, 126f., 143,

God, cont.
　159, 171–78, 182, 188,
　206, 216, 220–22, 228,
　230, 238f., 249f.;
immutability, changelessness,
　iii, 46f., 56, 59f., 61, 66,
　76–79, 83, 88, 91, 110,
　114, 124–28, 130, 171,
　174f., 206, 216, 218,
　221, 256;
impassibility, passionlessness,
　45–48, 64, 66, 73,
　75, 78, 83, 103, 124,
　126, 130, 182, 216;
limited power, 4, 42f., 125,
　132, 136, 163–68, 221;
Omega, Omega-point,
　184–86;
omni-amorous, omniloving,
　83, 230;
omnipotence, absolute power,
　ii, 38–43, 54f., 58,
　61–63, 66, 72–75, 79f.,
　81–83, 88, 90–92, 93,
　96, 104, 114, 119f., 131,
　158, 167f., 204, 210,
　216, 221, 223, 229f.,
　246;
omnipotence of love, 115,
　174, 178–81, 249;
omnipresence, 76, 83, 88,
　90;
omniscience, divine foreknow-
　ledge, 39, 60, 62, 77, 82,
　88, 91, 115, 248;

God, cont.
overpowering, 12, 32, 43f.,
　173, 192f., 207, 230,
　244, 254;
patriarchal, post-patriarchal,
　iii, 120, 153–60, 171,
　189, 216, 250;
power and love conjoined,
　19–21, 27, 29, 31, 41,
　45, 49, 55f., 93f., 111–
　13, 114–16, 118f., 134,
　158f., 172, 177, 185f.,
　190, 209, 211f., 221,223,
　230, 237, 241, 247;
power and love in conflict, i–
　ii, 46, 49, 56, 66, 73,
　78–80, 83, 90f., 96f., 109,
　119f., 132, 136f., 138,
　143, 148, 164, 167, 181,
　204f., 209, 212, 221,
　225, 227, 229, 246;
power in weakness, 27, 30f.,
　91, 112, 127, 181, 183f.,
　212, 230, 242–44;
preferential option for the
　poor, 205–07;
Primordial and Consequent
　Natures, 218, 222, 256;
"the One who loves in
　freedom," 89–92;
Trinity, iii, 38, 53–61, 65f.,
　73, 77, 112f., 119, 125,
　134, 155, 176, 205f.,
　216, 239, 250;
undefeatable, 13, 30, 181,

God, cont.
    224, 242f., 254;
    vulnerable (precarious), 11, 186–89, 212, 224;
    womb of God, 156, 206;
    wrath of God, 11, 13f., 17f., 47, 66;
    see also: *apatheia*, determinism, dipolar theism, initial aim, *kenosis*, love, power, Patripassionism, predestination, relationality, theodicy, time
Greek philosophy, i–ii, 37–49, 104

Holocaust, I, 141, 148, 164f., 246

imagination, 252
imago dei, image of God, 9, 27, 47, 133, 153
initial aim, 218, 228, 247, 255f.

Jesus, 27–31, 43, 45, 54, 58, 95f., 118, 131, 137, 149, 155, 167f., 171–73, 202, 206, 210f., 237f., 240–44, 251;
    crucified, 30f., 91, 113, 124f., 127, 134, 137, 183, 189, 204, 242–44, 256;
    "first Easter" (resurrection), 30, 38, 56, 204, 242–44;
    relation to God, 38, 243f.

kenosis, self-emptying, 110, 149, 181f., 192

liberation, liberation theologies, 10, 29, 127, 147, 156, 159, 163, 201–12, 227, 251
love, as *agape*, ii, 26, 64, 103, 135, 157, 159, 192, 230, 239, 251, 256f.;
    as *caritas*, 64;
    as *eros*, 26, 157, 190, 192, 230, 239, 251–56;
    as *hesed*, ii, 17-21, 26, 64, 241;
    as *philia*, 26, 239;
    divine: see God;
    human, 17, 30, 32, 65, 73, 78, 115, 223, 239, 254f.;
    phenomenology of, 187–91
Manichaeism, 57, 59
manipulation, 253f.
Marcionism, 38, 46
Medellin Conference (CELAM II), 201, 205
mystics, mysticism, iii, 109–20, 171, 249
neo-Platonism, 57, 59, 101
nihilism, 147
novelty, 218, 247, 251f.
open theology, 191
overman, overhuman, 147f.
Patripassionism, 125, 134f., 182, 216, 255
Pelagianism, 63
Platonism, 41, 44, 47, 59, 74, 101
potentia absoluta, potentia ordinata, 79f., 164f.
power, active and passive, 74f., 79;

power, cont.
  coercive power, compulsion, 44f., 180, 186, 190, 210f., 223, 225, 247, 253;
  erotic power, 155, 157, 190;
  persuasive power, 44f., 126, 158, 223, 225, 227, 253f.;
  power struggle, 254;
  relational power, 9, 224–27;
  unilateral power, 3, 224–26, 230, 241
  see also: *dunamis, exousia*, God
prayer, 165, 257
predestination, 62–64, 66, 78f., 81f.
process-relational theology, 217–30, 249
prolepsis, 28, 240
Puebla Conference (CELEM III), 201

relationality, interrelatedness, 155, 157–59, 216–19, 222, 225f., 228, 252, 256f.

salvation ("redemption"), 41, 55f., 62f., 65f., 78f., 89, 118, 134–36, 144, 190
Second Vatican Council, 201
size, 225f.
Stoicism, 101–05, 136, 216, 220f.

theodicy, 64, 96, 109, 163–65, 191, 204, 246f.

time (and timelessness), 59f., 61, 76f., 79, 93, 85f., 127f., 149, 248

weaving, tapestry, 72, 248f.
World War I, 124, 126, 130

zero-sum game, 226

www.ingramcontent.com/pod-product-compliance
Lightning Source LLC
Chambersburg PA
CBHW021140080526
44588CB00008B/148